THE SCREENWRITER'S SURVIVAL KIT

In a town without pity—namely Hollywood—all you need is a map, a guide, and a ticket to success. The first two you're holding in your hands, the third is up to you. From the screenwriter who broke all the rules and made the movie industry sit up and take notice, this is the book that will help you where the Guild can't. Will you make that million-dollar first deal? We can't guarantee you will. We wouldn't say you won't, either. But you will stand an excellent chance of always being able to have lunch in this town (or any town at all) again.

The Screenwriter's Survival Guide

or,

Guerrilla Meeting Tactics and Other Acts of War

Max Adams

WARNER BOOKS

A Time Warner Company

Warner Books, Inc., 1271 Avenue of the Americas, New York, NY 10020

Visit our Web site at www.twbookmark.com

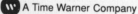 A Time Warner Company

Printed in the United States of America

First Printing: March 2001

10 9 8 7 6 5 4 3 2 1

Library of Congress Cataloging-in-Publication Data

Adams, Max.
    The screenwriter's survival guide, or guerrilla meeting tactics and other acts of war / by Max Adams.
        p. cm.
    Includes bibliographical references.
    ISBN 0-446-67622-5
    1. Motion picture authorship. I. Title.

    PN1996.A42 2001
    808.2'3—dc21   00-043538

Book design by H. Roberts Design

I know who you are.
I do not know how to identify you in the crowd.
But you are there.
And you know who you are.
This is for you.
Reach.

ACKNOWLEDGMENTS

incredible heartfelt thanks to Greg, who repeatedly told me I had written a book. (This is all your fault, Greg.) Kundalini Meej, who said I had better say "Kundalini Meej," so there it is. (What does Kundalini mean?) Laura, who, just by existing, forces me to be funnier than I am. Chris, who, just by existing, makes me think maybe I can do what I am not always sure I can. Patricia, Mike, Kitty, Jeff, Diane, Gayle, Bonny, Em, and all the GEnie-ites and Cat99ers. Who are the reason this book happened. Terri, who was the last person to say, "Write the book," before I finally said, "Okay, how hard could it be?" (Famous last words.) My interview subjects, who taught me one hell of a lot while I was writing for *FORUM* and *The Hollywood Scriptwriter*. David and Kerry for hiring me to do those interviews. Kurt, for being a voice of reason in the storm. Gale Anne, for being there during every career crisis. Karen, for always, always believing in me, even when I sometimes wasn't so sure. Gee Nicholl, for making the fellowship available that would save my tail, when I moved to Los Angeles. All the kids who set up the Austin festival I was "discovered" at. John Dougherty, for telling me to "write within my vocabulary." I didn't get it then, I sure get it now. Alan and Ramses and Dan, without whom I wouldn't have a career or a book. Peter and Sam for picking up the slack when they don't. John, for being foolish enough to buy the book. Dolph, Loki, and Jones, for laughing at all my jokes. And Chris's mom—I told him I'd mention her here and it's my book so I can do that (smile).

CONTENTS

1 Why I Wrote This

Sometimes, I suspect the entire reason I'm a writer is, when I was about six years old, my dad brought home an electric typewriter. It was mysterious. It was magnificent. They let me type on it once—and I discovered, right then and there, if you were going to type out a string of letters, it helped if you had something to say.

this is a book written by accident. I told a friend of mine that, and she laughed really hard and said, "Max, nothing is written by accident." But it was.

Six years ago, I bought my first modem and became part of a startling group of people. We were all driven. We all wrote scripts. We were all over the country. We were all killing ourselves to get "discovered." And we were all on the same electronic bulletin board. GEnie. It was a text-based system. Written by people on IBMs for people on IBMs. With something patched together loosely for anyone who happened to be on a Mac. I was lost for three days on that system. I didn't know much about modems and I knew less about electronic bulletin boards. But I was pretty damn alone, writing screenplays in

Utah. So I persevered. And ultimately stumbled across the screenwriter's forum.

I had won one small screenwriting competition, was reading for a place in L.A. that would ship scripts to readers out of state, had written four scripts, and was doing independent story doctoring on the side to subsidize my college tuition. I would come a long way, on that board. So would other people. It is one talented group. It includes Nicholl Fellowship winners, Disney Fellowship winners, America's Best winners, Austin winners, Warner Brothers winners. Hell, I think we've tagged every screenwriting contest that ever was, since those early days. Some of us are working professionally now, and those that aren't, well, I figure they'll get there.

The bulletin board's not there anymore, but when it was, it was a good place to be, if you were learning. I got a lot of advice. I learned a ton. And I gave a lot of advice. Long after the people I picked it up from were gone, I was sitting at a keyboard, for better or worse pounding out advice. What I'd picked up from other people. And what I was picking up, often the hard way, on my own.

Down the road, someone told me I had written a book in all those posts and letters. And then someone else told me. And someone else. And someone else again. Till I started to wonder. It sounded fine, this consensus I had somehow by accident written a book. But I hadn't saved any of it. Not a word. And I said so. Which is when people started sending me posts I'd written they had saved.

It was a lot. I had to buy a zip drive to hold it all. Which is just scary, thinking I thought at some point I had that much to say on the matter of screenwriting. But for better or worse—

What you hold in your hands is advice I have given that other people thought was important enough to save. It's feature advice. That only makes sense. I write features. TV people will have to wait till Jeff Lowell writes a book. (Jeff, get cracking.) But for better or worse, here it is. Advice from the front.

I hope it helps.

2 Starting from Ground Zero

NOTES INTO THE ETHER #34: Stories have always been my way of examining life without getting too close to reality. Reality, sometimes, is too much. Fictionalized, though, well, fictionalized, I can look at it. Without getting hurt.

there is this saying about seven degrees of separation—or maybe it is six degrees of separation, I have never been too great at math—but basically the idea is, somewhere someone who knows someone whom you know knows someone in Hollywood.

Maybe that is so for other people. It wasn't for me. I went to high school in a logging town. Movie people were just not thick up there. And while my stepfather's sister is married to a gaffer, the few questions I asked about maybe getting some help there didn't get a real response. So I was starting from scratch with no contacts and while that is harder? It can be done.

You will have to do it the hard way. You will have to get on the phone and call strangers and write letters and pound on doors. There are disadvantages to coming from outside the system. People who grew up here or have worked here understand a hell of a lot more about how this business works than I do. They have seen it in action, lived it worked it breathed it. Someone coming from outside has to learn from scratch. So here are some things that can help.

Don't act like you know what you are doing when you don't. Don't even bluff. Bluffing can make you look real smart, if you know just enough to drop the words that make you look like you know what you are doing even when you don't. The problem is, if everyone thinks you know what you are doing? It will never occur to anyone to offer you help or information, because they don't think you need it.

Ask for information. People like to appear smart. They like it when their opinions and thoughts are valued. So ask people for their thoughts and opinions. Ask them to talk about what they know. Tell them you don't know anything and would really like to hear what they do. You will learn a hell of a lot more that way than you will bluffing your way around like you know what's going on when you don't. And you won't make yourself look stupid in front of people who do know things, in the unfortunate event you bluff wrong.

This is called catch up. You started out behind. You have to play catch up now with all the kids who started out here. You can do this. It just takes more effort.

And don't play power games with the big dogs. The people in power in this town have been doing this a long time. Their power games are like the iceberg the *Titanic* hit. Everything you see is just surface, everything you don't is down there somewhere just waiting to sink some poor dumb screenwriter who thinks he or she is going to outwit a Hollywood power player. Don't even go there. These people are survivors. To even be where they are, that's a given. And they will win, if you try to out play them on their turf. So do your job, go home, be nice to people, stay away from anyone or anything that looks pathologic. And if you do get sucked into some sort of power play, i.e. trouble? Scream bloody murder for your agent and then don't answer your phone till the bodies stop twitching.

And if you don't have an agent? Don't answer the phone. Not till whatever is going down has gone down and you weren't in the middle of it. Seriously. Dirt sticks. Don't stand near the mud pit. That will just make you look dirty too.

All that said? If you're coming in from the outside, well, you just are. You can't change that. But these doors aren't locked. If they were, I wouldn't be here. In fact, no writers would be here. They all would have died off a long time ago. So take courage. Someone has to make it. It might as well be you.

3 Who Buys Scripts

CONVERSATIONS WITH WRITERS #64:

WRITER: *Maybe I shouldn't have mentioned in my interview that 30 hours ago, I was 1200 miles away and drinking myself into a stupor.*

ME: *Oh, I think that was okay. Where you lost points was when you told them about the headless Barbie collection.*

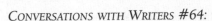 friend of mine had a script with a producer who was trying to set it up. To do this, the producer was sending the script to actors, the idea being, if the producer got a big actor attached, it would be a lot easier to get a studio interested in buying the script and making the movie.

My friend was talking about this on an internet newslist, and a few people on the newslist got very excited and started talking about a bidding war. A bidding war is a battle between entities—usually studios—that want to buy the same script. They keep outbidding each other until someone gives up and goes home, and the last man standing gets the script. It's good for writers because the bidding raises the price and the writer gets to take more money home. But—

Um, a bidding war? With actors?

I don't like to be the person to squash dreams, and I know people get excited about the concept of a bidding war. But, um, my friend's script was submitted to actors. Not studios. Actors. Like writers, actors are referred to as "talent." And, generally speaking, actors don't pay you. You pay actors. So—

No bidding war.

And that's important to know, if you are in this business to sell scripts. Just who buys scripts. And it's not actors.

This changes if the actor has a development deal at a studio and is wearing a producer hat, but in general, the reason you send material to actors is, if you can attract an actor and that actor agrees to attach to the material, in advance of a monetary offer (which you can't make, without a studio financially backing the project, and some actors will not look at material that doesn't have a dollar attached to the offer), that makes the script a more attractive project for a studio to buy.

And studios buy scripts.

See, if a studio gets a script, just a script? The studio is gambling it will be able to put together all the pieces, but sometimes a studio will get a script and then no one will want to direct or star. Oops. Now the studio has paid a whole lot of money for a project it can't make. Silly them. But once you attach an actor, well, you are partway there already, and then the studio can say, Oh look, here is a script that already has a star attached, and since there is one star attached already, others will attach on the basis of that and we will for sure get a director, so half our work is done and this might really be a movie.

Which is why "packaging" is so popular. A "package" is more than one talent entity (actors, writers, and directors are all "talent," though the term is most often used to refer to actors) attached to one project from the get go. It makes studio people who buy material happy and much more likely to purchase a project, because half the work to get this script turned into a movie is already done in a "package"—and studio people are the people who fight over scripts and bid in bidding wars.

There are actors who have development deals and producing agreements with studios and all that fancy stuff. But they operate out of discretionary funds that no one wants to spend because discretionary funds are emergency funds and that is another story entirely whereas? Bidding wars are funded by studios—*i.e.* suit people—not actors.

Another situation I watched go down on an internet newslist was, a friend of mine had a script with an agent and was wondering whether or not this agent was really behind the material one hundred percent, or whether to go looking for another agent who maybe would be more excited about the script and send it out to more places.

That's a very good question, and we'll talk more about that later. What is important here, though, is, someone on the list came back and said, "If he doesn't want to option or buy that script, yank it and send it somewhere else."

Well. Um. That's very nice advice, but agents don't buy scripts. Ever. Agents sell scripts. To studios. Then you pay agents a commission for making the sale. Don't ever mix that up or demand an agent make a monetary offer or else. That agent will think you are a crackpot and want nothing to do with you. Because—

Agents don't buy scripts. Studios do.

It is important you know that going in. Who really buys material. Studios. Studios buy material for actors to star in, for directors to direct, for producers to produce. They even buy material for writers to write. In each of these scenarios, though, pay attention to who is footing the bill. The studio.

The person who usually actually sells to the studio, though, is the producer. Not the agent, oddly enough, which makes no sense in a sane world, but we are in Hollywood. And in Hollywood, producers find material, take it to studios, and the studio buys the material for the producer to produce. That's why agents send scripts to producers, instead of straight to studios. It is a chain of command thing: The agent finds producers who like the material, the producers find the studios who like them *and* the material, and the studios cut deals with the producer and writer that the agents then negotiate.

Who knew?

And in general, producers do not buy material. This depends a lot on the producer, but here is how it usually works. A producer gets a script. The producer loves the script. The producer tells you he or she loves the script and would like to show it to a few people. You say that sounds okay. You have some little alarms going off, thinking, Fuck, someone is about to shop my script around and if they don't hit pay dirt, well it's shopworn material now. But you can't sell if you don't get read and you have qualified this person, you have checked their credits and they have maybe made some pretty good movies and your gut instinct is they are not trying to dick you around here. So you say sure. Then the producer takes the script to whomever he or she knows best at a studio and maybe would like to work with and says, "I like this script, I would like to make the movie, what do you think?" Now it goes one of two ways: the studio says "No way are you crazy?, no deal"; or the studio says, "Wow, what a great idea, we love this, let's cut a deal."

If the answer is "no way," the producer takes the script to the next studio contact on his or her list of "places that like me and will fund a picture I want to make."

If the answer is "hell yes, let's do it," the producer tells you you're in and the studio cuts the producer a deal to produce and you a deal for the script and everyone gets a check. Yay! Then everyone starts writing up budgets and casting lists and you learn the real meaning of "rewrite hell."

But pay attention to who just bought the script: the studio.

Some producers have a "discretionary fund." That is emergency money the studio put in a little account for the producer when the studio and producer cut their producing deal and the studio gave the producer those nice offices on the lot. Producers can spend discretionary funds on whatever they want, they don't have to get studio approval on material to purchase with discretionary funds. But, discretionary funds are limited, whereas studio pockets are deep. (Where the hell do studios get all that money anyway, is what I'd like to know.) And if a producer spends discretionary funds on a project and the studio says, "Well that's nice, but we don't want to make that movie," the producer is out his or her emergency fund, holding a script the studio won't reimburse him or her for or make.

Which is why producers don't like to spend their discretionary funds. They want to spend the studio's money. And why producers will ask you if they can show a script to someone at the studio, instead of offering to cut you a nice check for an option first.

Producers do buy and option scripts. With discretionary funds. But when a producer spends discretionary funds, it usually is an emergency. There is a hot script going around town the producer wants to buy (and so does everyone else, so they are in a hurry here), and whomever they need to get approval from at the studio just happens to be visiting Aunt Mary in Georgia and can't approve the studio buying the script for the producer. Oh no! Now the producer is going to lose out on the hot property everyone in town wants because they can't bid on it with the studio's money. Except, they can. That's what the discretionary fund is for. They are pretty damn sure the studio wants this project just like everyone else in town, they are pretty damn sure they will get reimbursed whatever they drop on it out of the emergency fund, and they don't want to lose it just because someone is visiting Aunt Mary in Georgia. So they jump. And use the emergency money to do it.

The only other times I know of that producers use discretionary funds are when a producer finds a new writer and wants to work with that writer and cuts the writer a small check, either for existing material, or for "future material to be named at another time," so the writer won't starve between now and putting something together they can sell a studio. (In other words, they are using small portions of the fund to keep their discovery alive until they can groom the discovery and go after big bucks.) Or when a producer is unhappy at a studio, the studio is not making anything the producer wants to make, or approving anything the producer wants to make, and the producer is getting ready to go to another studio where maybe the studio will approve some of the producer's projects. Then producers will sometimes use discretionary funds to pick up projects they know the studio is going to turn down, but that they can take to other studios and set up. That last one is kind of crafty and not very many people will tell you they are doing it, and more often, to keep things ethical, they just won't go near material they want until after they have moved, and then they will use the new studio's money to buy the material.

As far as producers wanting to send scripts around, well, if it's a good producer, this is a good thing. Because that is how you are going to get your material in to the buyer, the studio. You need to know where the producer is sending stuff. You need to keep a list. A good producer will tell you, too, just where material went. You may not always have enough knowledge to know whether the producer's choices were good, but you will have a list of where the material went. You will need that later, if nothing pans out and you end up talking to another producer down the line about the same material. The next producer does not want to walk a script in somewhere, only to be told people already read and passed on that script with another producer. That makes the second producer feel dumb in front of fellow professionals and you don't want to make someone who is on your side feel dumb. So keep track.

You do not owe a producer for showing a script around, however. Producers rarely show a script around as a favor. They do it because they think it's a good script and they can maybe make a movie and get paid in the process. That's business. Not friendship. Someday you may be friends. But for now, it's business, and until a producer has put money on the table, a producer is just feeling out the waters, seeing where he or she can go with this. That's great. That's fine. It gets you read. It might get you a deal. But that doesn't mean you owe the producer. Because the producer isn't doing you a favor and hasn't paid you any money. And if someone else comes along with a deal, you will give the first producer notice and the opportunity to respond to that with an offer of his or her own, which is a courtesy he or she has earned by virtue of expressing interest in the material and attempting to set it up. But you are not honor bound to pay homage to some vast commitment the producer has made to the script. The producer tried, but couldn't do it, and this other person could, so now it is time for the first producer to come up with an offer of his or her own, or graciously withdraw and wish you luck. That's business. That's how it works. Don't feel like a bad person for it.

One way to look at it is from the other side of where you sit. Where you sit, if the producer doesn't pull anything off, and someone else does or looks likely to, you will go somewhere else with the script. And from the producer's side, it's the same. He or she will show the script to a few people and keep going if it looks positive, but if the script doesn't move for him or her, or doesn't get a positive enough response for him or her, the producer will not be thinking he or she owes you for showing it around, and will not hand you a check, he or she will simply give back the script and move on. Both sides work this way: "It didn't work out, thanks for trying, it's time to move on." So don't think you're being wrong, or a bad person, in thinking that way. Just do what you need to do.

The other thing you need to know is, sometimes, when a studio or actor or actress or director turns down your script? It is not your script they are turning down. It is the producer who showed them the script they are turning down. It can be a real good script. People can really like it and even want to make it. But if they don't like the producer or want to work with the producer? Well, it takes a long time to make a movie. It sure helps if everyone gets along. And if they don't trust in or have faith in the producer, odds are they will turn the script down. Even if they like it.

There are exceptions. Sometimes someone will want a script so much, they will buy off the old producer. (You always wondered why there were so many producer credits on movies, huh? Well, there are more reasons, but this is one of them.) But sometimes they won't. Sometimes they can't. And sometimes it is just going to be too much trouble, so they pass. If you grant a producer no one wants to work with or has faith in permission to show your script around? Your script, no matter how good it is, can be dead going in the door just because no one wants to work with the person carrying it. Remember that. It's important. It is hard enough convincing people they should believe in and trust a new or untried writer. Don't add to that by giving someone no one wants to work with free reign with your material. This is the person who will represent that material to the buyer, *i.e.* the studio. Make sure he or she is good.

That means, when you are thinking about producers and studios and who buys and who doesn't and who can get material to those people who do buy, you need to be paying attention to who is legitimate.

In general, legitimate Hollywood players don't have to advertise, electronically or otherwise, for material. All they have to do is pick up the phone and call agents, and they'll be flooded with scripts. Keep that in mind the next time you see an ad for scripts in a magazine. People who advertise straight to the writer usually don't have the money to pay for scripts, or they wouldn't be running ads, they would be calling agents.

No doubt, there are people without money to purchase a script or the power to make a movie right now who will someday have both. If they're honest about that, okay. Everyone had to start somewhere. But when someone advertises as a "producer" or "production company" on America Online or in *The Hollywood Scriptwriter* "looking for screenplays," you're usually looking at someone who is trying to establish legitimacy by taking advantage of writers. Usually. Not always. But usually. That means they're lining up writers and making them jump through hoops for free so they can say they have twenty projects they're developing and look like big shots. Which is great for them, they get to look like big shots, but not great for the twenty writers doing free rewrites for someone whose only claim to fame is an ad in *The Hollywood Scriptwriter* or on America Online. Some writers are so desperate for (a) the dream and (b) legitimacy, they'll let quasi producers "option" material for nothing just so the writers can (a) believe they may be on the way to a produced credit here, or (b) say they have an option. Saying you have an option feels good and sometimes makes it look to other writers like you are in the big time now—well, not to other writers who know this scam and that you're really on the road to hell, but at least you can impress friends and family who don't—and 99 percent of the time, it's a rathole.

I mean it. A rathole. So don't go there. If you need to feel good about yourself, get a nice pedicure. Then qualify your readers and/or buyers.

This does not mean refuse to give material to anyone who isn't Steven Spielberg or doesn't have a studio deal set up on a lot. Many producers in this town operate independently and do not have offices on studio lots. They are still producers, still valid industry connections, and are still people who can maneuver your material into a studio sale. And, even when they aren't? Even if you are just talking to a story editor or an assistant, sometimes? These people are still contacts, people who can refer you to an agent, people who can get your material to people who can maneuver your material into a sale, people who you probably should be sending your script to. But do be skeptical of people who have never had a produced credit in their life, who talk maybe a little bigger than is quite believable under the circumstances, who mention just a few too many projects they are "working on developing," and who *advertise for screenplays*. Those people are maybe people who can do you more harm than good. Not always, but often enough that it should make you ask a few more questions than maybe you would be inclined to ask if it was Mr. Spielberg on the phone—questions that need to be asked before you hand over your script, not after.

4 Getting Read

EXCERPTS FROM CONVERSATIONS WITH NOVELISTS #47: "*Well I like Vanessa Redgrave too, I am not sure she would be the studio's first choice for the lead in a science fiction action/adventure movie, though. . . .*"

you wrote a script and now you need someone to read it because, face it, if no one reads it, no one's going to buy it. And if no one buys it, well, no one is going to make it. Which means no movie, and the point of writing a script is usually, you want to make a movie.

So you need someone to read your script. If you are in this business on the inside, you will just pick up the phone and call your good friends Arnold Schwarzenegger and Danny DeVito and presto, the script is read. If you're on the outside trying to get in, it is a little harder than that. You have to convince a stranger, who is bombarded with scripts daily, to read your script. There are three ways to make contact:

1. Cold calling.
2. Letter writing.
3. Faxing.

Which plan of attack you choose should be, always, based on your strengths and weaknesses. If you are good on the phone, you will get somewhere cold calling. If you are not good on the phone? Don't call. Write. If you don't know what you're good at, don't worry, you'll find out quick through trial and error.

Queries to whomever you know is a good gamble for getting your script read. However, if you're starting from ground zero, you don't know anyone. And while it would be great to be sending your scripts to actors and actresses and famous directors, it's a hell of a lot easier and cheaper to track down producers, thanks to *The Hollywood Creative Directory*, and agents, thanks to *The Hollywood Agents and Managers Directory*. So that's where you start. With two types of people:

Agents, because if a good agent signs you, that agent can walk your script in fifty doors and save you the bill getting that script through fifty doors yourself would rack up.

Producers, who are more likely to read a newcomer than agents (agents being huge on referrals to the point of refusing to even read an unknown writer without one) and can either buy (with someone else's money) your script (yay!), or refer you to an agent who can walk your script in fifty doors where someone else might buy it.

"Querying," by definition, means you are "enquiring" whether or not someone would be interested in reading your material. But you have to give someone a reason to read your material. Which means, you have to "pitch" someone, either over the phone, or in a letter or fax. And that's where most people run into trouble. Most people can't "pitch."

5 What a Pitch Is, and Isn't

EXCERPT FROM A PITCH MEETING CONVO #229:
EXECUTIVE: *It sounds great, what tone is it?*
ME: *What opened big last weekend at the box office?*
EXECUTIVE: JURASSIC PARK.
ME: *That is exactly it.* JURASSIC PARK.
EXECUTIVE: *Very funny.*

all pitches are Sales, with a capital S. There are different kinds of pitches. One is a sales pitch for an existing work, a script written on speculation you now want someone to read (and hopefully buy, or, in the case of an agent, help you sell). One is a sales pitch for a story that isn't written yet, you go in and tell people a story you want them to buy, as a project, and pay you to write.

The purpose of both pitches is to sell, and what you're selling is either you, the writer, and the script you've written; or you, the writer, and the story you want a studio to buy and hire you to write. So both pitches are about selling you, the writer; however, even though in both instances you are selling you, *you* are not the subject of either pitch. The story is the subject of the pitch. Always. And this is important to remember.

When you meet someone to pitch, or call someone to pitch, or write a letter to pitch, you do not talk about yourself. You talk about what it is you have written (the spec script) or what it is you want to write (the story you're pitching). This is a cardinal rule. That does not mean skip important criteria such as you have written ten blockbuster movies. If you've written ten blockbuster movies, you tell them that right up front so they will sit up and pay attention to what you have to say, figuring you are probably pretty good and they should be paying attention. But you don't ramble on about your family or your pet or your source of inspiration. See, nobody is interested in you, unless you have something they want to buy. Then they get interested in you. Then they are agog: "Wow, someone who created something I want to buy, who the hell is this person?" But until then, they don't care, they just want to know what it is you are selling and is it worth their time to even read it, or is it more dreck from the mill?

Hollywood people are busy people. Producers. Studio executives. Agents, who won't buy anything, but can sure help you sell. They are all busy people and just don't have time to find out who you are unless you have something they want. Which is not maybe the gracious way to put it, but definitely how it is. They aren't interested in you. They are interested in the material.

The only time this is not the case is when a studio cuts a writer a blind deal. A "blind deal" is a contract to write an as yet unspecified piece of material. Studios will sometimes do this, when they think a writer is up and coming, but they don't have a project they and the writer want to work on. People at the studio are pretty sure, though, if they don't come up with something quick, this writer is going to get snatched up by other people and get real famous and turn "expensive." So a blind deal is a deal a studio makes in advance of finding a project for a writer because it wants to contract the writer for hire while the writer's services are still reasonably inexpensive.

That doesn't happen unless people at a studio think you are an up and comer, however, and they won't think that until you have turned a lot of heads. Meantime you are stuck with the more normal scenario, you are selling you, but the subject of the pitch is not you, it is, in Hollywood speak, "the project."

There are two types of projects you will pitch: the existent project, *i.e.* a script you wrote on speculation and now want to sell; and the nonexistent project, *i.e.* something you haven't written yet, but would like very much for someone to buy and pay you to write.

6 Pitching a Spec Script

From the Files of "Please Engage Brain Before Speaking":
ME *(staring at* VARIETY *article): How can they be making a sequel to that? That was a really bad movie.*
PRODUCER: *I produced that movie.*
ME: *Oh.*

When you write a pitch letter, make a cold call, go into a story meeting, when you do any of these things, you have to be able to tell someone clearly and succinctly, going in, what your story is about. In one to three sentences.

The cool thing about having an existing script is, that's about all you have to do, if they are interested in the short description, there it is, thump, they can read it. But you have to be able to do that initial three line "here is what the story is about" pitch, to get them interested in reading the script in the first place.

Most writers can't do that. Can't condense a story that way. They have to learn. I don't know why this is. I have known good writers who could whip out a script that just zings and is wonderful. But you sit that writer down and say what is your story about? The head banging begins. This is not just with their stories. I've done roundtables where everyone was supposed to come up with one to three line descriptions of blockbuster movies. Movies like *Apollo 13*. Movies in big release. Movies everyone had seen. And people couldn't do it.

Well, I was not so hot at this myself, starting. But I have had a lot of practice. So here is a formula that works. it is not scintillating or brilliant. But it works, condensing story, and if you can't encapsulate your story in two to three sentences, work with it until you can. Go to movies and after the movies, do it. Read books and after you've read them, do it. Magazine articles, plays, songs, everything you see or hear, go home and do it. Because you will never be able to pitch, unless you can do this one thing. Encapsulate a story.

The formula is basic:

(Title) is a (genre) about (protagonist) who must (objective) or else (dire thing that will happen if protagonist fails).

In the case of *Apollo 13*, that breaks down to *Apollo 13* is a drama about three astronauts who must repair their spacecraft or they will suffocate in space before reaching home.

There are a lot of stories going on in *Apollo 13*. People on the ground running around trying to figure out how to fix the craft. People running around on the ground trying to figure out why no one is excited about "just another space mission." And there are a lot of characters. Wives, NASA directors and geniuses, reporters, lots of characters all caught up in the drama. But the primary story is about the astronauts, because the astronauts are the people with the most to lose. If they don't jury-rig that spacecraft, they will die. That is pretty much how it works in stories, your protagonist is almost always the person with the most to lose. So. If you are having trouble figuring out who a story is about? Figure out who has the most to lose. That is a big clue.

The "or else" part is optional. It doesn't always have to be there, but it's good to tag on because it clarifies what is at stake in a story. For example:

Raiders of the Lost Ark is an action/adventure about Indiana Jones, a procurer of lost artifacts who must travel to Egypt and find the Ark of the Covenant before the Nazis unearth it and use it to take over the world.

Nazis taking over the world is pretty big stakes. It could just be, This story is about Indiana Jones, a procurer of artifacts who must travel to Egypt and find the Ark of the Covenant. But you lose something without mentioning that the Nazis are going to take over the world if he doesn't. So, whenever the stakes are high, you put them in.

That formula applies to plot driven movies. There is a second kind of movie that is not plot driven. It is a situational movie, and usually character and situation driven. It still has a plot, but the lines are hazy, the stakes are wholly personal, it is not action driven, and so you have a second formula. Again, it is basic:

(Title) is (genre) about (protagonist) who (inciting incident that creates the situation the story revolves around).

These are the hardest pitches to sell, because they are vague and there are usually no big stakes involved. Romantic comedies that are straight romantic comedies—meaning not crossed genre with something else—usually fall under this category. *Moon-*

struck, which is a pretty good example of a straight romantic comedy, does and would translate to:

Moonstruck is a romantic comedy about a woman who falls in love with her fiancé's brother.

You can't spruce that up or make it more exciting, it is a simple story. A woman falls in love with her fiancé's brother. (Okay, so maybe Nazis won't take over the world, but who says growing old alone in an uncaring world until you die one day trying to get a can of green peas off the shelf isn't important stakes? Um, well, studio people. Never mind.) What makes *Moonstruck* special is, John Patrick Shanley wrote it and the characters and the way the story is told are wonderful. This is one of the reasons it is going to be harder to convince someone they need to read something this simple from you. You aren't John Patrick Shanley. Yet. And this type of story is execution dependent. The story premise is not unusual or sit up and take notice stuff, you have to tell it real damn well to make it special. People are less inclined to believe you can do that, if they aren't familiar with your work, and so less inclined to accept this sort of story from an unknown.

Stories are not always driven by their own genre, however. Genres mix. For example, *Romancing the Stone* is romantic comedy. But it has a story spine from a different genre: action/adventure. Watch:

(Title) is a (genre) about (protagonist) who must (objective) or else (dire thing that will happen if protagonist fails).

Romancing the Stone is a romantic comedy about a romance writer who must deliver a treasure map to her sister's kidnappers in South America, or good-bye Sis.

Sure, it's also about a woman who falls in love with a smuggler, but that is not the plot that drives the movie. The movie is driven by an action/adventure plot. Nifty, huh?

You might ask right about now, How come the sister isn't the protagonist, if she's the one who dies if things go wrong? Well. Because the sister can't do anything about it. That's another big piece of the protagonist equation. The protagonist is the character with the most to lose who can, through action, avert disaster. And if a character can't do that, act to avert disaster, that character is not the protagonist.

Lots of soft plot genres end up driven by an alternative genre's story spine because it is a hell of a lot easier to sell a plot driven movie than it is to sell a situation driven movie. And because it is a hell of a lot easier to drive a plot with action than it is to drive a plot with a situation. Trust me on that, I've tried both. If people are shooting guns, it's easier to move a plot.

You, in order to pitch, have to be able to distinguish between the two types of story, action driven and situation driven. Which comes with practice. An easy rule of thumb, though, is, use the first formula (which is action based) first. If no matter what you do, you can't make it work? Then maybe you have a situational story on your hands and should go for the second formula. It will not be as specific, and it may not even be the right formula, but it will still condense your story. Enough so you will be able to stutter it out on the phone to an impatient person who does not have an hour to hear all the details you crafted into your script.

And always tell someone your genre. Right up front in the first breath. This is entirely necessary so the person you are pitching knows what tone (more on "tone" later) they should be hearing the story in, in their heads. I used *Moonstruck* as an example. Unless you tell people up front *Moonstruck* is a romantic comedy, it will sound like a drama in their heads (a woman falls in love with her fiancé's brother), and they won't have the slightest idea you are talking about a comedy. That is the way comedy works a lot, the premise is not necessarily funny in and of itself, the way you approach that premise is what makes it funny.

So. Genre first. Then who the story is about (protagonist), what that person must do (objective), and what will happen if he or she fails (dire consequences).

Pay attention to that word "must." "Must" is an important word for a writer formulating a pitch. I have sat with writers for hours hammering out one logline. One. That's where the formulas come from. Hour after hour saying, "What must your protagonist do?, What is the objective, why is it necessary?, What will happen if the protagonist fails?" Till I had a frigging mathematical equation in my head to get there. (That is just scary, me doing math, but there it is.)

You can't say, "What does your protagonist do?" Writers with no practice at story condensing trying to tell you what a protagonist does go all over the map. Indy woos a girl, he travels to Egypt, he befriends a nice monkey, he rides a submarine, he teaches history, he outruns a big rock, he does lots, but—

He *must* get the Ark, or the Nazis will use it to take over the world. That's the crux of the story. You won't get that answer, though, unless you use the word "must." And sometimes, you have to think backwards. Ask yourself, What is the worst possible outcome of this story? If everything goes wrong, how will the story end? In *Raiders*, the worst possible outcome is the Nazis get the Ark and use it to take over the world. Then you know what the protagonist must do, get the Ark away from the Nazis to stop the worst possible outcome, Nazis taking over the world.

This seems obvious looking at a blockbuster that has been in release decades. It gets harder when you're dealing with a writer who has just finished a script and it is all layered with subtext and subthemes and subplots and you've never read it and you're trying to drag the crux of the story out of a groggy-from-writing-for-too-many-hours writer. And harder when you're the writer and have just invested a ton of energy creating all those subtexts and subthemes and subplots you don't necessarily want to let go of. And while the coverage people, *i.e.* studio or agency readers, can just sit down and say, "In this story, this is what happens," they (a) have read the script and (b) don't have anything invested in the subplots—and half the time they get it wrong anyway. (They do, I've read coverage, don't even try to tell me they don't.) So. Putting together a pitch for a writer, or as a writer, you have to say, always, what *must* happen? What's worst case scenario here and what is the only way to stop that from happening? That will usually get you a coherent sentence that describes a script's plot.

And that's your pitch.

Even with a stituational plot, like *Moonstruck,* that will work. What is the worst possible outcome of *Moonstruck*? The woman will lose both men. (Lose is always a big issue here, what do people have to lose? Don't say what will someone "do," "do" is just a bad word, say what will someone "lose.") Why? Because she cannot choose between two men. That's what she must do. Choose between two men. Why? Well there are lots of reasons, I mean, she is torn between security and love and all that, but bottom line, in most romantic comedies, a woman would just go for the nice guy with the job and wooden hand she is in love with. Why doesn't she? Because the man with the wooden hand she is in love with is her fiancé's brother. There is your story. She's in love with her fiancé's brother.

And don't get confused by the term "inciting incident." In *Moonstruck*, if we were just talking an inciting incident, it might be the finacé saying, "Hey, invite my brother to the wedding."

But we are not talking just "inciting incident," we are talking "inciting incident *that creates the situation the story revolves around.*" The story is not about a woman inviting her fiancé's brother to the wedding. The story is about a woman who falls in love with her fiancé's brother. That is the inciting incident for the situation the story revolves around, the woman falling in love with her fiancé's bro. And—

That is your pitch.

If people are interested in that, that short description, they will ask questions. That is great. You want people interested and asking questions. Answer the questions. Hell, you've written a whole big script, you know all the answers. This is the easy part. But stick with your pitch, the short pitch, going in. People have to know story premise, just to know what questions to ask. And if you haven't told them the story's premise? Anything you tell them, anything at all, doesn't mean anything because they have no foundation to relate it to. It is just "blah blah blah" with no story. Here is this great characterization, but what must the character do? They don't know, because you haven't told them. Here is this great detail in a scene, but what is it for? They don't know, because you haven't told them. Here are these wonderful emotions explored in the script, but what are they about? They don't know, because you haven't told them. That is like putting icing on a cake that is not there. They have no basis for interpreting anything you tell them, without a story premise to build on. So know your pitch. Use it. Then, if they ask questions, tell them more. But know your pitch. And say it first, going in.

7 Pitching a Concept You Want to Write

Arguments with My Horoscope #9,082:

HOROSCOPE: *This is just the kind of day you'll love.*

ME: *I don't see rain. Do you see rain? It's November. Why isn't it raining?*

HOROSCOPE: *Time for an impromptu party—*

ME: *You didn't get the no surprises thing last time, did you?*

HOROSCOPE: *Probably at your place.*

ME: *No! Not till I get the floors done.*

HOROSCOPE: *You and your friends share one of your silliest moods—*

ME: *Did I mention I'm having a really bad period?*

HOROSCOPE: *And the fun you invent, as always, is original and hilarious.*

ME: *Pepper spray can be amusing.*

When you go in to pitch a project that has not been written, that you want someone to buy and pay you to write, you still have to know the basic pitch. This is a (genre) about (protagonist) who must (objective) or else (what dire thing will happen if the protagonist fails). You have to be able to tell some-one that, going in, so they know what it is you're pitching them and have a bare bones comprehension of the story that is about to unfold they can relate to everything else you say about the story.

Unlike pitching an existing spec, though, if they like the idea, you do not have a nifty script you can just thump on their desk. So you can't just breezily say, "Hey, I'm glad you like the idea, would you like to read it?" You have to make them see the movie in their heads. They have to see it so vividly, they can go in and tell their bosses about it like they just saw a movie. So their bosses can say, "Well gee, that sounds like a great movie, let's pay someone a whole bunch of money to write it."

And that's hard.

I don't believe in doing a vaudeville act. I hear people take in visual aids and props and photos and news clippings and fancy hats—okay, I am big on hats, hats might be okay, wait, what am I saying?—and who knows what else to augment telling the story. But I am just not vaudevillian. I think, you have a story, you tell a story. That's what you do. Or, at any rate, that's what I do. I've sold a couple pitches, so it seems to work. But to sell a pitch, in addition to just "telling the story," or the basic idea of the story, you also have to know, emphatically, what a studio ex-ecutive needs in order to sell a pitch upstairs.

(That is where the studio executive is going with your pitch, by the way: "Upstairs." Once you sell the executive, he or she has to sell it to his or her boss.)

One thing you need to know is "mogul speak vs. writer speak." We'll get to that. But the rest is all about what elements of the story the studio executive has to have to buy a story.

Starting out, it's just like a spec pitch, you tell them what kind of story it is (they won't know unless you tell them) and what it is about. Á la, this is a romantic comedy about a lingerie buyer turned bounty hunter who must hunt down the guy who dumped her in high school. That part, the what it is about part, is a given, in any kind of pitch.

Then, however, you tell them about the main characters. The girl is such and such, brief portrait, the boy is such and such, brief portrait. The same kinds of portraits you paint in a character intro in a script, portraits that are fast and paint a vivid image, that show someone mentally just who characters are. Not physical descriptions. Not she's tall and good looking. Not he's tall and craggy. Those are paper dolls. Character descriptions:

"He doesn't send laundry home to mother, he doesn't wear a watch, and he's been trouble for the weaker sex since the day he was born."

"She's looking for love in a book and discards dating theories like last season's fashions."

"He has scars to prove he's been bad places and lived to not talk about them."

Those are important. Those are something executives can hang onto in their minds and give someone else later. Those fast character portraits. You don't want to go on and on, or it becomes too much detail. So you go fast, "here is the cornerstone of my person here, you can hang everything that comes later on this one aspect of character."

Then you tell them how the story opens, what the central dilemma is, give them three turning points in the second act, and then the conclusion. Then you answer questions.

That went by fast, but is important: how the story opens, what the central dilemma is, three turning points in the second act, and the conclusion. That is, for executives, a trailer. It's how they can see where the story happens, what the problem is, and how that problem plays out into story situations in a concrete way. That is what they can sell upstairs. That is what they need. And that is what they can buy.

You are still telling a story here. Don't just toss that stuff out there. You are supposed to tell a story. But when you are telling the story, those elements have to be there. Or executives can't buy.

And I say three turning points in the second act because you have to have at least three. Not only three. At least three. People walk into pitches with none. None is bad. None won't sell. So have at least three. And a couple more won't hurt you.

Also, a turning point is not merely "something happens." Lots of things happen in stories, but a turning point is, "something happens that changes everything." It's a revelation that puts the story in a whole new light: Luke finds out Darth Vader is his dad. Or a revelation that changes everything from an ability to act perspective: The marines discover they can't use their guns to fight the nice aliens because behind the aliens is a thermonuclear cooler it would be a real bad idea to shoot holes in. Or a physical event that totally changes the direction the story is going in: Nazis take the Ark away from Indy and seal him into a tomb to die. Those are turning points. After they happen, everything is different. And turning points drive story.

So. Opening. Central dilemma. Three turning points. Conclusion. That's what you sell when nothing is on paper. It's all you've got to sell. And without it, you don't sell.

I didn't know that, starting out, and didn't sell some very good projects because I didn't give executives the concrete elements they needed to buy a pitch. I could tell them what type of story it was, what the story was about, who the people were, how events would unfold, how the story would end—but I missed the three concrete turning points, which you have to emphasize in a pitch. For executives, a pitch without that is just some concept weaving along without wheels. A nice concept, maybe, a nice idea, maybe, but not something they can understand as a movie.

And executives won't buy something they can't understand as a movie.

This applies to books, too. It doesn't matter how smart your executive is, if you take a book in and say "I want to turn this into a movie," he or she will not understand how you plan to do this, unless you give him or her an opening, a central dilemma, three turning points, and a conclusion. Executives just don't think that way. They are not writers.

I've had notes on books I wanted to adapt come back from studios that said "The book is driven by internal monologue and we just don't see how that turns into a movie." Well, maybe that whole internal monologue outlines a plot, but you can't say, "Um, the whole plot is laid out in the internal monologue, I am just going to switch that to action." No one you're talking to in a meeting understands how writers do that, unless you're selling to writers. (That'll be the day.)

Instead, you have to take the action described in internal monologue in the book and tell it to the executive as action. The executive will sometimes not know that is what you just did, he or she will just think you are real clever for thinking up this bang up plot. I do not know why this is, it just is the way it is. And you have to be aware of that so you can present an executive a concrete movie description they can put their minds around and sell to someone else.

It is the same with a short story, a play, a cartoon, a comic book, any kind of adaptation. You have to walk in there and give an executive the movie's opening, central dilemma, three turning points, and conclusion. You can go into more. You can go through a movie beat by beat. (You better speed it up if you're doing this and start losing someone.) But those elements, beginning, central dilemma, turning points, and conclusion, have to be in there. Emphasized. Always and forever. Or dollars to donuts, an executive will not see the movie, and you won't sell.

You have to know more, of course. You have to be able to answer questions, after a pitch. Like character motivation and maybe some fun other moments in the as yet unwritten script, and why certain things that you have just told someone come to pass. A little backstory. People who like your pitch are going to be interested and want some detail. It's good when that happens. It means they are investing in your story, getting involved in it. And sometimes questions are good. They make you think about things you haven't thought about before. They can help your story.

Other times, questions can be tedious and dumb. Someone will be asking for too much, they will be asking, basically, for a whole damn script. Which executives just can't have, in a pitch scenario, unless they pay you to write a script. There is no script. It is a pitch. Doy. You can tell people a lot. Why characters do what they do, why they are who they are, why this situation happened that created this turning point in the script, what the big turning points are, how it all comes out in the end, some fun stuff along the way— all of that you can tell someone. But you cannot tell someone word for word how you are going to write each scene description in each scene and what the damn headers are going to be.

In those sorts of meetings, meetings where it becomes obvious someone is just asking questions to be arbitrary or that they do not understand the difference between buying a pitch and buying a spec (um, one is written, one is not, doy), smile pretty and get out. You can't read pages from a script that isn't written yet and that is just how pitches work and anyone with a brain knows that and anyone who doesn't, you don't want to work with anyway so no big loss. You will tell the story to someone else who does.

8 Writer Speak vs. Mogul Speak

CONVERSATIONS WITH WRITERS #98:
WRITER: In this week's rash act, Ryan will scream upsetting
  obscenities and throw baseballs at a 400-pound grizzly bear.
ME: This doesn't have a happy ending, does it?

Writers and "movie makers" speak different languages. If you don't know this, it can get surreal holding a conversation with someone who is using writer terms, but is not a writer, because you are both using the same terms, you are simply using them to mean different things. I'll give you an example:

When writers talk about tone—it is wistful, it is dark, it is suspenseful, it is eerie—writers tend to describe work in terms of an emotion evoked by the piece. They are telling you the flavor of the piece in their heads, in an emotional context.

When a movie maker asks you tone, like an executive or a producer, and this applies to agents too, they mean, "What movie that made a lot of money at the box office is this like?"

If you don't know this, it is going to be hard to sell any pitches, because a studio executive will ask you about tone, and he will want to hear it is *Men in Black* in tone, while you will be saying, "It is suspenseful and fun."

This one miscommunication probably cost me five pitches. They were really good projects, too. I just didn't know what the hell I was doing. An executive would ask me, "What is the tone of the movie?" I would say, "It is dark and wistful and kind of fast paced." The executive would say, "That's great, but can you tell me the tone?" I would say (looking at the executive like he was from Planet Zorg), "Um, sure, it's dark and bittersweet and moves real fast." And the executive would say, "That's great, um, um, well I'll get back to you." And we would both walk out of the meeting wondering what the hell the other person was talking about.

I think this is one reason many writers think studio people are completely stupid and unsane. (Okay, some studio people are completely stupid and unsane, but not all of them.) "Why the hell do they keep asking the same question after I already told them?" Well, because you are speaking a language they don't understand, and vice versa.

The same problem crops up when an executive or producer type asks writers what a story is about. Executives and producers mean, "What is the crux of the plot?" But "What is it about?" means a lot of different things to a writer. "What is it about?" encompasses theme.

Wow, can *theme* get you into trouble. The executive asks a writer what the story is about. The writer says, "Oh, it is about our fear of rejection." The executive looks blank. The writer eyes him. Wow, what a moron, but okay, here goes—and launches into more and more about people's fear of rejection. The executive is eyeing the security button. Hmm.

What the executive needed to know was, the story is about a man who falls in love with a super model. That's what the executive was asking to hear. That's plot stuff. And ultimately, the crux of the plot. What the writer was answering was a theme question. To writers, stories a lot of the time are about theme. To executives, they are not.

Sometimes, when you wax theme oriented answering "what is the story about?" executive and producer types humor you. Oh those wacky, starry eyed writers. It is just endearing the way they carry on. And they see it as passion and they want you to be "passionate," always, about material. But—they can't sell "It is about fear of rejection" upstairs. They can sell "It's about a man who falls in love with a super model." But not "fear of rejection." "Fear of rejection" is intangible, not concrete, that damn "A" word I can never think of. Where is my damn thesaurus? "Abstract." Executives and producers cannot sell an abstract thematic ideal in Hollywood terms, because an abstract thematic ideal does not translate to a trailer in people's heads. No one can see the movie. It just isn't there.

When I got to Hollywood, I stopped even using the term "theme" right after I went to a meeting to talk to three people who assured me they were literature Ph.D.s from Harvard or something (we are all friends here and really smart, ho ho, let's get deep—if they had been cops I could have slapped a lawsuit on them for entrapment), and then when I used the word "theme," glazed over. Then my agent got a call saying they liked me bunches, but thought I was too intellectual for the project. Too intellectual? Jeez!

I didn't use the term "theme" again in a pitch meeting until it turned up as the flavor of the day question. Not too long ago, too. I've been asked about "universal theme" now at three separate pitch meetings (by executives!), so I'm going to guess this is getting asked a lot these days. It's a smart question, I wonder who came up with it before it ran like wildfire through the ranks? At any rate, people are looking for it now. "Universal theme." Wow.

I wouldn't take it too far and open a pitch with "theme," I wouldn't even bring theme up in a meeting, unless we were in the questions section and someone sprang it on me and then sat back to see what I would say. (They get so crafty in those meetings sometimes.) You should know, though. In the back of your head, if you're pitching, know what it is everyone on the planet is struggling with that is somehow touched on in your story. That is "universal theme." Also referred to in literary circles as just plain "theme," but it sounds flashier and more important to executives with "universal" tagged on there.

In one of my stories, the "universal theme" was, everyone is so dependent on formulas and shopping lists these days, everyone is looking for love by the numbers in self-help books instead of in their hearts. (Okay, universal themes always sound cheesy, so shoot me.) In another, it was, everyone is so afraid of failure, we've stopped trying to succeed in order to avoid it.

Everyone is afraid of failure, everyone wants love. Those are universals. Know that stuff about your stories so you can answer the new trick question.

But don't open with it. Just remember the keywords are "universal theme." That's when they want to hear that. Not when they ask "What is the story about?" Whenever they ask "What is the story about?" they are talking about concrete, action and verb driven plot.

And when people ask you questions in studio and production offices, remind yourself this is not a writer you are talking to. This is someone from the business building. They think in concrete substantial terms. Their questions revolve around concrete substantial answers. Tone is "what other movie this is like that made a lot of money." "What your story is about" is plot. Who do you see starring means, not who were you thinking of when you wrote it or who do you really like who you think is talented, but *who made big box office last week who could play it?*

There are myriad examples of "mogul speak" vs. "writer speak." They will change with every story and every meeting. The important thing to remember is, executives want answers in concrete, plot specific terms. And examples that relate directly to box office. Keep that in your head, and you will be okay.

Also, there are catch phrases and terms in Hollywood. The latest one seems to be "edgy." That's a catch all term. People pick those up and use them to turn down projects they don't have good reasons to turn down. "Um, I like it, but it is just not . . . edgy."

One reason for this is, everyone is pretending this is a science and they have reasons, outside of what they like and what they don't like enough, for turning projects down. "Edgy" is today's reason. Tomorrow's may be different. It sounds good, for someone to say, "Oh that's soft, it needs edges." But that doesn't mean anything. Saying, "More people have to die to make my boss think this is hip and will sell" means something. "It needs more edges" does not. It is just an excuse. They don't have a good reason for not making the movie. They just don't really want to. Hey, it happens.

It can also mean, though, that they can't conceive of you being capable of writing something cool and hip like the story you just told them. Sure, you told them the story, but they don't believe you. Why? You look wrong. This is an image oriented town. Movies *are* images. Smoke and magic. And how you look counts. If you hear "edgy" one too many times as a turn down? Look at the material. If there's nothing wrong there, take a glance at the mirror. If what you're wearing would fit in at the next PTA picnic? Go shopping. It can't hurt. It might help.

9 The Pitch Letter

MEEJ MYSTERY QUOTES #12: "The part I like best is the second paragraph: 'My opinions are my own and formed by those women I include as my friends, as well as the Arturlians from Mangus XI in the Alpha Quadrant.'"

if you are just setting out to make all these great contacts and get your foot in the door and get read, you need to write a pitch letter. That is a letter so entrancing and wonderful it convinces someone you've never met they must read your script instead of the fifty other scripts they got pitched today. Don't panic. You're a writer. You just wrote a whole script. You can for sure write a letter.

When you write the letter, the person you're writing needs to know you have a script; you want them to read it; what the script is about; why they should read your script instead of the other fifty scripts they got pitched today. And how to get a hold of you, if he or she decides to read your script.

That last bit means put your name, address, and phone number on the letter. This sounds obvious, but I've interviewed agents who told me they got query letters from people and were interested except, uh, no return address or phone number on the letter. Oops.

If you have stationery with all this stuff already on the sheet, great. If you don't, write your name, address, and phone number at the top of the page. This is a business letter and that is how it's done in business letters. If you have to be different, write it at the bottom of the page. Write it on the side of the page. Write it somewhere, anywhere. On *the letter*. People throw envelopes away. And you want people to be able to contact you and ask for the script. That is why you're writing the letter. Make sure they can do that.

As far as stationery goes? (My editor made me put this in. I think the stationery dilemma is the dumbest dilemma in the world, myself, but he made me do it so here goes.) If you have pretty stationery? Great. Fabulous. Hats off to you. If you don't? Who cares? Look, obsessing about stationery is a way to distract yourself from what is important. And what is important is story. So don't obsess about stationery. No one in this world is going to read your script or make your movie because you have pretty stationery. They just aren't. Stationery doesn't carry that much weight. And no one is going to turn down a great story premise because you sent it in on plain white copy paper. I mean, type it on nice clean paper, sure. And lose the Crayolas. But that aside? The people you are writing care about what matters. Story. So should you.

Pitches, both on the phone and by letter (we'll get to phones later), are part skill, and part numbers. If you're new, you don't know what people are looking for, because, well, you don't know the people. Maybe this guy you're writing will for his entire life make action/adventure movies and you sending him an action/adventure pitch makes perfect sense. Then again, maybe he has made all the action/adventure movies he ever wants to make in his life and has decided to do something new. You don't know, so you play the numbers, meaning the more pitches you send out, the more likely you will hit people who will be interested in your story and read your script.

People starting out quite often address letters to "Dear Agent" or "Dear Producer." Never do this. It is like addressing a letter to "Dear Resident." No one at studios or agencies reads "Dear Resident" letters. Those go straight in the trash. Which means someone (hopefully not you) just spent $33.00 on postage to send out one hundred pitch letters that will never get read. Don't be that someone. Always address a pitch letter to a specific person. That is why you bought directories. They are in the back listed under "Resources for Screenwriters." Use them.

Also, do not address people as Mr. or Mrs. or Miss or Ms. in pitch letters. First of all, that gets you in trouble with women right off. You don't know if they're married or single or a Ms. or the Dalai Lama or what. So Mrs. and Miss and Ms. are just confusing and a waste of time. Then there is gender. I get letters addressed to Mr. Max Adam a lot. I'm a girl. Ask me how well that goes over. At the very least, I know whoever is writing me doesn't know who the hell I am. That's a bad start. So don't assume gender. Don't waste time trying to figure out whether someone is married or Big Foot. Write Dear Chris Columbus and keep going.

Now the letter has your name and address and phone number on it and you have addressed someone specific. Tell them you have a script you want them to read—that is your number one goal here, to tell someone you have a script you want them to read—and what kind of script it is. I don't mean "good." Of course it's good. Mom told you so, right? Mom wouldn't lie. I mean "what kind of script it is." As in genre.

Actually, I'm lying. People have asked me what kind of script I had and I told them "good" and they sometimes laughed and told me to send it. But I did that on the phone, I could feel who

I was talking to, you are writing a letter, it's harder to play fast and loose in a letter. So—

Tell them genre going in. This is important, because if you don't tell them the genre of the material, they won't always be able to tell just from a title and brief story line. (Especially with comedy. No one would know *Moonstruck* was comedy unless you told them up front.)

Dear Big Wig Producer, I would like you to read my script, *Best Adventure in the World,* a feature length action/adventure script about a man who must beat up some real cool aliens to save the world. (Now, if you have them, you put your credits in.) I am a Nobel Prize–winning writer five times over, have a Ph.D. from every film school in the nation, and the President says I can really write a script. (Now you tell them how to get a hold of you.) If you would like to read my script, please contact me at (Your number goes here). Sincerely, (Your name).

That's a query letter. It is straight forward and to the point. It tells someone what you want, what you have, and how to get in touch with you, if they're interested. You can open saying how much you like their work. Flattery never hurts. (Make sure you are talking about their work, though, and not someone else's, or you have an enemy for life.) You can close saying thanks for their time. Being polite never hurts. But in a nutshell, what you just read is the bare bones query letter. It shouldn't be longer than three pages, ever. Technically, it shouldn't be longer than one.

(This is where my editor says, "How can it be three pages? How can it even be more than one page, if they're doing what you say?" My editor is so cute. He thinks people are going to listen and do it right. Make him proud.)

It is hard for writers, who have just poured heart and soul into 120 pages of deathless script full of brilliant characterization and action and visuals and detail and subplots and subthemes, to condense a story down to one or two brief sentences. To even believe they really should. They are so often just convinced, if they put in that one extra detail, hell, those twenty extra details, maybe even thirty, it will make all the difference in the world. But—

All the detail in the world will not convince someone to read your script if they just aren't interested in making a movie in your genre or about your subject. It won't. Really. You just can't convince vegetarian pacifists to make a movie about cattle farmers invading Russia. It's not their thing. And they won't know your genre or your subject, if your story description is so bogged down in scintillating detail, they flat out can't find a simple "this is what the story is about" in there somewhere. Preferably at the top. So be brief. If they want to know more, they will call.

Also, notice your number went in that last line in the letter? Any time you say "Call me direct," it's a good idea to put the phone number right there where you say it, at the bottom of the letter either under your name or in the last sentence. I know this sounds dumb, the phone number is already somewhere else on the letterhead, but it's a good rule of thumb because it means they don't have to look around for it. They can call on impulse. It is right there. It's easy. This is all about making it easy for someone to ask for a script. So make it easy.

Making it easy also means, do not give someone five phone numbers including your office and invalid aunt's and directions as to what time of day on which day of the week they can reach you at which number. Put down your home number and start checking messages. Some of these people call late, and those calls you'll get. If you have a day job, you can call people who call during the day back. You just don't want all that stuff going to an office. Bosses don't like employees spending the boss's time on movie calls. Receptionists make mistakes and you don't want Bob in accounting fielding your script calls. And, if you leave the job, well there goes your contact number. Keep it simple. One simple number someone can dial and get you at—and if you aren't home, they'll leave messages. Really. They will. These are business people who are used to message machines, they know how those work. And if you've got a cutesy kid voice on the machine at home? Take it off. You want a straight forward recording on that machine. Something that says "I'm Bob Smith, take me seriously."

It's considered a courtesy, when you query someone, to include an SASE with your query (Self Addressed Stamped Envelope). This makes it simple for your intended victim to jot you a note and drop it in the mail to you, and it saves the company you're contacting postage on hundreds of queries they receive and maybe don't want to foot the postage or phone bill for responding to. Some people take the SASE one step further and send a self addressed stamped postcard, with boxes for "send the script" and "don't send the script" right on the postcard, so someone can just check a box and drop it in the mail. Both work, as far as SASEs go.

Thoughts on SASEs tend to be mixed. One writer I know flat out refused to send SASEs. His feeling was, if they want the script, they'll call, and if they don't, why pay postage for them to tell you no? He has a point. On the other hand, many smaller agencies and production companies are bombarded by queries and don't want to pop for postage to send you a letter of any kind, including a "send the script" letter. You know if they really really wanted that script, they would call, but people fence sitting, you maybe want to nudge in your direction sometimes. So—

It's a judgment call. How confident are you? And how much postage change have you got? I used to get positively annoyed when I would get a letter back from one of the bigger companies that didn't use my SASE, but instead came on company letterhead in a company envelope with company postage affixed. (They threw away my SASE? That was postage!) And ultimately,

I quit using SASEs. It just wasn't worth it to me to pay for no's.
I was only interested in yes's, and figured, if it was a serious yes?
They'd pay for the phone call to say it. That attitude, however,
might have cost me. And it might cost you. The smaller companies can't all afford to be sanguine about postage and phone bills,
and if they're on the fence, well, they'll fall your way faster with
a SASE enclosed. So think about it. Weigh the options. And decide what's best for you. Or, go the fax route. Which eliminates
the SASE question altogether. And either way?

Include your phone number on every letter.

And when these people call you back? They do not care why
you wrote the script. They do not care about your friends, family, and neighbors. They do not care about your dog Spot, no
matter how cute Spot is. (And I am betting he is pretty cute.)
What they care about and need to know is what the script is
about (the plot, not metaphorical overtones or great thematic
meaning of the cosmos) and why they should read it instead of
one of the other fifty scripts people asked them to read today.

Less is more. Which does not mean turn into a wooden pup-
pet or refuse to answer friendly questions. But let people calling
you ask what they need or would like to know. Don't spew. And
don't get cute. Tell them the ending. People are not generally inclined to read something *just to find out how it ends*. They will more
likely dump your call. So don't withhold information. Tell them
whatever they would like to know. And then write the next letter.

There is a sample letter in the back of the book. It is addressed
to producers, but with a title change it is essentially the same letter you send agents. Good luck.

10 Cold Calling

ANONYMOUS DEVELOPMENT PERSON #648: "Utah? Does that mean I should talk slower?"

everything that applies in the pitch letter applies on the phone: You want them to read your script, the script is such and such genre, here is what the story is about (think plot), these are your credentials, may you send it? *Less is more.*

The difference between just writing someone a letter and talking to someone on the phone is, one, the phone is a lot faster, as far as response times go you will know real fast whether to send or not send; two, you can feel the response you're getting from the person you're talking to and react to that, which helps people who are good talkers convince someone to read a script. Also, I tend to think industry types think it is pretty ballsy of someone to cold call them, and if you can actually speak English and charm them in addition to that, they find it mildly endearing.

There's another big difference, though, between phone queries and letter queries: You can't choke in a letter, that is safe and under your control, but you sure can choke in a phone call, because a phone call is live.

Also, phone calls, while they get you a fast yes or no? Are time consuming. One letter you are going to send a hundred people takes the time it takes to write one letter. A hundred phone calls takes the time it takes to call a hundred people. So. For phone calls to be worth your time, you have to be hell on wheels on the phone or really need a fast yes or no.

This is one of those know your strengths moments. If you are good on the phone? And a phone gets you a lot more yes's than a letter ever will? Go phone. If you choke on the phone, but are real good at letters? Go letter. And if you don't know? Try both. You will find out real quick which one works. For the phone to work at all, though—

You have to get someone on the phone. The person you're trying to reach will be (a) an agent; or (b) a producer.

Cold calling agents: In most cases, the person answering the phone is the receptionist, so ask to speak to your intended victim. You'll be put through to that person's office, where you will either (a) get voice mail, (b) get an assistant, or (c) get the agent. This depends on time of day, who's in, and the size of the agency.

No matter who you're talking to, never say "I'm looking for representation" as an opener. That phrase right there is the kiss of death. Don't ask me why, it just is. Better to ask if the agent is taking on new clients. If you're calling blind, it's a good idea to find out if this person reps what you write. It wouldn't do you a lot of good to pitch a features agent a telescript, because that agent doesn't represent television writers. And sometimes, all the research in the world just won't tell you this stuff, you are out of avenues of information and just finally have to call and ask. So call. And ask. If the person says he/she doesn't rep what you write, ask who at the agency does. If the agent says he/she is not taking on new clients, or won't take a script without a referral, ask if there is a junior agent at the agency who might be willing to read you and/or is looking for new clients/building a client base.

If you don't get through to the agent, ask the assistant these questions. And be nice to assistants. They're tomorrow's agents and today's door to the person you're calling.

If you get voice mail, don't leave a message. Odds are they won't call you back, if they don't know who you are, and you want a person. (Also, that person will not be thrilled to talk to you later if they know your name because you left fifty annoying messages on their machine.) Call again later, and keep calling, till you get a person. This is if you're hell bent on the phone route.

If the person you're speaking to tells you to try a junior agent at the agency, call back, ask for the junior agent (by name, don't say "Hello, I'd like to speak to the Junior Agent please"), and tell him or her that "so and so told me you might be looking for clients." Just saying the name of the agent or assistant who told you to call this person validates you to some extent, because it means the first person you spoke to maybe didn't think you were a crackpot.

It is also, if you're new to this, a good idea to have your pitch, or an outline of your pitch and/or story, taped by every phone in the house. This way, if you get through to someone and they say, "Tell me what your story's about," you won't go blank and make an ass of yourself. Making phone calls to total strangers is hard. People blank. It's called choking under pressure. Do yourself this favor and if worst comes to worst, you can read your story off that sheet of paper straight into the phone. This is also a good idea, anytime you're querying by letter, because if some-one calls you when you aren't expecting it, you can grab that sheet off whatever phone you answered. (I learned this the hard way the day I climbed out of a shower wet and naked to answer the phone and went blank, talking to an important agent.)

Cold calling producers: Pretty much the same rules apply, calling producers, as apply calling agents. Know who you're calling. Also, with producers, it's good to have some idea what they have produced in the past, so look them up in a directory ahead of time. When you call, you will talk to either the producer, or the producer's assistant, or, at a large company, you want to talk to the story editor or director of development. (The director of development is in charge of the development slate, the story editor is in charge of assessing material before it goes up the ladder for consideration for the development slate, not all companies have both, most will have at least one. Shoot for the top and work your way down.) You will know who these people are at these companies because you are savvy and have a copy of the *Hollywood Creative Directory,* which lists companies and their employees all out for you.

(If by now you are real tired of seeing me drop these directory titles and still have no idea what I am talking about, turn to the Resources section and look them up.)

When you pick up the phone to call a person about a script, you have one goal. To get your script read. That is what you are calling for, to ask this person to read your script. If you get only one thing out of your mouth on the phone, it should be "I want you to read my script." Always have that in your head, that you want this person to read your script, that you are asking them to read your script. This sounds simple. It is. But in the heat of the moment, people forget. Don't you forget.

From the callee's perspective, there is only one reason industry professionals such as themselves should read your script:

because you can write and it is a good script. Anything that might suggest this? Professional writing credits (I do not mean your letter to the editor was published in *Guns & Ammo*, I mean you got paid to write something that appeared in a professional publication), any writing awards, any educational background, anything that might suggest you are qualified to write a script and it might just possibly be good and they could be making a mistake not reading you, you tell them. It will help. If you don't have any credits? Skip over that little fact, concentrate on story, and work on getting a few in the meantime.

And bear in mind, confidence counts. I called an agent a very long time ago. I was tired. I had made a lot of calls. Half the places I had called were no longer in business (I had a bad and old list). Half of what was left didn't even rep features. It was late (which is why I got the agent and not her assistant). I got this agent and asked if she repped features (I was learning). And she said yes. I asked if she was taking on new clients. And she snorted and said only if they were as good as Woody Allen.

I was a dumb college student who had written one script and didn't know much about writing and sure as hell hadn't had anything in print or won any awards, and I had a pretty good suspicion I was not as good as Woody Allen. But there was only one good answer, so I gave it to her: I told her I was as good as Woody Allen. She laughed. But she told me to send the script.

So. If all else fails? Bluff.

And when it is taking more courage and confidence than you sometimes think you have to pick up the phone and call one more stranger? (And sometimes it damn well does, cold calling is not fun.) Ask yourself this: What is the best possible outcome, if you call, and what is the worst?

The best is someone will say send the script, they will read it, they will love it, set it up somewhere, make the movie, it will be a blockbuster and you will make millions and millions of dollars as the author of the next *Lethal Weapon* type franchise.

The worst is, they will say no, they're not interested, and not read your script.

Now ask yourself, What is the best possible outcome, if you don't make that call?

The best possible outcome, if you don't make that call, is they won't read the script. Not making the call just got you the worst possible outcome making the call could get you. Make the call.

# 11 Faxing

EXCERPT FROM A PHONE CONVO WITH A PRODUCER #232:
TELEPHONE: *Ring ring.*
ME: *Hello?*
PRODUCER: *Hi, how's it going?*
ME: *Great.*
PRODUCER: *Cool. What page are you on?*
ME: *I don't know, I'm working out of sequence.*
PRODUCER: *Oh, well, cool, keep up the good work. Is there anything you need?*
ME: *Yes. Send dog food and cigarettes.*
PRODUCER: *You're so funny. Call me when the script is finished.*
TELEPHONE: *Click.*

He thought I was kidding?

faxing is just faxing a query letter instead of mailing it. There are a couple of reasons to fax. One is it's fast, it goes right to them, there is not a lot of waiting around, you know, in most cases, within three days if they're going to ask for the script, with faxes.

Another is the SASE (Self Addressed Stamped Envelope) dilemma is totally eliminated in faxes. You can't fax a SASE. Nobody can even call you rude for not trying. It just doesn't work.

You send a fax and it has your number on it and is quick and if they want the script, they can call. That's straight forward and you also don't have to worry about what sort of letterhead to use or should you use fancy paper (don't worry about fancy paper ever, it's not the stationery you use, it's the concept you're selling and how well you write a query that will make the difference in getting read), faxes all show up on the same paper. End of story. Pretty straight forward, yes?

But faxing doesn't work for everyone. I have no idea why, some people just appear to write letters that translate better as faxes than others. So. If you're daring and want to give faxes a try and are not afraid of the phone (faxes can only be responded to by phone and some people have good cause to be afraid of the phone and should keep this on the "correspondence" plane whenever possible—*i.e.* use SASEs), give faxes a shot. If you don't get a good response, try the old fashioned way: the Post Office. If that doesn't work, try cold calling. If none of it works, try a new letter.

In general, a good response rate to any query is 30 percent. And I mean Good, with a capital G. You send out one hundred letters to total strangers and thirty of them ask to read the script, you are a query God. Most people don't get that high. I don't think I've ever seen anyone go higher than 33 percent, though I read in a book somewhere someone's students were getting higher than 50 percent. I think that someone was confused, but I could be wrong. Bottom line, from what I've seen both doing it and watching other people do it? If you're getting a 30 percent yes-send-the-script rate from strangers? You're great. If you're lower than 10 percent? You could stand some improvement.

I'm not kidding about a hundred letters, either. The people I know who broke through from the outside and are solid working professionals in this industry today sent out hundreds of letters. Not one or two. Not fifty. Hundreds. So buckle down.

There is a drawback to faxes. Especially if you have a fax machine at home. Faxes are fast. Once they're sent, you can't take them back. And something about their presentation exaggerates mistakes.

In the bad old days, I had a friend who was sending out faxes and getting a hell of a hit rate. This may have something to do with the fact assistants, while real willing to say no to you on the phone, "screening," which is of course their job, are less inclined to toss a piece of paper with their boss's name on it in the trash. Something about the authority of true correspondence sometimes just overrides that. So faxes get through sometimes where calls can't. Because faxes just appear to have the authority of true correspondence and—faxes possess an air of immediacy given only to faxes. Both of which can get a fax past an assistant who might happily otherwise hang up on your call and trash your letter. That's my theory, anyway.

And this friend was getting a good hit rate from faxes, and fast. Faster than letters ever get. And faster than phone calls, because calls are time consuming, and faxes aren't, once the fax is written, you send and you're done, no talking your way in. So I thought I would try it. And I sent out six fax queries. This was a new approach, I was half blind from updating the database and too tired to finish it, so I started small, just pulled a few off the top, to see what the hit rate was, and then maybe take it from there. And off went six faxes.

About a week later, I wasn't hearing anything. For faxes that's odd, usually you hear something in under a week. And I and the people I was hanging with were hell on wheels with queries, we

FAXING ■ 57

sent them out, we got responses. I should have gotten at least one out of six. So I pulled out the fax, to see if maybe I could jazz it up . . . when what to my wondering eyes did appear? Not any damn miniature sleigh. A great glaring typo. It was a bad typo, too. It was the kind of typo that could be a typo? Or could be you just didn't know how to conjugate a damn verb.

A typo looks bigger in a fax than it does in a letter. I don't know why. It just does. Maybe it's the onionskin paper.

The only saving grace was, I only sent six of those.

The moral might be, don't spend five hours reading small print before you proof a query. Or don't send large batches of the same query out the same day you write it. Both those work and are pretty good advice. I was lucky. I only sent six. I fixed it and sent out the rest and got a pretty good response rate and sent out lots of scripts. But I am still appalled at the thought I would have sent a hundred of those out, if I hadn't been too tired to finish the database that night. It is grace of God stuff I didn't. So be careful with faxes. Don't send a fax the first day you write it. Sleep on it. Then look at it. If it is okay? Then fax it. But not before. 'Cause mistakes are glaring in faxes. I didn't get an answer from a single one of those first six companies. Not one. Which for me by then didn't happen—unless there was a six-foot typo in the middle of the fax.

12 Happy Birthday, Read My Script

FROGS DON'T DO THIS #342: Wow. You are so hospitable. Do you put mints on the pillow, too?

People want to get read and think up a lot of ways to do it. One way is trading on friendships and associations. If you write to a USC alumni, it doesn't hurt to say you went to USC. If you went to high school with someone, well that works too. Everything I'm telling you in here will say over and over again get read, get read, get read. That is your goal, to get read, always and forever. You want to breathe it, eat it, drink it, sleep it, live it: "Getting read." But I knew someone who went to high school with someone who got important, lost touch for a couple decades (I said decades, there), then saw in some magazine that the important one's birthday was coming up, and decided he was going to send her a birthday card and, in the card, pitch her his script.

Um, don't do this. This is one of the only times I will tell you to not do something to get read. So listen. Don't do this.

Birthdays are personal. People are vulnerable on birthdays.

They are wondering if anyone loves them and is going to re-member their birthday. They are wondering if they will get nice presents. They are wondering about getting older. There's a lot of stuff going on with a birthday. And it's all personal.

Now you send a card with a pitch in it. On this personal day.

It is obvious, because you have not been sending cards every year, but now this person is important you are and you just hap-pen to have a script under your arm doing it, that you are send-ing a card because you want someone to read your script. Have no illusions it's going to look like sending someone this card and looking up their yearbook quote is just an out of the blue "gee I wonder how So-and-So is doing" thing. If it were, there wouldn't be a sales pitch in the envelope.

Let's say I am the recipient of the card. I am feeling vulnera-ble wondering if anyone remembers my birthday and loves me and is maybe going to get me a nice present. I get your card. But is it a card? No. It is a sales pitch. Do I feel loved? No. Did I just get a nice present? No. I am thinking, Christ, the only people who remember my birthday are users who want something from me.

Personally, I don't want someone thinking or feeling that when I pitch a story.

People in positions of power get hit on all the time. By friends. By family. By neighbors. By strangers. Think of it this way. You win the lottery. You are excited and happy. This is pretty wonderful, you just won a lot of money. Then, people start walk-ing up to you on the street, asking to borrow money, strangers start calling, asking you for money, old boyfriends call, guess what?, they need money, every time anyone in your family needs anything, they turn to you—for money.

And then your birthday rolls around and you get this nice card from someone you went to high school with and think,

Wow, that is really sweet, and open it up, and inside it says, "Can I have some money?"

Cut them some slack. For crying out loud. It's their birthday.

If you want to look sincere, send a card. Alone. No pitch. Just say "Happy birthday, been a while, wondered how you were doing." If further contact develops out of just being friendly, great. If not, pitch them another time. Not on their birthday.

The next pitch "disguised as a nice gesture" is the congratulatory note. "Congratulations, read my script." That's nice. Um, would you be congratulating me if you didn't want me to read your script?

People will never know. Not when a nice gesture is accompanied by a sales pitch. Maybe you would have congratulated them, even if you didn't want to sell them something. But trying to sell someone something in the same breath as happy birthday or congratulations reeks of insincerity. And the sales pitch, even if you meant the congratulations well? Will invalidate the congratulations in one breath.

That does not mean you shouldn't send people birthday cards or congratulate them. You should. Just don't pitch them at the same time. Pitch them another time.

And finally, there is the pitch disguised as "asking for advice." One way to gain a little time with, and attention from, busy people is to ask for advice. Advice is easy. People give it away for free. Every day. And often, they are more prone to give you time to help you out if it doesn't entail you asking anything directly of them. Like for a read. And if you do it at their convenience. That means don't back someone into a corner when they are doing something social and fun, on the assumption them having fun isn't important and you can just barge on in. How would you like it, if every time you tried to take a break, someone was shoving work questions in your face? You wouldn't.

Their fun time is not your time. Ask when it would be convenient.

If you ask for advice, however, and the second someone has settled into being comfortable, you use that as an excuse to thrust a script at them? It won't go well. They know they were just set up. They offered to give you time and you took advantage of that and threw a script at them. Now they're stuck fending off the script. Or taking it against their will to be gracious. Guess how fast they want to get out of the room/off the phone/away from you?

Fast. So if you say you'd like advice, that's what any meeting or phone call stemming from the request should be about. Advice. Or the request, in hindsight, looks like a ploy—and not a very advanced one. And not one that will ever get you advice again.

Who Gets Read

Conversations with a Hollywood Six Year Old in a Movie Theater:
Me: What did you think of the movie, Honey?
Six Year Old: I think it's derivative trash.
Me: Yipes.

People pound Hollywood doors every month, every week, every day, every minute, every second—and they all have scripts and they all want to get read. There is not enough time in the day to read all those scripts. So some people get read. And some don't.

Pretty much, it all comes down to, who does someone feel like reading today? Maybe nobody. Maybe they feel like taking a chance. In which case, whoever sounds the best is going to be the one.

You're a producer. Writer A tells you he's a dry cleaner and he has a wonderful script you should look at. Writer B tells you he's a production assistant and he has a wonderful script you should look at. Writer C tells you he's a pharmacist and has (you can't see this coming, right?) a wonderful script you should look at.

Odds are, the production assistant wins. A production assistant has actually maybe read a script. He at least knows what a script is supposed to look like. You can't assume that with the dry cleaner and pharmacist. You can make a hopeful leap of faith with the production assistant. So odds are, he wins.

Story didn't enter that equation. Maybe someone told a better story, and could pull ahead on that alone. But it helps to let someone know you have a clue what it is you're wanting to send them.

This is a real old bio. (My career is over with the printing of this bio, probably, but there it is.) I was working real hard here to let people know I had a clue.

> I'm a reader for Writer's Workshop (formerly American Film Institute's Alumni Writer's Workshop) and I do freelance consulting on the side: one of my clients won the '92 silver medal in the Houston Worldfest screenwriting competition. I've been asked to participate as a reader in the FORUM's ladder project. I've taken screenwriting courses through University of California, Forbes Institute, Robert McKee, and University of Utah (most of the U classes are in production these days). One of my scripts took first place in a national competition, another is doing the Hollywood shuffle, and Dave Trottier of Forbes Institute is using material of mine in his course materials. I'm also a staff interviewer for SCREENWRITE NOW!, a publication of The Freelance Screenwriters FORUM, and I've worked in partnership with the Utah Film Commission as a press liaison for the Sundance Film Festival.

I look at that now and am sort of horrified, but it got me in doors. I was just hammering again and again that I had seen scripts, I knew what they were, I was a better bet than the pharmacist or dry cleaner, that the person I was writing should read me. And read me first.

That is your goal. Get read. And get read first. To do that, it helps to have points, any sort of points, in your favor that will push you ahead of the pack and make you look like maybe a better bet than the pharmacist or dry cleaner. So go out and find something you can do that is going to make you a better candidate to get read and use it to get read. You won't sell a script if you don't get read.

Format

L.A. MOMENTS #792: Taunted and force fed the phone number of Trashy Lingerie by someone to remain nameless, I hesitantly lifted the phone and dialed. (They answer the phone "Trashy!") And asked about the red pinafore in the window.

"Um, pinafore?" asked the guy.

"Red. Plaid. Pleated skirt."

"Oh!" he said, comprehension dawning. "You mean the parochial schoolgirl costume."

(!!!)

format was the hardest thing for me to find out about, when I started writing scripts. Don't laugh. Format and brads. I had no idea what brads were, but every book said I had to use them. (Brads are fastening devices, two flat metal legs attached to a round metal head larger than a standard paper hole punch. You stick the legs through hole punched pages and bend the legs apart and voilá, attached pages.)

Format was hard because no one had time to sit down and explain it to me and I had never seen a script and didn't know where to get one. I was in Orange County, I knew no writers, I was starting from scratch, and I was clueless. So it is a damn good thing I stumbled across this book that explained all about it: *The Complete Guide to Standard Script Formats, Part I: The Screenplay,* by Cole/Haag. It covers all aspects of format, and I mean all, in depth and in easy to understand language; however, unless it has been updated since the last time I saw a copy (which is possible), it has two areas you should ignore.

First, the book tells you to signify sounds and specific view points by writing "we SEE such and such" and "we HEAR such and such." Ignore that. It's outdated. If something makes noise, write a normal sentence and capitalize the sound: "The stereo plays soft MUSIC." (Even capitalizing sound is not something everyone is doing these days.) If something is of interest within the scene, don't write a "We SEE" cue. Write what's happening in the scene—"Tom crosses the room"—and leave it at that.

Second, the book tells you to include whoever (characters) or whatever (a brooch, etc.) the camera is on when the scene opens in the scene header. This is not a good idea. A lot of readers skim scene headers and won't thank you for forcing them to stop and read them. Put people and objects in scene directions, not scene headers.

Cole/Haag is the format bible, get it, read it, use it. And no way can I top Cole/Haag, but I will add a couple things.

Scene continueds at the top and bottom of every page are out of style. Dump them.

A lot of people aren't using continued cues for dialogue that breaks for scene description anymore, either, although you still use continueds for dialogue that breaks across pages.

Please don't use a bunch of camera angles in a script. Look, you are telling a story here. Not playing with an erector set. Just tell your story. And if there is a visual way in which you want it to be seen? Write it in a visual way.

```
INT. BEDROOM — DAY

Carrie's eyelids flutter, snap open.
Snap wider open. Holy shit! She stares
around the room. Empty, barren, all the
furniture gone, who the hell knows
where, just gone —
```

That "scene" just opened on a woman's closed eyes, her startled reaction, then shifted to the room around her. It didn't read "Close Up On A Woman's Eyes" or "Pull Back To Show Room," but that's what it did. On the page and in the head of anyone reading it. It just did it without jerking a reader out of the story with a bunch of camera cues. That is something you want to avoid, jerking a reader out of a story. And something camera cues, no matter how well intended, do. So try to avoid them. Especially if you aren't very familiar with them, because, while camera cues don't read well? Camera cues used incorrectly read less well.

You can cheat margins some, for page length. Some. Don't go tossing an extra inch on all sides to make a script longer, that will look pretty weird, but a quarter inch here and there, no one is going to have a heart attack over.

You will see a lot of variations in scripts you read, some wild variations, but variations are red flags. Signs to a reader you may not know what you're doing. So avoid them. When you are famous and wonderful and everyone wants to hire you, those little variations (and sometimes big variations) will be seen as "eccentric." While you are starting out, they will just be "mistakes." It ain't fair, but it's the way it is, so get Cole/Haag, read it, use it, and try to do a good formatting job.

You have the option of buying a format program. Those can be expensive and I have never used one. I wrote style sheets into a Word program ages ago and they are just as fast for me. But some people swear by format programs, and writing style sheets is hard for someone not versed in computers, almost impossible for someone on an IBM or clone, and you have to know what format is to do that in the first place. So, if you have a little extra cash? Maybe you want to get a format program. It simplifies the process. Even with a format program, though, you still want to get Cole/Haag. All the format programs in the world won't teach you how to use format, they will just make it simpler and easier to use it, once you know how.

There's a sample formatted script page in the Resources section. Good luck.

15 Submissions and Presentation

Scripts are printed in 12-point Courier font on three hole punched paper and secured with brads (two or three, makes no difference—two is a sort of a standard, but no one's going to rip you for using three brads to secure a script, no one that matters). Every written medium, from plays to short stories to novels to screenplays, that is printed for submission, is printed in 12-point Courier font. That is what typewriters used to use and we are all still pretending we use typewriters. Some of us even actually do. Twelve-point Courier is what is on a computer, by the way. On a typewriter, that translates to 10-point Pica font.

Do not use non-proportional font. That is font that changes spacing on the page to fill in the right margin, creating block paragraphs that make business letters look "crisp." Well, business letters are short and scripts and manuscripts are not and it sucks reading non-proportional font for extended periods of time and all editors hate it and all readers hate it and just don't use it or else.

It's not a bad idea to use a stiff cover and back sheet (three hole punched and secured like the rest of the script). First and last pages tend to rip free after heavy handling without cover sheets to protect the script and keep it intact. Cover sheets can be heavyweight paper or clear plastic. Heavyweight paper is the industry standard and plastic is slippery so I would stick with heavyweight bond. This is also known as "card stock cover," and if you go down to your local stationery store, they will show you some so you know what I am talking about if you have never heard of this stuff before. Basically it is stiff paper, stiffer than construction paper, and pretty tough so it holds up to heavy handling.

When you purchase brads, try to find Acco #5, 1¼" brads. They're sturdy and long enough the script won't fall apart the second you open it (holding self-destructing scripts together to read them is annoying), but not so long they'll stab your reader (try not to stab your reader, you want your reader to like you). If you can't find a store that carries them, find a store that will order them. It is an incredible pain to read scripts that fall apart or stab you. And it is not that hard to find good brads. If I could find them in Utah, it's just not that hard. It's a little thing for you to do, but a big thing for your reader. Truly.

The cover (that heavyweight paper we were talking about) is blank, or has the script's title on it, and that is it. You can use a distinctive font for the title on the cover sheet, if you must, but that is the only place you will ever use a distinctive font in a script. Information like your name and contact info goes on the script's title page. Scripts in offices are stacked or shelved and people write the title on the script's spine in magic marker, so having a title on the cover is not going to make much difference, one way or the other, the only person who will see it is the person who takes it off the pile or shelf to read it.

Don't write the script's title on the script's spine yourself. People in offices do that and if you do it, it will look like a recycled script. (We are all pretending we don't need the money here, so the less often it looks like you're sending something used, the better.)

Don't use some sort of permanent ring binding on a script, people can't write the name of your script on the spine if you do that. And don't use those big metal rings playwrights use, this isn't a play, it is a script, and those are a pain for people who aren't used to them and not the easiest thing in the world to stack or shelve.

The cover color is up to you. I wouldn't go with puce myself. But other than that, whatever makes you happy is usually fine. Some agencies have standard covers. CAA was red with a white logo. William Morris is blue. You can use one of these colors in an attempt to mimic an agency, but, um, you aren't fooling anyone so subliminal messages aside, go with what you like and we will all just pray that it is not something too bizarre.

William Morris also prints scripts on double sided pages. Don't do this. They are William Morris. You are not. You do it the old fashioned way, printing one sided pages.

Try not to go crazy on title pages. A title page should have your title, name, and contact info on it. Sometimes it doesn't hurt to put "WGA registered" down in the right bottom corner, just because sometimes you are dealing with paranoid readers who insist on WGA registration before they'll read a submission. (There is a sample title page in "Resources.") Other than that, leave the title page blank—

Unless you are adapting or basing your work on another existing work. Then you would add "adapted from the novel, title,

by So-and-So," or "based on the novel, title, by So-and-So" beneath the script's title and your name. (I am assuming here, if
you are basing a script on a pre-existing work, you are either the
author of that work or have purchased rights from the owner. If
you haven't, go write something else, that's not yours and you
can't sell it.)

The bottom line in presentation is, keep it simple and don't
get so fancy you outsmart yourself. You're not selling stationery
or window design, you are selling story. And the less that dis-
tracts from story, here, the better off you will generally be.

Greg Beal (thanks for letting me use this, Greg), the Program
Coordinator for Nicholl Fellowships in Screenwriting, drew up a
list of "ten things that might make a reader think a little less of
your script before it has been 'cracked' ":

1. Art on the script cover
2. Hard, slick, Acco covers with long metal connectors
3. "Permanently" bound scripts
4. Commercial, "college paper" covers
5. Wimpy brads
6. Long, "dangerous" brads
7. Cut, "dangerous" brads

(Notice how many times "dangerous brads" comes up? I'm betting he's been stabbed by a couple scripts.)

8. Overly thick scripts

(I quit a reading gig once because they sent me a 190 page script
and I thought, Do I really need to read a 190 page script? No. I
would rather quit. And I did. People hate huge scripts. Agents,
producers, readers, other writers, everyone hates huge scripts.)

9. Overly thin scripts
10. The color of the card stock cover just bugs the reader

Okay, number ten is maybe not your fault, how could you know the reader was struck by a powder blue van earlier that morning? But try not to be aberrant.

Bottom line, everything listed there was something that made an impression on someone before they opened the script. Did you get that? Before they opened it. Those are red flags. Odds are you will still get read, even with red flags, but why cover yourself with red flags? Just keep it simple and ship it in.

When you mail the script, put a cover letter on it. The purpose of the cover letter is to remind the person you are sending this script to that they asked you for it. This is because the person who said he or she would read the script does a lot of things in a day and will probably not leap to his or her feet at the sight of your script and cry "Oh here is that script from that nice person who called me from Idaho, I have been waiting for this all week!" I mean, maybe they will, I don't know, but what are the odds?

A cover letter says, "Hi, we spoke Thursday, thanks for requesting my script." That is important, to say right off that the person you're sending the script to asked for it, (1) because the person may need reminding, and (2) if one of those sassy assistants sees right off in a cover letter that his or her boss asked for the script, the sassy assistant is less likely to assume the script is an "unsolicited submission" and toss it. Which some places do, with unsolicited submissions. Toss them, or send them right back to the sender.

Now you name your script and get out of the letter: "My action/adventure, *Best Action Adventure in the World,* is enclosed, I look forward to your response. Sincerely. Your name."

Don't synopsize your script in the cover letter. You want them to read the script, not a synopsis. You can say what you said in the query that got them to ask for the script in the first place, "about a guy who must save the world from real cool aliens or else." Which might remind them why they asked for it.

Please don't tell people what to do with your script when they are done reading it. If you want it back, you include a script-sized SASE with enough postage attached to ship a script back. (It's going to cost you less, printing another script, usually, than it will to pay postage to get used copies back.) If you don't want it back, don't tell people what to do with their trash, that's rude.

Do not send your script "signature required." Many smaller companies have P.O. boxes and someone will have to stand in a Post Office line to pick up anything mailed signature required. How friendly will that person be after standing in line for an hour for a script they are wondering whether they should have asked for in the first place? Also, if you do certified mail, it makes it dumb to call later to find out if the script arrived. You already know it arrived, you have a piece of paper in your hand that says so. Well. That call you make later to find out if the script arrived is a savvy way to remind someone you are waiting on a read without appearing pushy. So don't cost yourself that and don't make people wait in Post Office lines. It puts them in a bad mood and bad moods is not the goal here. Getting read is.

On the outside of the envelope, write in big letters "Requested Material Enclosed." Lots of people in mail rooms are snooty about unsolicited submissions—these guys went to Harvard and their parents are miffed they decided to work in mail rooms in Hollywood instead of taking nice banking jobs with ten figures attached so these guys are stressed—and will ship anything back that doesn't specifically state it is requested. Even if it is requested, if it doesn't say so outside on that envelope (and sometimes even when it does, sigh), you will just get it right back in the mail. So always, always mark submissions "Requested Material Enclosed."

There is one envelope hated by everyone in the industry. Maybe even everyone in the world. It is the padded paper envelope full of weird gray filler that, the second you start to open the envelope, flies all over the room like some sort of weird mutant alien mushroom spore.

Don't use this envelope. People will hate you for it.

Do use Tyvek, which is lightweight and water and tear resistant and, I suspect, probably could withstand nuclear attack. (I have heard one editor say he didn't like Tyvek because it was slippery. I don't care. It costs less to post and cannot be destroyed.) Do use nice manila envelopes. Do use nice manila bubble wrap envelopes. Do use nice cardboard priority mail envelopes provided for free by those nice people at the post office.

Do not use alien spore envelopes.

I use labels. You can print them out from a data sheet and you know post office people can read them no matter how bad your handwriting is. So I think they are nice. But you don't have to have them. You aren't selling calligraphy here, you are selling story. So that is up to you. Write it in, print it in. It doesn't matter. As long as post office people can read the address and deliver the package, the address is doing its job.

Don't overseal envelopes. I have gotten envelopes that were sealed like time capsules. These envelopes were so sealed, I had to get utensils out of tool boxes to dent them—and injured myself opening them. Look, don't do that. First of all, nobody likes you if they have to hunt up power tools to open your package. Second, people get hostile if they sustain injury during the great breach of the manila wrap. This is not a message for alien civilizations post the apocalypse. This is a script. It is your script, sure. That makes it special to you. But all it has to survive is the post office. Not World War III. So take it easy on the tape.

Finally, a word on presenting you. A lot of people send résumés out with scripts. This could be a good thing, I guess, if the résumé says something so spectacular it just wouldn't fit in the query letter that got you the read in the first place or the cover letter you are sending now. But whatever that spectacular thing is, it had better be about writing. Because that is what you're selling here. Writing.

I taught a pitch workshop. Everyone had to send in a writing sample and a lot of people sent résumés with their samples. Everyone got in. I'm not mean. I just want to know who I'm dealing with. But one of those résumés said "massage therapist." Which is when my hair turned white and I jotted a note to me to say something about résumés in this book right now.

Don't send a résumé to Hollywood that says massage therapist on it. No one will take you seriously as a writer if you do this. They may ask you for a massage. They won't take you seriously as a writer. Don't send a résumé that says banker, or butcher, or candle stick maker. You are selling yourself as a writer. Everything you send should say "writer writer writer." Anything that does not say writer? It may have its place, but this is not that place. Take it out of the envelope. Put it in a little drawer. And lock the drawer.

16 Simultaneous Submissions

THE WAY THINGS WORK #42: What guys never seem to understand about women going to the bathroom together is, one of those women has the keys. See, this is the whole thing. One woman goes to the bathroom, and the other women are worried she might be sneaking out the back, and they KNOW she has the keys and if she goes out the window they will be stuck with whoever she just snuck out on (who won't be fun AT ALL, if she doesn't come back). So they follow her pretty quick.

Simultaneous submissions are the norm in Hollywood. This is a given. People coming from publishing, get used to it and stop quaking. You never have to tell anyone in this town you are submitting to other people. They know. They expect it. And the only time you don't submit to other people is when someone has an exclusive option or you have an agreement (not made lightly, either) they have a specific period of time in which to show a script during which you won't show it to other people. Period. The end.

This goes for producers, who know the rules, and double for agents. No agent has the right to demand you sit on your hands waiting on them to read a script. They take too damn long to read newcomers, and they know better with established writers. If you offered to wait, they, being agents, might take you up on it, so don't offer.

The only time you tell someone that someone else has the script is when you've got an offer from one party, and you need an answer from the other in a hurry before you make your decision. Then you tell party A that party B has made an offer. This is a courtesy you give party A that allows A to turn the script around in a hurry and decide whether A would like to make an offer too. And you don't give them a long time. They get twenty-four to forty-eight hours, or a weekend, if it's Friday, and then they are out of there unless they are talking offer. The end.

Studios and large agencies sometimes move slowly. But they can move very fast when they want to, and when they want to is, when someone is about to scoop them on a script.

Once in a while, a tricky situation will develop, where you are talking to one production entity about a possible deal on a script, and another one asks to read it. Well, okay, it's not tricky, but it comes up enough I thought I would say something. People are always in a quandary in this scenario. Are they doing something underhanded, sending out a script when someone else is talking about buying it. Well. No. The key word there is "talking." "Talking about buying it." You do not have a "deal." If you had a deal, they wouldn't be "talking." They would be "buying."

Send the script. Best case scenario, both entities want the script, and the price goes up. Worst case scenario? The deal everyone is "talking about" doesn't happen, and the other person you sent it to doesn't respond to your material. Either way, the more people who are reading and liking your work, the better.

And even if a production company buys your script, if someone else asks to read it? You send it. A script you've written that is no longer for sale is called a "writing sample." "Thanks so much for your interest, we just set that up at such-and-such studio, it's real exciting, would you like to read it as a writing sample?"

# 17 Releases

SAFE RESPONSES TO REALLY STUPID SUGGESTIONS #22: "That's Interesting."

release forms are standardized (sort of) legal forms studios and production houses sometimes ask you to sign when you submit material yourself instead of through a recognized industry representative. They were invented by legal types after too many people sued studios for real or imagined similarities between movies studios/production companies made and material submitted to those same studios and production houses. And they basically say you promise not to sue the studio or production house if such similarities occur because you understand they have a lot of projects in development and there is a good likelihood some of it is similar to your material at least in part if not in full.

I've signed a lot of release forms. They basically suck, but without a signatory representative, when someone asks you to sign one, you do it because you want to get read. The good news is, if someone actually steals your material and you go to court, release forms don't protect the person who stole your material because the understood purpose of a release form is to protect the studio from a nuisance suit, not to allow the studio to steal your material. And that is the knowledge you sign the release form with, and therefore what you are agreeing to.

Nifty, huh?

Release forms only show up when you are asking to submit to a company on your own or through a non-recognized entity—like a non-signatory agency or a law firm nobody wants to acknowledge—instead of through a recognized signatory agency. The company people send the release to you when they request the script, and you submit the script with the release form. You never offer to send a release on your own when querying a company. You only sign a release when and if you're asked to. And then, only if it is an acceptable release form.

There is only one release form I ever refused to sign. Most release forms look scary, but don't mean much. This one, though, had two clauses so bad, I wouldn't do it, so I struck through those clauses, signed it, and sent it in. The company sent my script back and said (in a real snotty way, too), my lawyer had apparently struck the clauses without their agreement and unless I signed the form in its entirety, they wouldn't read the script. So they didn't read the script.

I'm not going to tell you what company it was because I don't want to get sued for saying nasty things about some production company in print and I have to work in this town (um, Scott Bakula's company and I still have a copy so go ahead and sue), but here are the clauses I wouldn't sign (sections excerpted: 5, 9):

> 5. "1 hereby grant to you a non-exclusive right to use any or all protected material for any and all purposes, in perpetuity,

without any obligation to give any credit to me. If you use any of the protected material, you agree to pay me the "reasonable value" (as defined below) of such nonexclusive right to such use of such material, and I agree to accept such sum as payment in full for such use. Because I recognize that determining the monetary value of unsolicited material involves uncertainties and subjective factors as to which reasonable persons may differ, and in order that we both enjoy the benefit of a certain, fair and reasonable determination of value for the said material, I agree that the reasonable value of the protected material shall not exceed the applicable minimum flat-deal compensation for such material set forth in the agreement between you and the Writers Guild of America, Inc. (in effect as of the date of this submission). The "reasonable value," as used herein, shall be determined as of the date of this submission.

9. You and your assignees may assign your rights under this Agreement, in whole or in part, in any manner and to any person, corporation or entity that you shall determine.

Now, that looks like I'd be signing over the material, relinquishing rights to any screen credit, agreeing to accept WGAw minimum (which is not great), if they decided to pay me at all (since when do people negotiate sales prices before they read material?), and they could give the material to their neighbor's cat, if they so choose, sans compensation, agreement, credits, or consent.

Pretty bad, huh? It's dumb, too, once a company buys material, they automatically have the right to sell it or assign it to anyone else they want, including the neighbor's cat, sans your consent, that is just the way it works—but they are supposed to buy it first, not make you sign something that implies they can have it for free unless they feel like cutting you a check for WGA minimum.

But cheer up. That is as bad as it gets. And anyone who asks you to sign something that bad doesn't deserve to read your material, so don't send it to them. I didn't. And most other releases you are asked to sign, even if they don't look great, will not ask you to agree to bad sale terms in advance of them even reading your script, and will not be a license for them to steal your material. So go ahead and sign them and send them in and just tell yourself someday, you are going to be a great big screenwriter and won't have to put up with this crap, but for now, you are getting there and this is just the road to doing that.

If the company doesn't send you a release form and instead asks you to just send one along? (These things used to be so standard, there were print shops in L.A. that sold them by the dozen, and probably still are.) You can just type one up and use that. Assuming you know pretty much what it is supposed to say. If you don't, there is a generic release form I used to use in the Resources section that you can use as a guide, making one up.

18 Coverage

LETTERS TO WRITERS #423: You have to love this guy, he writes longer sentences than Faulkner, which is not only impossible to do, but heroic. Do not skip the footnotes.

Coverage is a report a reader writes on your material after reading it. (Well, let's hope they read it.) Not everyone who tells you they read your script actually did. Often they gave it to a "reader" for "coverage." Then they read the coverage and base their opinion of your material on that.

It is a one sheet that synopsizes your story in one to three sentences, has a small section for additional comments ranging from "This is the dumbest thing I've ever read" to "This writer is brilliant and you should keep an eye on her." The reader then recommends the company pass, consider, or (much more rare) buy the material. And at the bottom of the page there is a grid box that lists characterization, dialogue, structure and story out separately and grades them each from "poor" to "fair" to "excellent." That's the one sheet. Attached to that, there is often a one to five page story synopsis the reader writes up for big wigs so they can skip the script and just get the gist in one quick synopsis. And that is coverage.

Some readers are paid professionals and part of an actual guild. They are good at this, they have a lot of practice, and they are trained professionals. Others are assistants or development people working their way up the ranks, some of whom know story, some of whom don't. And some readers are unpaid interns who know squat about story and should go back to New York before they, um, fuck up any more writers' careers. Okay, not all unpaid interns know squat about story, and some people who are highly paid and are supposed to know a lot about story don't and, um, yes, fuck up writers' careers just fine too—so I don't mean to pick on the interns, I am just making a point. And that is sometimes a reader will be quite good, and sometimes a reader won't. Mileage varies and you are pretty much dependent on luck of the draw. But readers have a purpose. There is no way executives and producers and agents can humanly read every script that comes in over the transom. It can't be done. So they need help. And that help comes in the form of readers. And that means we all have to live with coverage.

Don't panic about coverage. When people look at a script, it gets coverage. Even if an executive reads the material himself or herself, more times than not that executive will still send the script to a reader for a second opinion and voilá, coverage.

That is just the way it is. You can't get around it. So you have to believe in the script. You have to say, It is a good script, and the coverage will be good. That is not always the case, even with a good script, but people have to see it and read it to buy it and make it, and they just won't all read it themselves, so it has to go out there and that means it has to get coverage.

And sometimes the coverage will be positive. And sometimes it will be negative. But either way, coverage is not do or die.

If the execs like the script enough, they will sometimes overlook negative coverage. (My editor boggled and said, "Why would they do that?" Um, because they like the project and want to. This is not a science. People do things for arbitrary reasons.) Likewise, if they don't like a script enough, they have been known to disregard positive coverage. So don't sweat it. The coverage at this point, if they've told you they like it and want to discuss it further, is being done so that (a) they have an educated (let's be optimistic) analysis of the piece as a whole and can make story suggestions to you based on that, and (b) so that they can show it to other people and say, Look here, this script is great, look at how the reader raved about it.

Where I worry about coverage is CAA. CAA coverage is forever. Seriously. This is pretty well known. I have known people who have stolen script coverage out of CAA, literally engineered covert operations to get coverage out of that agency's files, because it just doesn't go away. Ever. I'll give you an example.

After I signed with CAA, I told my agent about *My Back Yard.* That's the script that won the Nicholl Fellowship. A few people think it is a pretty good script. He came back and said it had been covered at the agency. (It had, I had gotten it to Martha Coolidge's agent a year previously. You got that, right? A year previously? I hadn't even known it was getting agency coverage at the time, but that coverage was still on file.) The impression I got from the conversation was, the coverage had not been stellar positive so it was a dead issue. I told him I didn't care what a reader said about the script a year ago, six Academy readers said it was a good script and I would appreciate it if he read it himself. And he did. But I have not forgotten that. CAA coverage lives forever.

It is not the same at studios. Studios do coverage, sure. But it is not forever the way it is at CAA. (Well, at any rate, that is the impression I get.) And sometimes people will tell you not to send a script to a studio because it will get "studio coverage" and "you know all the problems with that." That sounds very ominous, and usually the way it is done is you find some nice producer who loves the script first, so going in to a studio, you already have people on your side making you look good before the script gets read and any coverage at all. Great. But if you have a channel in to a studio? Studios buy scripts. Studios make movies. Think about it. You can't skulk around worrying about coverage more than you are worried about getting the script read by people who might like it and buy it and make it into a movie. That is insane. Send it in. You wrote it. You presumably believe in it. Send it. This is an opportunity to jump the producer's reader, to jump the agent's reader, to quite possibly go straight to an executive and jump his reader, before it even gets coverage. And even if it goes out for coverage first? Maybe it will get positive coverage. Maybe everyone will love it and buy it and make a movie. You have to believe that. Honestly, you really do. Or you shouldn't be in this business.

And if you sign with an agent down the road who wants to go out fresh and avoid past coverage? You change the script's title and send it out again. That's not so hard. Changing a title is easy. So don't worry about coverage. Worry about getting read by people who can either make your movie or help you get read by people who can make your movie.

19 Submission Records

CONVERSATIONS WITH PEOPLE WHO WANT TO SEE YOU FAIL #326:
ANNOYING ONE: So what ever happened to that script that won
   that other contest?
ME: I still have it.
ANNOYING ONE: It didn't sell?
ME: I want to make it myself.
ANNOYING ONE: That means it didn't sell, right?
ME: That means I want to make it myself.
ANNOYING ONE: But it didn't sell, right?
ME: Oh look, there's Cher.
ANNOYING ONE: Where?!

there is an old technique for remembering what you sent
where when and to whom. It's called keeping records.

   You have to do this. It is the only way to keep track of whom
you queried, whom you submitted to, who has responded back,
what the response was, and how long you have been waiting on
a read you maybe need to follow up on.

   You may be real good at record keeping. And you may not.

Either way, you have to have a system. If you have one, great. If you don't, here's my old system:

When you make a query, write down what project you are querying about on an index card. Beside that, write the date. Beneath that, write where you sent it and to whom. Put it in a check file.

Have you seen a check file? It is an envelope-shaped manilla accordian file with pockets for each month. Put your dated index card in it, in the pocket for the month your query is mailed. Put the card on its side, to the right of the pocket. That way, the index card sticks up a little over the top of the pocket and is easy to see right off.

When you get a response, pull out the card and write down the response and the date. Put the card in the pocket for the current month, on its side to the right, if it is a yes, and to the left, if it is a no. And send the script if it is a yes.

After a while, you can see, for each month, how many no's you got on the left, how many queries and submissions are out on the right, and how long ago each spurt of activity took place.

This is not a high-tech system, it is a cardboard check file and index cards. But it is fast. Easy. And allowed me to keep track of scripts, short stories, essays, plays, articles, queries for all of the above, submissions for all of the above, contest submissions, publication submissions, and follow up calls on everything, for a good long time. Because each time you do a follow up call, you pull that card and write down what was said on the card and put it in a new date pocket. And when an index card is filled up? Staple a new one on top of it and keep going. That way you build up a stack of cards that records every interaction you have had with each specific company.

You do simultaneous submissions in Hollywood. So you have a lot of cards for one script. But you only send a company one script at a time. So the card stacks are not for one specific script. They are for one specific production house or studio or agency.

If you query that production house or studio or agency again? It is for one of two reasons. Either you decided you were getting too many negative responses to your last query (which means it wasn't working) and enough time has passed you think you can get away with a new query for the same material to the same places? Or you have new material you want to query the old places with. Maybe they have read you and said no to the last one, but are interested in anything new you write. Maybe they said no, they had something too similar on the books and wouldn't even read the last one. Maybe they just said no, don't send anything, period. But for whatever reason, you like them. And want to try them again. In which case, you staple a new card on there with a new date and query info, and file it in the current month.

I am sure hoping some of this makes sense. It's hard to explain, if you haven't seen a check file. Maybe you should go down to Office Depot and look at one. Then it might fall into place. At any rate—

Looking at the check file, just at the months that have cards on the right, you can see immediately that you have stuff on the "sent" side that has not gotten a response in a while—because it's in a pocket two months old—and do follow up in any down time you have to spend on marketing. And you can see immediately that you have one huge month of no's right there. Which maybe you should consider and do something about. It's all real clear because no's are on the left, queries and submissions are on the right, and in dated accordian pockets.

If you get real advanced, you will also start using different colored cards for different scripts, and you will start printing cards off a database, the way you print addresses when you're doing a hundred people query using a database. But you may want to start small. I did.

And you may want to use some completely different system. Which works too. Hey, cardboard is not for everyone. But use a system. You have to know what you've got out there, whom you talked to, when, and what responses were. Otherwise, you will start making dumb mistakes. Like querying people who already either have the script, read the script, or turned down the read for a real specific reason you should remember. Or, worse, finally finding a producer who wants to take the script around, only you don't have any idea where that script has already been so you can't tell the producer and save him or her the embarrassment of walking it in some place people have already seen it and passed on it.

That's important. So keep submission records. I don't care how, just do.

Most people starting out don't have databases. They write a script and think the first person they contact will read it and buy it and make the movie. But that doesn't happen very often. It does happen. But not very often. So. Eventually. If people keep doing this. They may build a database. I was on script number seven, before I did. Someone who liked technology more probably would have built one sooner. And I was a broke college student and built it from scratch using a nifty book that explained how to do that—on Microsoft Word. On a Macintosh. Which won't translate for anyone on any other kind of computer. Using any other kind of software. So I can't tell you how to build a database. It would be a waste of time.

I can tell you what needs to be in your database.

Producers and agents need to be in your database. Their names, companies they work for, titles, what they have worked on or who they represent, that all should be in there. And you get that from *The Hollywood Creative Directory* and the *Agents and Managers Directory*. And you have to update this database. A lot. Because people in Hollywood change jobs a lot. That is why those directories come out four times a year. Because people in Hollywood change jobs so often.

So—

If and when you are ready to build a database so you can send one hundred letters to people without hand typing each and every name and address onto each and every letter you are sending each and every time you send a new query—which I did for a very long time, scary, isn't it?—build it according to whatever newfangled machine and software you have. And then. Each time you are about to send out new material? Double check addresses and names. In the directory. But also. Call places to make sure they are at the same address and the person you are about to query still works there. People move that fast in this town. And if they aren't or don't, ask where they went. Sometimes, losing a contact at one company just means gaining one at another. And if your contact is gone, ask who the new story editor or director of development is and add that person to the base.

Making calls will save you a lot of headaches on "return to sender addressee unknown" queries. May move you into new territory at new companies—most people change companies to move up. And can keep you in at old places, if you can make the leap from old story editor and/or director of development to new story editor and/or director of development.

Databases. Who knew?

20 The Cost of Submission

YOU'RE NOT IN KANSAS ANYMORE, TOTO #87: Um, Nick of Time is about a little boy lost in a mall? Either someone didn't do their homework, or that was one hell of a rewrite.

I figured out once what it was costing me to mail each script. At the time I lived somewhere where copies at a shop ran 6 cents per page, making it cheaper for me to run copies off on the printer. That came out to around 3 cents a page. $3.60 per script, if your script is the standard 120 pages long.

You can get priority envelopes from the post office for free, if you aren't addicted to Tyvek (which is water proof, tear proof, and the greatest thing under the sun for mailing if you want to keep what it is you're mailing intact), you can save some there. $3.20 postage to mail the script priority. A little spit and a few incidentals like stationery and you're off at somewhere around $7.00 per script.

If you're sending out one copy per year, that is nothing and we will all toast you in the old age home when you make your first sale. If you query one hundred companies and get a good response rate of 30 percent, you are sending out thirty copies right off the bat, and that is $210.

It depends who you are, if you are a professional with a big salary, that is not a lot of money. If you are a struggling college student with very little income, it is plenty. And doesn't include postage and phone bills you racked up getting thirty companies to say they would read your script. And doesn't include the $96 it's going to cost in SASEs, if you send envelopes along for the scripts' return. (I worked that one out once and decided it was cheaper just to print new scripts. This is because the bigger companies don't use your SASE, they dump it and send stuff back in their envelope on their dime.)

And none of this includes what it costs in man hours, first writing the scripts, then making the calls and writing the letters, and then printing and sending the letters, and then packaging and printing the scripts and shipping them out.

It adds up. But you're dealing with Hollywood. Looking stingy is not exactly the way you want to go. It might look desperate if you said, Well hey I am waiting for a copy of the script to come back because I can't afford to print another one. It might look desperate if you were using fourth class postage. It might look desperate if you did a lot of things. So you send nice new script copies and you pay full postage and you just don't bitch about what it costs to anyone on the phone. Because you really can't afford to look desperate in this business.

On the other hand, you can't afford to foot the bill for shipping scripts to Bozos just to be "nice."

So don't ship scripts to Bozos. If you talk to someone you don't think is a good avenue, well don't tell them you think they are a Bozo. That's not politic and you could be wrong and you just don't want to hurt anyone's feelings. But forget to mail the script. It is that simple. It is costing you, sending scripts. It adds up. You send to ten people who just don't need to read the script, that's $70. Forget to mail a couple scripts, and you will save a few bucks.

Faxing costs, if you have to send stuff back and forth or if you want to fax query and don't have a fax machine. Because you have to pay for it at a copy place. (It costs anyway in phone bills, but it is a lot more at a copy shop.) You can get around this with fax software and a modem. Learn how to use the software and fax via modem. The copy looks real pretty on the other end and it saves time printing out letters and saves paying someone else to fax something for you at a buck a page. (Proof a hard copy of the fax before you send it, though.)

Receiving faxes is something you might want to be able to do, because sometimes people will fax you release forms. Find out the fax number at your local copy shop, talk nice to the owner and say sometimes you will be receiving faxes there, give them your business card so they can contact you, if something comes in. You will pay for the pages, which sort of rankles, paying money for release forms you would rather not have to sign in the first place, but being able to receive faxes is a good option to have.

And when you send a submission? Always send a good copy. That means good print. I don't even know if there are dot matrix printers out there still, but unless econofast is good clean copy, don't use it. I know it's cheaper and faster. Don't use it anyway. It will save you ink and time, but sometimes cost you face.

I once sent a draft copy of a script to a writer friend. Draft copy was the quality of printout I selected when I was still in the process of maybe doing rewrites—it was lighter print and didn't look great, but for drafts, it was okay. And hey, this was just going to a writer for his opinion, right? Draft copy time.

Here's where I got into trouble. My friend thought it was a

great script and sent it to his agent. He also mentioned to me I ought to get myself a better printer, 'cause most people would consider my printer's quality amateurish. Um. Well. No kidding. If I'd known he was going to send it to an agent, I would have printed a better copy. But that's the point. If I'd known.

You never know. With that in mind, when you send a script out anywhere, to anyone, send out a good copy. Period. The end. The only exception to that might be when you send a copy to your mother, but even Mom might surprise you, so do it right every time.

Also, while we are on the subject of expenses, since I have brought them up a few times, you should have business cards. Something nice. Something plain. With your name and a contact phone number on them. You can buy nice plain white business cards in printer-ready sheets at most large office supply stores. They're relatively inexpensive and you just print them as you need them. These are nice to include in correspondence and, if you meet someone, it is just nicer handing over a card than it is scribbling your name on a napkin.

With cards, like with everything else, keep it simple. Do not go berserk. Your name, maybe your address, definitely a contact phone number. You don't need a title. You're independent. And a business card that says "screenwriter" in big fancy letters, coming from someone who's never sold a script, well, I don't want to say it looks dumb, but, uh—less is more.

21 Following Up, Staying in Touch

Notes into the Ether #400: There is nothing more horrifying to me than seeing Mr. Potato Head sing about french fries. And what was the deal with the Little Mermaid encouraging people to eat fish sandwiches?

i f you call offices to check in and make sure a script arrived, you maintain contact with the individual you initially convinced to read the script. Which is a plus. You want these people to remember your name. They are the only people in Hollywood you know, going in.

This is also not a bad tactic, if you are with a fringe agency. A fringe agency is a small agency no one has ever heard of that you sign with because it is a Guild signatory agency. There's a barrier you hit, making submissions to production companies on your own: the "no non-signatory submissions" barrier. To get around this, writers sometimes sign with an agency that does not do a hell of a lot for them other than give them a signatory cover to send a script in under. Which is better, sometimes, than nothing. But if you sign with a fringe agency, well, some of these agencies are fringe agencies for a reason. So you need to make sure, going in, this agency is actually sending out your material. Which means you call the company the script is purportedly being submitted to. That maintains contact for you, a good thing, and lets you know pretty quick whether or not a fringe agency is actually making submissions on your behalf. Something you want to know before, not after, everyone you contacted has forgotten who you are or that you ever sent them a letter or talked to them on the phone, *i.e.* before you have to start all over again from scratch. So give it a week, then call to make sure the script arrived.

You don't want to be pushy or rude about this call. This is not a confrontation. You are just calling to find out if something showed up. "Hi, I'm so and so, I (or my agent) sent a script in last week, I just wanted to make sure you got it." Someone, either the assistant or the person you sent it to, will usually be nice and look to see if your script came in. They keep a list. If the script didn't show up, you want to send another copy. Or, if you have an agent who allegedly submitted the script for you? You now know something important about that agent. Call the agent, tell the agent the script didn't show, check with the company the following week, and if the company still doesn't have the script? Lose the agent.

If the company got the script, you say, "Great, thanks a lot." And get off the phone.

You *can* push your luck. Depending on how frenzied the person on the phone sounds (if they're frenzied, get off the phone), you can ask how soon they think someone will be able to get to the script. They'll either think you are incorrigibly pushy, or tell you.

Once a submission is made and you know it has arrived, you wait. How long depends on your level of patience and how long someone told you it was going to take. When I started out, I was getting some reads that took upwards of six months. (This was always at agencies. Producers never took that long to read a script.) As people got to know me, that time went down, and I've gotten reads that were twenty-four and forty-eight hour turn-arounds. On average, however, I'd figure two to three weeks is a good estimate for an average read time. Then you want to call in to check on the script and see if anyone has read it.

If you wait any longer than three weeks, turnover is so high in this town, it's possible whoever said they'd read the script has changed jobs. Which means you'll have to start over with who-ever took their place and make a new submission because your script is, count on it, lost. If you call any sooner than two weeks, you risk being an annoyance. Which you seriously don't want to be. So wait two to three weeks. But then, definitely, call. At the very least, your call will remind people you're waiting on a read. Sometimes they need reminding. Or you may find out they read it and have just been too busy to get back to you, at which point they will usually give you feedback. It may or may not be good feedback, but it's feedback, so smile, don't argue, listen to what they have to say. Then, if it's no good, toss it. If it is good, use it.

Most of the time, all you are going to get out of a submission is an opinion from the person you submitted to. We'd all like a sale here, but this is a numbers game and unless you are just loved by God, your first submission is not going to result in a sale. But opinions can be good things. For one thing, if ten peo-ple read the script and tell you it's pretty bad, you have a good idea you need to maybe take another swing at the script or maybe take another class. If ten people read it and tell you it's good, well then you know you are on the right track. And, if they like your work, people will usually tell you to send them the next thing you write. Which is a contact and an open door. Which is one less door you have to knock down next time you write a script. And there will be a next time. Unless, again, God loves you way too much to be healthy.

Also, since agencies are much harder to get read at than production houses, a producer who likes your work can be a real asset because producers know agents and can refer you in at an agency. And once you've got a decent agent, it all gets a lot easier. Not easy. But easier.

And don't pay attention to odds. Odds are pointless. You do what you have to do and don't worry about odds. They're against you anyway, there is no point figuring out how much against you. You just keep submitting. And you hope this is "the one" every time you send a script out. And you keep working so you don't get too wrapped up in waiting for responses from specific people. And each time a new door opens, you get happy. Because it is one less bell you will have to ring next time. And maybe, just maybe, you just found the one person in Hollywood who will say yes and make a movie happen for you. It could happen. Keep submitting. And keep following up.

22 Selling Ideas

NOTES INTO THE ETHER #87: *Did you ever notice publishers never print a retraction at the beginning of a book? "The publishers do not necessarily agree with or condone the viewpoints expressed in this book"? People do this with advertisers. In all mediums. Magazines, TV. There it is: "We don't necessarily believe anything we're hearing here." But not with writers. Is that because no one in their right mind would agree with a writer, so they don't even have to say it? I wonder how crazy they really think we all are. . . .*

People get paid a lot of money in Hollywood. That seems to be general knowledge. And is maybe why so many accountants get off the bus here every day. The "million dollar spec sale" has turned heads. And now a lot of people want to work in Hollywood.

Except not everyone wants to work. Some people just want to cash in. These tend to be the people who show up asking, What if they don't want to write the script? What if they just want to sell the idea?

Well. I guess it happens. But it better be a damn good idea.

I mean, there are some pretty smart people in this town, and they are coming up with good ideas every day, it has to be as good as those or better. And if you are more of an idea kind of person than a writing kind of person? Maybe you should be a producer. Producers come up with ideas, then they find writers to flesh out those ideas, then they take the writer to a studio and talk the studio into paying them to produce and the writer to write those ideas. Producers do that. Maybe that's your calling, if you are this great idea person.

But again, it better be a damn good idea.

Sometimes writers sell an idea. The writer pitches it. Of course, when the writer pitches it, it is a bit more than an idea, it is a full fledged story now with characters and a beginning, middle, and end. And those turning points that are so important for making the executives see trailers that aren't really there. Writers can do this because they make this stuff up in their heads. Nifty, huh? And the studio buys the pitch. And pays the writer to write the script. But that only generally happens to writers everyone knows can write a script. And the reason everyone knows the writer can write a script is, the writer has written scripts before. And people have read them. See, that is living proof someone can write a script. They've done it. And people have read it.

For sure, it is unfair, giving jobs to people who have shown you they can do something, instead of to people who are just real sure they can and tell you so. But that is how it works in this town and that is probably not going to change. So here is the deal. If you want to just sell ideas and not write the scripts, be a producer. And if you want to sell ideas and write the scripts? Um, go write some scripts. It's pretty simple. You just sit down at the computer and whip one out. Get cracking.

 Protecting Ideas

GOOD ADVICE NOT TAKEN #53: "Wear Sunscreen."

You cannot copyright an idea. You can copyright the execution of an idea. As in a script. But not the idea itself. Which means anything you want to stamp yours, legally, you have to write. On paper. Then you own, if not the concept, at least the script. Which is as close as you're going to get. And then you can register it and copyright it to your heart's content.

Registering, you do with the Writers Guild.

Copyrighting, you do with the U.S. Copyright Office.

You can also copyright and/or register treatments and outlines. (Treatments and outlines, by the way, are not what you send people, when you are querying them about reading your script. That's a query, a one page letter that merely says—briefly—what the story is about and tells someone how to contact you. A treatment or outline is several pages long and gives story beats and character descriptions and basically outlines the whole story, beginning, middle, and end.) It's not a bad idea to register treatments and outlines, either, if you're working on material in its conceptual stages with other individuals. Basically the rule of thumb there being, never give a producer or executive an outline or treatment on paper unless he or she is paying you for it, but if for some reason you have to break that rule? Register it first or at the same time you hand them that piece of paper.

Everything with screenwriters is verbal, until someone pays you to put something on paper. That is the rule. If you break that rule, protect yourself. Because once something is on paper, it's very easy for someone to photocopy it and hand it to someone else. Like another writer who will get paid to write your story, off your treatment, instead of you. And while producers and executives will ask you (all the time, those crafty dogs), for a brief outline? Just a little something on paper? Maybe a copy of your notes? They heard the story. They know what it is. They are supposed to remember it. That's their job. Those are the rules. And they know that. So don't be belligerent about it, but don't feel bad about saying no.

It's not nuts to be story paranoid. Stories get stolen. I know people who've been burned. I've been burned. I've seen written treatments by one writer peddled to another writer by a producer, and sometimes the rights issues on those stories and treatments are pretty cloudy.

So yes. It happens. People get robbed.

The thing is, you can't sell a story if you don't pitch it/write it/get it read. It's a catch 22. Do you want to sit on your material to protect yourself from theft? In which case you will surely never see the movie. Or do you want to take your chances and try to get a movie made? In which case you are going to have to be brave and send your work to people. Me, I lean towards option number two, myself.

And, on the bright side, producers mostly have better things to do than steal your material, and people will mostly behave in an honorable fashion because they don't need lawsuits. Not always. But mostly. So curb your paranoia, go ahead and register your material, then cross your fingers and send it out.

That's if you've written it. If you've written it and registered it or copyrighted it, you can, to some extent, protect your idea by protecting the execution of that idea.* Which is a *script*. If, however, you haven't written it, you just have an idea that is hugely high concept? And you are brand new and have never been produced? You can't copyright it. Ideas are up for grabs. And very few people are going to pay you to write it, because you have no track record. So I would not take that big concept into a meeting, and I would not take it into a classroom. I would not bounce it off the local bartender down at the pub and I would not bounce it off other writers who maybe have more clout than you and could walk it into a pitch meeting. I would keep my mouth shut till I had written the script. Then register or copyright the execution of that idea, which makes it yours, and go pitch the *script* all over town.

---

*Copyright is considered legal and binding every time you execute words on a page. A more formal copyright can be obtained through the U.S. Copyright Office. Script registration is a service offered by the Writers Guild of America, West, for about $20, which validates a completion date of material, but does not guarantee content or carry the legal ramifications or rights and entitlements of a formal U.S. copyright. Which is way too complicated for this humanities major to fully understand, let alone explain. For more information, contact the U.S. Copyright Office or the Writers Guild of America, West. They are both listed in "Resources."

24 Business Meetings

MOMENTS OF THE SURREAL FROM HOLLYWOOD #267: So, I meet a producer for lunch at this little hole in the wall cantina. The producer is very up on using actors' names to describe a picture, as in, It's Mel Gibson this, it's Mel Gibson that. This is making me amazingly uncomfortable. After about the fourth time he says it's Mel Gibson this, I have to say, Uh, Mel Gibson is sitting at the table right behind you. . . .

there are three primary kinds of meetings. The meet and greet meeting, where you go in and say hello and get to know each other. The you pitch them meeting, where you tell them a story you want them to get behind, back, or buy. And the they pitch you meeting, where they pitch you a story they would like you to write.

If you're new, you are probably not going to get a lot of the third kind of meeting. And if you do? I should probably just say please do not leap out of your chair and yell that this is the stupidest idea you've ever heard in your life. Be gracious. Say it sounds interesting. Go home and laugh it up with your dog. But don't tell anyone to their face something is stupid. It might be their idea and that will hurt their feelings and then they won't bring you their next idea, which might be good. Ideas, after all, are just that, ideas, some are good, some aren't.

Also, with these types of meetings, one of two things is going on. Either these people really like you and you are the only person they are telling this idea to, *i.e.* you get first pass? (Which is the best.) Or they are talking to a whole lot of writers about this idea, waiting to see which one will come back with a story line they want to use. That last one can cost you, because each time you come up with a story line for someone else's idea, you invest time and emotion in it. And you have to come up with a whole pitch here and pitch it back to them. And then, if they like it and want to go with you? You still have to go pitch that to a studio. That's a lot of work. And, if they don't want your take, if they like someone else's take better? (Even if you have first look and are the only writer they are talking to, they may not like your take and just pass and go looking for someone else.) Well, you are out in the cold after investing a lot of story work and emotion in a script you are never going to write.

It's very possible to spend a whole career chasing other people's story ideas, coming up with pitches and story lines that will never be your own because they are based on other people's ideas—and never working on your own because you are spending all your time on other people's. Which makes writers insane. So don't do that. Keep thinking about your own ideas, while you are talking to people about their ideas, and don't chase just anything. Only chase the things you like. Because ultimately, that is the only way it will be worth your time investing yourself in someone else's idea they may or may not ultimately offer you as a project—a project you will then still have to sell to someone at a studio. Even if it is set up at a studio already, you will still have to sell the studio on your take. And the studio may say no, go get another writer, we don't like this take. It happens.

The meet and greet meeting usually comes after someone has read a script of yours and liked it, so they are inclined to like you. This is good. They will either take you to lunch and buy you food (food is nice), or you will set up a meeting at their office and "visit" there.

Lunch meetings are interesting. You can sort of gauge how much a person likes you by the type of restaurant they take you to. Like, um, if it's McDonald's? No offense to McDonald's, but that is not saying a lot about the esteem these people hold you in—unless they are really broke. Then it says more about how they are doing in the business than about how much they like you, they may like you a ton and just not have the bucks. Lunch meetings are always at one o'clock, that is just the designated Hollywood hour for lunch. They last an hour unless you are having such a good time you want to talk more and no one has an important engagement scheduled after.

One important aside note about lunches: Don't order the pasta. It is just too hard to eat most pasta in a delicate way, and you want to be concentrating more on what you and the other person are saying than on just how the hell you are going to get this tricky food into your mouth without disgracing yourself and staining your nice clean T-shirt—a T-shirt you probably need to wear into the next meeting, marinara sauce or no. Also, beware of designer salads, which chefs like to serve in death defying hunks that would daunt guys who scale Kilimanjaro. Ask how the salad comes. If the waiter looks pale, ask to get it sliced up. Or get something easy. I know it sounds stupid, but you will be glad you did this when you see that poor writer at the table next door staring at his or her salad in horror.

And you don't pay. They pay. Those are the rules.

There are only so many lunch slots in the week, though, so most times you will go to someone's office. Someone, usually the assistant, will offer you a soda or coffee. Take it. That is what it is there for and you will need it because you will be talking. A lot. You will usually wait a little, then get ushered into "the office." (You can tell a lot about a person from their office.) Or you will get ushered into a conference room. You will chitchat with the person you're meeting. This is friendly get to know you talk. You can even talk about yourself a little here without getting into trouble. That is what the chitchat is for. Then they will tell you what they do and about the company they work for and what sort of projects they are doing and looking for. You will tell them about what you've written and what you want to write. It will be especially nice if you have common ground or interests outside the office or conference room, because an hour can go by slow if you have nothing in common with a person you want to like— for both of you.

The "you pitch them" meeting starts out pretty much the same. You go in, everyone grabs a soda, you chitchat a little. The difference is everyone knows you are here to tell a story, so when you get done chatting, you tell a story. Meetings last an hour. The pitch should be between ten and twenty minutes. So, chitchat for fifteen, tell a story for ten to twenty, answer questions, shake hands, go home. Simple—

Unless you are crazed with anxiety and nervousness. Look, don't do that to yourself. You don't want to be crazed with anxiety and nervousness in a meeting. There is just no point. For one thing, this meeting is not the make or break moment of your career.

Writers going into meetings who are new at it are often incredibly nervous, thinking, This is it! Pass or fail, this is my entire career riding on this one person's opinion! Well. That is just not the case. You are going to tell a lot of stories, you are going to tell the same story many different times, sometimes well, sometimes not so well, and, ironically, the first person you tell the first story to is probably not going to have any impact on your career whatsoever, because that person will probably be so far down the food chain, well, it just won't matter. Even if they were inclined to say nasty things about you, you are so far down the food chain yourself in the beginning, bad mouthing someone no one's ever heard of won't make them important so they won't do it and you're entirely safe early in your career. Later, maybe you have to worry about that, not now. But—

Writers don't realize this because we are heliocentric, this is so all encompassing within our lives, we forget, people we are meeting have other things to worry about, including, but not limited to, the other five writers they are meeting today. Which is not especially flattering, but the truth.

The people you are meeting are also not gods. They just aren't. When someone new to this walks into a meeting, the people they're meeting often take on the aspect of gods, at least from the perspective of the new writer, because those people look like they hold the keys to heaven. And that causes nervous sink syndrome. Nervous sink is bad. So stop it. Right now. Look at the person across from you as a person, not as a life raft or dog biscuit, and just tell a story you really love, simply and succinctly, and you have a shot at making a pretty good impression and won't steam up all the windows in the office, which will make you very popular at least with the guy who has to service the air-conditioning, if no one else.

There's an expectation studio people walking into meetings have, that the writers they are meeting know what they're doing and can tell a story—and by the time you're doing a lot of meetings, this is generally true. Because you have done it enough times, you just are okay with it. You have to reach this basic understanding, though. It is just not make or break here. It is a pitch. And a pitch is telling someone a story. And you are a story teller. So relax. A story is a basic thing: This is a romantic comedy action adventure about this protagonist who must accomplish this thing because, if they don't, this terrible thing will happen. Here is who it's about. Here is how it opens. Here is the problem. Here are some exciting events resulting from that problem. Here are the big turning points. Here is how it ends. That's a pitch. It's simple, it's clean. Ten minutes in the short version, twenty minutes in the long version. And you're done.

The main problem writers who can't summarize a story have is, they are ensnared in detail and trivia. I ask a writer, What's your story about? The writer starts with Genesis, proceeds through the Second World War, and at some point after that, starts explaining to me who the protagonist is, except wait, this is not the protagonist at all, this is instead a cab driver who's going to pick up the protagonist—and all the time I'm sitting there asking, Uh, could we cut to the chase, as in, what is your story about? And they aren't telling me. They are telling me everything else but what the story is about.

Well, that doesn't work. Not in a meeting. People's eyes will glaze over and they will start wishing they were on the phone doing something important instead of trying to drag a story out of you. I think the initial habit of overtelling a story stems from an attitude along the lines of, This person I'm talking to can't possibly understand what I'm doing unless I explain the Bible to him/her first. Whereas, in actuality, people in this town hear so many stories, every day, year in year out, you can generally assume they actually do have the ability to follow a story and quite often will jump ahead of you. What they don't have the ability to do, however, is wade through extraneous detail. That confuses them. So lose that and you will do okay.

And, if you miss a story beat along the way? Don't panic. This is story telling here, there is no law saying you will get shot for picking up a story beat later in the telling. Just go back, "Oh and what I didn't tell you earlier is this one thing happened that is important now because this new thing happens because of it," and you are back on track and everyone knows what is happening.

And tell the story to everyone in the room. There will sometimes be several people here. You. The executive. Maybe a junior executive. Maybe a producer who is backing you on the project. Don't ignore anyone here just because you think they are a peon. That's rude and not very smart. Today's peon is tomorrow's studio head.

In most cases things will go just fine. But in some they don't. It happens. The meeting gone bad. There are horror stories about that. I've seen it. It's not pretty. But don't choke. Bluff it out. Keep telling your story. The guy is snoring? Keep talking. (Okay, I am actually inclined to kick anyone who snores during a story of mine, but I am trying to be a good influence here so disregard that.) The phone keeps ringing? Maybe back track a little when they get off the phone so you don't lose the flow and keep going. The person doesn't get your story? Well, then they don't. Be polite. Smile. Shake their hand. Leave. Try not to ask if they are the stupidest person in the world. You can tell your agent that, you can tell your mother that, you can tell your dog that, but you don't really want to say it to the person. It won't make you popular.

And don't get overly excited with casting suggestions. Don't even make casting suggestions unless someone asks you who you see in the lead roles. Which sometimes they will do, at the end of a pitch. If that happens, well it's good, hopefully they are really thinking about this as a movie and mulling over in their head how they would go about making it and that is why they are asking. (Sometimes they just didn't get the characters and are asking for names to get a handle on that, but most times that's not it and you're glad they're thinking "How would I make this a movie?") Only name people who have recently come out in hit movies. These names change monthly, so stay abreast of who is in what recent flick and how well it is doing at the box office. Remember that executives and producers are trying to put a trailer together in their heads that they can sell someone else. A trailer starring someone they can put on a movie poster. A trailer starring a "star." That's what they're asking you for. A made up trailer and made up movie poster to sell an executive, or in the case of an executive, their boss. Give that to them. The same people may or may not be around by the time you get around to making the movie, but that doesn't matter, right now you just want to sell the concept so you can write the movie.

And then, when it is all over? Go home and write. That's what you do. Write. Don't get caught up in the meeting circuit to such an extent you forget that. You're a writer. You write.

25 Guerrilla Meeting Tactics

QUIET DRIVE DOWN RODEO DRIVE? You haven't seen those steely nailed women in their foreign cars, have you?

When scheduling meetings, pay attention to geography:

Burbank = Warner Bros., Disney

Studio City = Universal Studios

L.A. = Paramount, Fox, that strange building that houses Jim Henson Pictures

Culver City = Columbia/TriStar/Sony

Santa Monica = MGM/UA, Beacon, Artisan, a few odd office structures outside the lot system

You can bounce with relative ease between Disney and Warner Bros., even between Disney and Universal. Likewise, you can go from Paramount to Fox in under half an hour. But you cannot easily bounce from Burbank to Santa Monica. That's at least an hour freeway. Clump meetings according to locale, to save driving back and forth. The one exception is Fox to Sony. That's a straight shot down Motor Avenue (an anomaly), which makes it under half an hour.

All of which means, have an HCD (*Hollywood Creative Directory*) and map beside you every time you talk to someone, and confirm with them what lot they're on. Always.

Figure an hour per meeting. Figure fifteen minutes to get past gate guards, find a parking place, and find your building. If you're going from lot to lot, it'll take half an hour between lots, another fifteen to get parked and find yourself, and take advantage of the extra time between (if there's any left, sometimes complications arise) by finding a bathroom.

The easiest, simplest way to do meetings back to back is do them on the same lot, walking from building to building. This is not always easy, some of the lots are big and easy to get lost on; however, if you stick to this plan, you can literally do meetings back to back. Meetings are generally scheduled on the hour. Lunches are all at one. The biggest mistake you can make is going back and forth between Burbank and Santa Monica—traffic can burn you if it decides to go bad (which it does, every day, about three o'clock). When I was coming in from out of town, I'd designate each day a specific locale. Like Monday would be Burbank Day, Tuesday would be Santa Monica Day, Wednesday would be L.A. Day, etc. You get more meetings in that way, because you aren't driving back and forth. And I still do it, like, if I have a meeting in Burbank, I will kick and scream to keep from doing another meeting the same day in Santa Monica.

You start with whomever you speak to first. Say it's someone on the Sony (Columbia/TriStar) lot. They get their pick. Once that day's chosen, you build all Sony meetings around that meeting, and other studios, you give them the choice of other days. Then, once someone in Burbank has picked a day, that's the Burbank Day. You fill in a calendar with everyone hitting close to each other geographically. If you're building a Santa Monica Day and someone in Burbank says they absolutely positively have to have that day, you tell them you're in Santa Monica all day and schedule them late or for dinner. Whatever you do, don't schedule one meeting in Santa Monica at ten, the next at twelve in Burbank, the next at two in Santa Monica. Bouncing back and forth like that will waste serious time and make you psycho.

Also, while here, you want to have (if you don't have one, rent one) a cellular phone. This is so, if you get stuck in traffic, you can call and say you're going to be late, or, if you get lost, you can call someone to talk you in—this is important, because many areas in L.A. are not payphone friendly, and I'm serious here, there are areas in L.A. where getting out of your car means risking your life. So get the cell phone. You can rent a cell phone at just about any rental car place, I think the rental truck places all have them too, and it is worth the investment.

Things you should always have with you in the car: Dollar bills to tip valets with. Quarters (five dollars, minimum) for parking meters. Chapstick, the beverage of your choice (in large quantity), aspirin or its equivalent, sunglasses, a change of clothes (especially fresh socks, I know this sounds bizarre, but changing your socks can give new momentum to the day), business cards, two cans of Fix-a-Flat, breath stuff, deodorant, safety pins, a Thomas Guide and a Los Angeles street map, masking tape, Post-it notes, a pen or pencil, a toothbrush and toothpaste, dental floss, some form of lozenges, hairspray, lipstick. (The lipstick and hairspray are optional for men. Ahem.)

Special travel tips: When you arrive in a new city, regardless of where you are staying, it will make your stay better if you immediately buy yourself two nice pillows. Pillows in hotels suck. Pillows provided by friends vary. It makes a difference, on the road, sleeping on nice pillows. It's expensive. But you're worth it.

You won't necessarily need one, in hotels with wake up call service, but if you're staying with friends? Bring your own alarm clock. It makes life a hell of a lot easier.

If you're staying in hotels? Hotel soap sucks. Bring or buy your own.

Always carry something to snack on. Not necessarily sugar. Sugar can put you over the wall, but trail mix, or peanut M&Ms, which at least contain nuts, and so protein. There are times you will need something to eat, and be on the run, and it's good to have something on hand between meetings so you don't pass out in anyone's office.

When you arrive at a meeting with a couple minutes to spare? Use the bathroom. You are a long time between facilities. You take a complimentary beverage at every meeting. Grab the bathroom before the meeting, not during.

Know whom you're meeting with. Sometimes, meetings can all start to slide one into another, so in the morning, before you start the gauntlet? Or the night before? Make notes for yourself. So, before you get out of the car, or walk in the door, or whatever, you can look at your notes, and say, "Oh yeah, okay, I'm meeting with so and so, who works with so and so, and they've done such and such." Have that, walking in the door, and have it at your fingertips, because you will get tired. And disoriented. I have been between meetings on lots at five o'clock, and been leaning against a wall so tired I wanted to cry. Having that, though, that list, so I could look at it and reorient myself and know whom I was walking in to talk to? Helped. A lot.

The cell phones I rented at car rental places were something like five dollars per day, you got a specified amount of free use every day, and then they charged around a buck a minute. This is a royal pain, if someone just digs putting you on hold. Tell them you are on a cell. Sometimes that will slow them down.

If you bring in an out of state phone, know people here are weird about area codes (like anyone was born in L.A. besides me and David Valdes, who are they trying to kid?) that aren't L.A. or NY based. And a lot less likely to call them. I don't know why. Almost no one has my cell phone number, though. It's not for people to call me. It's for me to call them.

It takes me up to two hours to get to the airport during rush hour. Forty-five minutes to an hour to get to Santa Monica at a non-rush hour time of day. I have traffic demons. Maybe you don't. Keep traffic in mind, anyway, when you're estimating driving times, because, no matter how much God loves you, if you're in L.A., you will, eventually, hit L.A. traffic.

I would not personally want to drive in every day from Ventura, Pasadena, or anywhere else that sounds good on the phone because it is inexpensive, but turns out to be hella far away. You might save five dollars a night on your hotel bill. You will pay for it with freakish amounts of time in L.A. traffic.

Set up as many meetings in advance of a trip as humanly possible. Three weeks notice helps. Airfares are cheaper if you stay over the weekend because businessmen all want to fly home Friday night or Saturday morning. Three meetings a day is reasonable. I've done a week of fives. By Friday I was too tired. Way too tired. Also, know in advance a lot of meetings fall through. People will try to hold your slot, if they know you're coming in from out of town. They can't always do it, though, so schedule business stuff up front and save personal stuff for times that go free because meetings fell through.

Don't worry about telling people what kind of meeting you are going to have. This is not something you tell them. This is something they tell you. Call and say you'll be in town on such and such dates and would love to meet. Don't designate office or lunch, just suggest you meet. They'll pick lunch or the office depending on when they can meet. And what they want to spend on you.

You get a Thomas Guide (the Thomas Guide is used by all limousine and delivery services in the city) because it blows up street images section by section making it possible to find an exact location on a map easily, using indexed street addresses and zip codes. As opposed to the larger fold out city maps which, while indispensable for an overview, suck eggs finding exact locations. You want both. Unless you have some internal bird-type guidance system built in. Then more power to you.

The Los Angeles County Thomas Guide is around $19. That is a small investment to make to ensure you will be on time for meetings because you are not helplessly lost in a (very large and sprawling) strange city. Anyone planning on a career in this business can pretty much count on visiting Los Angeles more than once in their lifetime, so buy one.

Parking in Beverly Hills is 25¢ cents per 15 minutes on the meter, $2.50 to $5 with the valet. Rolls of dimes and quarters are advisable, but not all parking meters take coins smaller than a quarter. Some office buildings do not have building lots, so in those cases you will need those quarters. It is always cheaper to pay the meter/valet than it is to pay the ticket. So. When you are weighing that extra twenty-five cents in your hand? Think fifty dollar ticket and stick the quarter in the meter.

26 Meeting People in General

TRAPPED IN A REST AREA BATHROOM STALL #12: Help!

People do not like to feel used. They want to feel special and like human beings. It's selfish, sure, but that is how people are. Bear that in mind the next time you are eyeing people up who can do something for you professionally. They are not just objects that can do something for you professionally. They are people. Or at least they think so.

I have seen this a lot: A writer is meeting someone for coffee. It is an important someone. The writer wants them to read a script. Hear an idea. What have you. The writer wants something. Usually to get read. And is fretting about the best way to make that happen. Should the writer leave the script in the car? Have it at the table? Have it in their bag? How soon can they give this person the script?

I know writers get anxious to get read, but relax. Drink coffee. Make it decaf. Have the script in your car or your briefcase or your purse or a paper bag, if you must. But don't shove a script in someone's face before they have a chance to sit down, shake your hand, and say hello. I mean, it would be nice if they could remember your face, instead of just a flurry of pages and a thump. You know? The hope is you actually see people you meet as people, not just rungs in a ladder, and will treat them as such. Otherwise, you just might as well mail it.

Technically, mailing a script post lunch or coffee is more tactful and classy, anyway. As opposed to having a script tucked under your chair, just waiting for a moment to flip it out. If they tell you they will read the script, they will not forget that during the two days it takes the post office to get the script to them. And you will look less desperate and more gracious and maybe even enjoy chatting, if you are not consumed with worry over the best possible moment to whip the script out.

And sometimes, the best way to get to people is to stop asking for things. Everyone in this business is constantly asking for something. It is not often someone comes back and is just saying, "Hey, thanks, let me buy you lunch." This will backfire, though, if you offer to buy someone lunch and then throw three scripts on the table before they get a nice glass of ice tea, so try to be sincere about it.

Bottom line, remember to be human. Remember this is not all about shoving story ideas down someone's throat. Sometimes it really is just about keeping acquaintances alive, staying in touch with people you like, and going back to say thanks.

And never ever insult someone's work and then ask them for something. One aspiring writer e-mailed Joe Straczynski, the creator of *Babylon 5*, and informed Mr. Straczynski *Babylon 5* sucked, but this aspiring writer thought he could help Mr. Straczynski out maybe fixing it up.

He was not offered a job on *Babylon 5*.

An indie producer publicly savaged me and my work, then wrote me saying he thought we could do "our" careers a little good working together.

We aren't working together.

An "I'll write the all American novel when I stop talking about it" type approached a friend of mine at a conference and told her her books were drivel. Then he asked her to read his short stories.

She is not reading his stories.

Do you see a pattern here? Insulting someone's work does not make you appear worldly or superior to the person whose work you're insulting. It just hurts their feelings. And they won't give you a job. And they won't work with you. And they won't read your stories. Ever. Because nobody likes to have their feelings hurt.

A better approach is honestly complimenting someone's work. This means maybe you should gravitate toward people whose work you actually admire. That is not a bad idea, you might actually enjoy working for or with someone whose work you admire. And if you admire their work, well, you can be sincere. This is a town seriously lacking in sincerity. We could use more of it.

And if you can't say anything nice at all? There is an old rule about that: Don't say anything at all.

27 The Screenwriter's Uniform

LETTERS TO WRITERS #557: Scoff if you will, but a tiara in the right hands can be a dangerous weapon.

The screenwriter's uniform is (and this is unisex): jeans, high top sneakers, a plain T-shirt, and a loose casual jacket. That is standard, across the board screenwriter attire. For lunches, for dinners, for drinks, for office meetings. Not, maybe, for premieres, but for just about everything else, that is *the uniform*. And the sneakers are always frighteningly clean, as in "they may be sneakers, but by gum they glow like they just came out of the box." (Don't ask. Glowing sneakers is a Hollywood thing.)

Guys? No ties. No suits. I'm not kidding. If you wear a suit and tie to a meeting, people will mock you.

Girls? No dresses. Actresses wear dresses. Screenwriters wear sneakers and jeans.

You can vary on this some. There was a Hawaiian shirt craze for a while and lots of guys wore those. Every once in a while someone wears cowboy boots. That works. Especially if you're from Texas. That makes you "colorful." I cheat and get unusual

French and Italian sneakers. (I was seated at the wrong table in a restaurant once, and the way the producer spotted me was, out of the corner of his eye, he saw my sneakers and said, Good God, those are Max sneakers, and came and got me.) Women can substitute leggings for blue jeans (wear a jacket that covers your butt if you do this). But it is a uniform.

In the industry, everyone has a uniform. The executives wear suits. The actresses wear flowing skirts. The gaffers crease their jeans. And writers wear jackets and jeans and high tops.

If you spend money on your *look,* you want to spend it on a good watch, expensive sunglasses, and a good haircut. Those are the accessories (along with the glowing sneakers) that indicate you are successful and not needy. (That's important. Needy kills in Hollywood.) Though, because you are an eccentric, *i.e.* talent and a "writer," you can go the "interesting" watch route instead of the "expensive" watch route, and people will think that is nifty too. In any event, money here, if you are a writer, is spent on accessories that say you have made it. Not Armani suits.

There are individuals who don't wear the uniform. A woman writer I know wears heels and pearls and dresses nicer than most execs. That's what she's comfortable in and by now everyone knows that's her and if she walked in wearing jeans, they'd call the FBI. But—

If you walk into the room looking like an actress or executive, people are, on a subliminal level, I think, less inclined to perceive you as a writer. Whereas, if you walk in looking like a writer, *i.e.* wearing the clothes that stamp you "writer" in this town, they will. That's important, starting out. To be perceived of as what you set out to be. In this town, perception is a lot. We are a town of images. And if you want to be a writer? I would say, dress like a writer.

Being a writer is great, too. We can sleep till noon, we don't punch time clocks, and we don't dress up for nobody. And we want to keep it that way. Writers worked hard for the privilege. Our predecessors spent harsh hours drinking red wine and sleeping in jackets for that just right look. We go in a little scruffy and eccentric and keep that alive. It's only right. It's tradition. Almost always. Except—

When you go to an *event*. Then you dress up some. Not a lot. But some. And since you are not always sure when something will turn out to be an *event,* it doesn't hurt to carry fashion back up in the car. I'll tell you a story.

I was in L.A. (this was the road trip days) making mad morning phone calls to try to line things up in extra blank calendar spaces before I got out the door. The phone was ringing back at me, things were insane, but I finally dashed out the door later than I should have, to drop scripts and meet people, and then I realized (a bit late, since I was already zooming along in the car) I had this spotlight luncheon thing going at a restaurant called L'Orangerie later that day. Does that sound casual? Not especially. But it was too late to turn around and go back to change, and I was in jeans, and a T-shirt with a beer logo on it, and my Kings hat and tennies. So I asked myself, "Well, how bad could it be?" and kept going.

Pretty bad. When I got to L'Orangerie, there were ten valets parking cars. That was not a good sign.

When I got inside, everyone was *dressed* and the waiters were in tails. I wondered if it could get any worse.

Yes. It could. It did. They were serving champagne. Oh boy. But—

I am a child of the road. Which means I pretty much never leave the house without emergency fashion provisions. In this case, black leggings in my bag and a jacket in the car—a jacket I had to wrest away from valets, when I realized I could be in trouble. So I walked through to the bathroom, stripped off jeans and put on leggings, turned my T-shirt backwards so the logo didn't show, twisted the shirt around my waist for that tailored look, dumped the hat, donned the jacket, and voilá, I could sort of blend.

It is difficult to look comfortable on a hot day in a heated dining room wearing a jacket. But that is a damn sight less difficult than looking comfortable wearing a Gila Monster Beer T-shirt in the middle of a French restaurant. At least for me. And it must have fooled someone. The New Line rep asked for a script.

I was still in the uniform. Leggings, tennies, jacket—it was simply a spruced version of the uniform. And sometimes you'll need that. So carry emergency fashion provisions in the car at all times. The rest of the time, don't sweat it, you look fine.

28 The Dating Metaphor

THINGS TO DO WHEN YOU SHOULD BE WRITING #8: *Bundle all recyclables. In Christmas paper. Make pretty bows.*

hollywood is the largest living dating metaphor on the planet. And in Hollywood, the writer is the girl. That's why writers don't buy lunch or dinner or drinks at meetings. Producers and executives buy lunch and dinner and drinks at meetings. Even the agents buy. Always. Because the writer is the girl. That is why writers do not call producers or executives. We wait for them to call us. Because the writer is the girl. (This is where my editor has a heart attack and says, "Hey, didn't you just tell everyone to pound on doors and make phone calls?" And I say "Yes, but that is starting out, which is a terrible place to be, and the second you can stop doing that, you sit back and quit it immediately, because you are—repeat after me—*the girl.*") And why writers never look desperate, or sit by the phone waiting for it to ring. That is just no way for a girl to appear popular. And if writers don't have dates (read jobs), we lie and say we do. Because the writer is, always, first and foremost in Hollywood. The girl.

That is also, by the way, why writers are treated like second class citizens, artistic morons, and dummies who can't be trusted to handle real business matters, and why writers get the shaft in Hollywood. The writer is the girl. Not to make any sort of feminist statement here or anything, but. Um. Ahem.

Girls don't have it all bad, in this world. We have feminine wiles, which I figure it is every girl's God-given right to use, seeing as we pay a price for that in cosmetic bills. That is what legitimate real life bona-fide girls have going for them when everything else goes to hell. The ability to get someone else to pick up that big heavy refrigerator. And be happy doing it. Hey, I'll take that, if that's the only game in town. Why not?

Guys, on the other hand, don't necessarily know how to "be the girl." That's got to be real interesting, being a guy writer in Hollywood, when most guys are probably being the girl for the first time in their lives. Oh well. Welcome to my world.

Everyone knows the old dating rules. Especially real girls. We break them, but we sure as hell know them. Anyone who was raised by wild apes can go and buy a copy of *The Rules*. Someone was actually kind enough to put them down in print. (The mind boggles.) And all those dating rituals, all those rules of protocol, are in full swing and practice in Hollywood. So read them. And if you are the writer? You are the girl. You remember that, and that the executive/producer/whoever is your date? Things will maybe make a little more sense and you can operate within the system and maybe make it work for you, instead of against you—if you just understand what the system is. And that's the system. I kid you not. A dating metaphor come alive. Yikes.

Oh, and your agent? (Okay, look, any agents reading this, just stop right here, this is for writers, not you, skip ahead to the next chapter or something, you'll like it, it is all about agents—sheesh, nosy!) You don't necessarily want to tell your agent this, but your agent is your mother. Like your classic *Glass Menagerie* mother, who wants her girl to get to dance with all the best boys and have gentlemen callers and be so popular everyone could just die?

That's your agent. And this is your coming out party. Don't say that to his face. Just remember that you are the girl, and all of this might make a little more sense.

29 Agents

agents represent you, your work, and your skills to the working Hollywood community. They send your material to prospective buyers and employers. They set up meetings between you and prospective employers. They negotiate your contracts (read how much you get paid and when). And they collect your checks. Good agents know everyone in town and can get your work and face out there faster than anyone else on the planet, barring a good manager. And if you're on your agent's favorite list, your agent will do his or her best to make you very popular and very employed. Both good things. And agents do all this for 10 percent commission, which means, if you don't get paid, they don't get paid. Also a good thing. All of which means—

A good agent is a good thing to have.

Getting a good agent is the tricky part. There are different places you can look agents up. One is *The Hollywood Agents and Managers Directory.* Which you should have. Go look in "Resources." It is right there. Another is the Writers Guild of America West's list of signatory agents. Which you can ask the WGAw for, and they will send it to you for a couple bucks and a SASE. And you want a signatory agent. That is the only kind of agent you want. However, don't assume, because an agency is on the WGAw signatory list, people at that agency are competent and ethical. Unfortunately, that's just not so. (If anyone at the Guild would like to argue that with me, feel free to call.) The horror stories about certain agencies on that list abound. And inclusion on it does not accomplish anything even resembling insurance an agency is "good."

What Guild signatory status does accomplish, however, is acceptability for submission purposes. Most of the time, studios won't look at scripts submitted by non-signatory agencies. Sometimes they will. But most of the big dogs won't. And even if they will look? Studios that have signed contracts with the Guild are not allowed to negotiate contracts with non-signatory agencies. So. Looking is great. But they can't negotiate a contract with or buy from a non-signatory agent. All of which means. If you want an agent to represent scripts in Hollywood? You must be with a signatory agency.

You do not want personal representation by a guy in London, though. Not even a signatory guy in London. Not if you are trying to sell to Hollywood. A guy in London won't do you any good in Hollywood. He is too far away.

I am using London here as a metaphor for "far away," but I actually knew a screenwriter who was getting read by an agent in London. The idea being, someone thought maybe her script would do well in a foreign market so why didn't this nice foreign agent take a look at it? That's nice. But. Even if it looks like a script would be better off in Europe? (Which is stupid, but that's beside the point.) A big agency could send it to the European packaging department to see about funding it through foreign channels. And you, you want to be represented by someone here. Someone who can benefit all your work, not just one piece, and whom you can phone without paying intercontinental phone rates.

When I say here, I mean California too. While everyone says there are phones and faxes and anyone in any state can represent you? You want representation in California. Period. The end. Los Angeles, California. (That goes double for writers out of state. If you can't be here, your rep better be.) People in Los Angeles know more about what is going on. They go to lunch here, they go to dinner here, they go to the gym here, they go to film openings here, they go to parties here, they talk to people *here*. Every day. In person. Up close and personal. That's an edge. You want that edge on your side.

There are a lot of things going on with a career. One is talent. I mean, you have to be good. But being good is not enough. You have to be read. Because it does not matter how good you are, if you aren't getting read, you aren't going to sell. And agents will help you get read. If they read you. And sign you. And they have their reasons for both. Not all of which have much to do with talent. Some of those reasons have a lot more to do with how easy you are going to be to represent. Why did CAA sign me? I'd had a script sitting at CAA for a year that no one had bothered to read at the time. (No, not *My Back Yard,* another one, I had scripts all the hell over.) But the timing was right—and I had a deal on the table.

No matter how many agents tell you they don't want sullied material? (And they will all tell you this.) Work that has been read by people around the town? That you just shouldn't even be talking to producers, only agents? Because agents want never read before material only? (These are the same agents who only take people on referral, right? Who is going to refer you, if no one can read you but agents who only take people on a referral you don't have because, according to the agents, you can't let anyone else read you?) No matter what agents say, it makes a hell of a difference to an agent, if you walk in with a deal on the table. Which I did, at CAA. That's why CAA signed me. And later, why did William Morris sign me? Well, because I was a steal from CAA and I had a go picture at Columbia Pictures. That sort of stuff just tends to make you popular.

Which brings us to two items: luck and timing. I am awful damn lucky my picture didn't die at Columbia. It could have. And then where would I be? No place good. But it didn't. It was a go picture, it was going to shoot. That made me a better commodity. Is it that easy, for someone who no one's heard of? No. Because it takes a lot of money and effort to launch an unknown. Agencies messenger scripts. It's around $15 a pop to do that. (Bigger agencies have in-house messengers and don't pay a service, but paying someone by the hour also costs.)

Think about that. What it costs an agency to launch an unknown writer. At $15 a read, a lot. And think about the mentality in this town. It is easy to bet on a horse you've seen come through the gate. But if you've never seen that horse run? You're going on guts and instinct with a lot of money on the line, betting on a new writer, and you can't step back and say, "Well, here's justification for my bet, he/she won before."

A lot of agents passed on me, in the early days. Today, I'm sure some of them are sorry. That doesn't matter. What does matter is finding the person who will fight for you. Who believes in your work so much, they will spend $15 per submission. And make a lot of submissions. Because they think that is coming back to them. That's work on your part, finding that person. It isn't all writing. A lot of it is sending letters, making phone calls, beating every odd stumbling block that comes your way, till you cut through that morass of red tape and get read, and then keeping going till you cut through all the "no" readers to the one who says yes. That person is out there for you. But you have to find him or her. And if you aren't repped yet? It's because you haven't found that person—that person who's going to say yes to you. Part of that is luck. You can't effect luck. Part of it is effort. Effort, you can effect. So get out there and get read. Write letters. Make phone calls. Just get read. Not just by agents, either, by producers. Because they are referrals. But right now we're talking agents.

The old trick to calling agents is, call after 5 P.M. The reason this often works is, agents work long hours, and often pick up their own phones after normal business hours are over. (All those people who say no one on the West Coast works hard? I've been on the phone after midnight with my agent. If that isn't working hard, I want to see your time sheet.)

Assistants come in by nine (okay, it might be earlier, but no one calls me before nine on pain of death, so that I wouldn't know). Agents aren't always in that early, they're often doing breakfast meetings or on the car phone between breakfast meetings. First thing in the morning is not the best time to call—especially first thing Monday—because they're usually playing catch up and damage control on everything that went awry yesterday or didn't get taken care of before the weekend that's high priority. Later in the day, when the fires have been put out, is better. They've dealt with a whole lot of people all day they maybe didn't always want to talk to, and will opt out sometimes for easy calls later. You are an easy call. Take advantage of that.

When you get an agent on the phone, do not say you are "looking for representation." That term is the kiss of death. Always, without fail. Don't ask me why, it just is. So don't say that.

Ask if the agent is taking on new clients. If the agent says no, ask if anyone else at the agency is, and then call up that person and say "So-and-So said you might be taking new clients." Using that name tells the new person you're maybe not a crackpot, since someone he or she works with gave you his or her name.

Never say you are a "new writer." That term is just scary to agents. Tell them you are a writer, you're agent hunting and would like to send them a script. And if you're "between agents," never bad mouth the old agent to a prospective new agent. Just say it didn't work out. Otherwise, you have an agent listening to you say bad things about the old agent, wondering if he or she is next.

Unless someone is asking questions, this is not the time to launch into your life story. The more you tell an agent about yourself, the more chances you give yourself to stick your foot in your mouth. Try to keep it simple. You want to know if they're looking for new clients, you have a script you would like to send them. This is what the script is about (briefly). These are your qualifications/professional credits. May you send it? Thanks a bunch, you'll put it in the mail.

Why you wrote the story is not important, unless they ask. Then tell them. What the story is about is important, and they will definitely ask—unless you told them you are a "new writer looking for representation" and they ran screaming from the phone. Writing credits count, college course work, reading experience, publication (not letters to the editor, I mean real published credits someone paid you for) count, so if you've got 'em, flash 'em.

Don't tell an agent your mother, your husband, your wife, your family, neighbors, friends, or college professor like your script. Unless your professor is a big film school professor. Then the professor counts. Don't tell an agent your creative writing classmates think you write in a real "visual" manner. Do tell an agent So-and-So Producer at Such-and-Such Film Company liked the script. Though that, too, could get you into trouble, because if So-and-So liked the script so much, well why didn't So-and-So buy the script? Walk that line carefully. (Personally, whenever someone asks me why someone didn't buy a script, I tell them because that person is a moron. But not everyone will get away with that, you have to say it just right.)

Every agent in town will tell you they don't recommend a script lightly, that because of this, when they send a script out, it gets taken seriously. Um, taste is like a sense of humor. I never met a person who didn't think they had one. So, while on the surface, that sounds good? The only real way to know if an agent is sending out material people consider good is to ask producers. Producers will tell you which agents' clients they read first. And then you'll know.

The first question an agent who likes your material will ask is, "What else have you written?" While you are waiting to find out what an agent thinks, maybe you should write another script so you can tell them.

Never include a synopsis with a script. You don't want people reading a synopsis. You want people reading your script. The only time this doesn't apply is when you had to stick a short synopsis in a release form. Well, then you had to, but never do it on purpose and always make it short.

Also, know some big agencies will ask you to sign a release. This is dumb, but they will do it. Sigh, sign it, and send it.

Never, ever apologize for your material. An agent taught me this back in the modeling days. When you're looking at photos, you don't say, "Well, I'm not too fond of that one, it shows the bump on my nose." Before you point that out, maybe that was this person's favorite photo. After you point it out? They will see "bump" every time they look at it. It works the same with scripts. Don't make apologies or excuses for the genre or story or structure or cover or anything. Act like that script is the greatest thing since sliced bread. I don't care if you are eaten up by self-doubt that would shake Moses' self-esteem. Recite the alphabet, sing Abba tunes, spit on the floor, I don't care what you do, just do something to stop yourself from making derogatory or apologetic comments about your own work. Other people will find many flaws in your work without any help from you. You don't need to point out the ones they might have missed before you got helpful.

Some of the bigger agencies, places like CAA and UTA, have a committee system. One agent cannot autonomously decide to take on a new client, the whole committee has to vote on it, and the consensus to sign the client has to be unanimous.

The downside to the "committee" is, it is harder for a new writer to get on at a place where everyone and Grandma has to like you.

The upside is (at least in theory) once you're in, agents at these places "share" clients, as in everyone at the agency represents you and looks for opportunities for you and pushes your name out there in Studio Land, not just the lone agent who signed you. This is not always how it actually works, but in theory, it is nifty.

Simultaneous submissions are the norm in Hollywood. You don't send to one person and wait, you send to anyone and everyone (well, anyone and everyone professionally viable) who asks to see the material. Sometimes this results in you having a script at more than one agency, and Agent A calls and says they want you while you are still waiting on a response from Agent B.

This can work for you, if you call B and say you just got an offer from A and are wondering if B still wants to play and if so, you need a response. That will in some cases get B to read a little quicker. But B is going to ask who just offered to rep you. And that's where this can really backfire.

See, you can't do this, if an agent in some podunk town in Arkansas just offered to represent you, to get someone at a place like William Morris to read your material faster. It doesn't work that way. The agencies both have to be on some sort of related professional playing field that is recognizable to both parties. Or it doesn't work.

And if you were to call Agent B, who is a big shot agent, and say, "Hey, Agent A, who is a podunk agent, wants to sign me, turn it around in twenty-four hours, Bub, or you are out of luck," well, you have just insulted Agent B and made a real ass out of yourself because you just shouted loud and clear you have absolutely no idea who the players are in this business and who the players aren't.

If, on the other hand, you were to tell someone at William Morris that Endeavor just offered to sign you, that would possibly make people move.

There are stratospheres in the agency hierarchy and you acknowledge them, or you lose whatever bargaining power/credibility you have. You stay in the correct stratosphere, agents will understand this is put up or shut up time and either move in your direction or release you to get on with your business. You imply an agent at an unheard-of out of state agency is a threat to a power player, though, well, you are obviously lost.

This is not to say, if a boutique agency like Warden White were to offer to sign you, you couldn't turn that around to use at one of the big agencies. That you can do, because both places are recognized as professional entities with pros and cons, and a monster like CAA is going to understand that perhaps they could lose out to a Warden White simply because, at WW, a newer writer will get more attention. So that works. And WW is going to understand the stakes just went up in a big way, if CAA just offered to sign you, and will probably respond by reading the material.

The trick is to be in this position in the first place, where one real player has just stepped forward and said "We want you." You have to have that one real offer to make other agencies sit up and take notice, because in Hollywood, everyone wants what someone else wants. It's like a law.

As far as keeping a podunk agency on hold while you wait on an answer from a big agency? Well, it probably won't go so well. I had a script at CAA for a year that no one read, remember? And while you're stalling, the smaller agent is going to figure out you are holding off because you are waiting on someone you like better. (This is like making someone wait on an answer about going to the prom, while you stall to see if the football captain is going to get around to asking you—the guy who asked first will figure out pretty fast you are just stalling him while you wait for the football captain and will not be happy with you.) And meanwhile, um, why did you send to this podunk agent in the first place, if you didn't really want to sign with that agent?

As far as waiting for that better offer goes, I don't believe in waiting on agents. Agents are famous for "this weekend" every weekend till the sky falls. At least when you are new, they are. So get the material out there, don't worry about too many yes's un-less they actually happen. If a nice agency offers to represent you, don't stall, take it. And don't send material to agents you don't actually want to sign with.

Agents will tell you not to send material to other industry professionals until after you have an agent, that agents are not in-terested in material that has been "shopped" because they can't present it to the town as fresh new material.

I have been to conferences. I have watched agents talk. I have read the interviews. They all say they want pristine mater-ial. Something no one else has read. Something they can take out to the town clean. Well—

It sounds good. It really makes sense. If I was an agent, that is exactly the attitude I would have. But here is the problem.

Agents are harder than hell to get read by. I played this game. You write or call an agent, the agent comes back at you, "We don't read anything without a referral."

Um, who is supposed to refer you? If you aren't allowed to send material to anyone who isn't an agent because the material is supposed to be pristine, then who does that leave you? Agents? They won't read you unless you are referred in. And you can't get referred in, because you aren't allowed to send material to any-one who isn't an agent. Nifty system, huh?

When no one had ever heard of me, producers took me to lunch. Bought me dinner. Gave me sodas. Let me sit in the com-fortable chair. On the power of a blind phone call. I was a college student in Utah and couldn't afford to drop a thousand bucks on a trip to Hollywood and have no meetings. But my then agent dropped the ball and there I was in Hollywood with no meetings. Desperate times call for desperate measures, so I pulled out the Hollywood directories and made calls. I would call and say, "Hey, I am an out of state writer, through this fluke of fate, I happen to be in town for the week, would you like to meet?" Thirty-one people said yes.

Thirty-one *producer* people.

Agents don't do that. You call an agent and say you are in town by a fluke of fate, they will tell you, write a query letter. I'm not kidding, I've had it happen. ("Um, could you maybe read that query letter by Friday? That's when my plane leaves." What are the odds?)

Now I am a pretty good talker. I can talk thirty-one producers into meeting me with less than a week's notice. And those producers had never read a word I wrote. I drove scripts to gates and dropped them off and people read me overnight before meetings. But I had a hell of a time getting read by agents. "Not without a referral." What does that say?

Well, for one thing, it says agents are fucking difficult to get read by. More importantly, it says all this stuff about don't send your material to anyone but an agent because the agent wants something no one has ever seen before? It's a lie. A serious in-your-face lie. An agent won't read something no one has ever seen before. But an agent will read a script a producer tells them is good.

So. Ignore all that talk about only showing your stuff to agents and go get read by producers. Producers are your referrals to agents.

The next big lie is, you can't get read or make a sale without an agent. I've been read at plenty of production companies sans an agent. When I got my first offer, I didn't even have an agent. It damn sure helps if you have an agent. But you do not absolutely positively have to have an agent to get read or make a sale. What you do need agents for, though, is—

To set the table. It is not deemed socially acceptable to say yourself that you are a genius or the second coming or Shakespeare. You might be, but you are not supposed to say it. That is just not delicate. But your agent can say it. Your agent can call people up and say you are a genius and no one will blink. Cool, huh? And that will not hurt you, having someone out there saying you are a genius and telling people you are great. Agents do that. And it's great.

Agents also talk money. We are "writers," we are not supposed to be interested in filthy lucre, we are supposed to be starry eyed artistes. (Some people will tell you screenplays aren't art, but these tend to be the same people who suck the life out of starry eyed "artistes" and ask them to work for free, so kick them in the shins and keep walking.) In Reality Land, we all want to maybe put dinner on the table once in a while, but in Fantasy Land, we are not supposed to be even interested in money because we are so caught up in the emotion of it all. That's an illusion, but people like it and it makes us feel holy or something so we all play along. So who asks about the paycheck to keep the illusion intact?

Your agent. Your agent talks about money and negotiates fees and is a damn sight better at it than you because he has a lot of practice and you don't. And if someone doesn't pay off? He sues the bones off them till they do. Yay!

Agents are not miracle workers, though. They are deal makers. Some will get you work. Some will merely negotiate contracts while you go out and get work. And some, well, some are just signatory covers. Regardless, once you sign with an agent, you can't simply sit back and say, "Now I have an agent, I don't have to work this anymore." Um, are you unsane? This is *your* career. That is why you get 90 percent, and your agent gets 10 percent. You have a lot more to lose here. And a lot more to gain. So which would you rather have? One agent working on your behalf? Or one agent and one crazed obsessed writer working on your behalf? I tend to think the latter accomplishes more. I could be wrong. But—

There are a lot of Guild writers out of work. I went to a meeting. All they could talk about was how many Guild writers were out of work. So. If your agent can be the end-all be-all of your career, great, more power to you. But if he can't? (And your agent is, truly, human, I know people say different, but we are not talking Moses here, we are talking agents.) I would not sit around saying, "Whew! At last I have an agent, now I can drink ice tea and watch Oprah while the offers roll in." I would stay out there and hustle.

I mentioned it helps, getting an agent, to have a deal on the table. It does. You show up with a deal, that is a 10 percent commission right away for the agent and he didn't have to send out a script or make a phone call to get it.

If you don't know the story (and why would you?), *Excess Baggage* was a spec script I entered in the Austin Heart of Film Festival screenwriting competition in 1994. It won that competition, was read by the then President of Production at Columbia Pictures, Columbia optioned the script, then signed Alicia Silverstone to star in it in an acting/producing deal, seven writers rewrote it, and it was released in August 1997.

Since it won a big contest, sold to Columbia, and signed the at-the-time hottest young actress in town, you would think *Excess Baggage* was maybe semi-marketable. But a lot of agents passed on *Excess Baggage*. The California agent who'd been dicking me around for a year told me it wasn't marketable. I left her and got on with an attorney whose reader didn't think the script had much going for it (did I mention some readers are really stupid?), but the attorney was willing to send it out for a submission fee—which I would have done, except then I got slammed by places that refused to read a script submitted by an attorney instead of an agent. So I signed up with a guy in Texas who was a signatory. (I did a lot of things here I am telling you not to do, maybe there is a reason I don't think you should do them. Ahem.) He wasn't an effective agent, but he was a signatory cover I could send in under. He thought the script ought to maybe be rewritten to be more marketable, too, but he quit giving me notes and started sending it out when he started getting requests for it. (Agents get happy if people call and ask for stuff without them having to do anything to make that happen.) That relationship, though, wasn't leading anywhere. And I was a finalist in Austin and doing pretty well in the Nicholl competition and figured I needed a real agent and the attention the contests were starting to get me was only going to last so long and maybe I had better try to use that while I had it. So I left the Texas agent. Went to Austin. Won. Columbia decided to option the script. And then I signed with CAA. Because then, CAA was interested in me.

Prior to that, I got turned down a lot, agent after agent telling me *Excess Baggage* wasn't marketable. But what they meant was, I wasn't marketable. Okay, maybe some of them were stupid and actually thought that script wasn't marketable, but the wall I tend to believe I was hitting was, they didn't think they could sell an unknown writer from Utah without way more effort than they were willing to put into it. That's what they were turning down. Me. Not the material.

You will get turned down a lot. That is just the way it works. It's a given. But?

In the end, all it takes is one yes. One yes, and you are in there. Some people thought the script was good. Some people thought it wasn't. One person thought it was worth paying for and making into a movie. And once that one person says, "How much?" a lot of doors open and suddenly everyone (regardless of what they may have thought before, or at least regardless of what their readers may have thought before) thinks it's faboo and wants to buy it too. Seriously. There was a bidding war. Studios fought. Over my "unmarketable" script. Very bizarre.

In just under five years, I had five agents. Most of them of short duration. One I got via a query. One I got via an interview. Three I got via referrals. CAA was via a referral from someone who wanted to buy a script. And because of contest wins and because the agent and I met in Austin and liked each other. But I wonder if the contest wins and liking each other would have mattered as much, if the President of Production at Columbia Pictures hadn't called and said, "I read this script and think I am going to buy it."

Agents don't tend to say this (it would be the height of tactlessness to say "Oh we won't look at new writers unless they make a sale on their own") but a lot of writers who get picked up (we're talking new, breaking in writers) bring a deal to the table at the time they're signed. It looks sometimes in the press like this agency discovered this writer and then found and negotiated this great big deal for the writer, but that's not what happened. The writer found the deal and *then* got discovered by the agency. And then the agency did the negotiations. In other words, these writers go out and find someone to buy their movies and then go looking for an agent. Except that isn't exactly an accurate portrayal either. In actuality, these writers were probably looking for an agent the whole time they were killing themselves to sell their stuff. It's just no agent in town would read them without a referral. And then no agent in town would sign them without a deal on the table. So the writers sent to producers until someone bought something. And then agents would talk to them.

Go send your script to a producer. Send to agents too. As often as you can. But send a lot of scripts to producers.

30 Bad Agents

FROGS DON'T DO THIS #32: I wonder how long it will take them to figure out there's a problem with a premise about aquatic animals raising a baby land creature. . . .

You will notice there is a lot of stuff in this book about agents. That is because writers are crazy for agents. At least half the time you are fielding questions about anything screenwriting, it is questions about agents. How do I get an agent is the biggy. Getting an agent is really hard. Once you find someone who will sign you, the first impulse is to collapse in relief and thank God that is finally over. The next is to cling to that agent, come hell or high water, because you never, ever want to go through the hell of looking again.

Which is, I think, why so many writers sign with bad agents. Because it was so hard to find one in the first place. And also why so many writers stay with bad agents. God no, look again? It's understandable, from an emotional viewpoint—but professional suicide.

Sometimes, agents are not actually "bad agents," they can

actually be real good agents, just bad agents for you. Compatibility is a factor here. Do you work well together, do your personalities mesh, does the agent *get* your material? This stuff counts.

Other times, agents are just plain bad agents. They don't know what they're doing, they behave in unbusinesslike ways, they don't send out material, or they send it to the wrong people, they don't have any contacts, or their contacts are all bad, or just in the wrong field for you, they are sometimes crackpots who like calling themselves agents and have somehow finagled signatory status out of the Guild, but it's just a title to feed a vainglorious ego and they aren't agenting at all, or maybe they are actually pretty good at agenting, but withhold royalties from clients and are just basically thieves—whatever the scenario, they are just bad agents.

Whether you are dealing with a bad agent, or an agent who is just bad for you, makes no difference to you. You have a bad agent. Bad agents don't return phone calls in a prompt and courteous manner. Bad agents don't get around to reading your work. Bad agents don't promote your work. Or you. Bad agents don't set up meetings. Bad agents fail to follow through on things they say they will do. And fail to follow up on anything you do yourself. Bad agents lie to you. Bad agents lie to people about you. Bad agents are not helpful. At all. And bad agents hinder you. In a lot of ways.

For starters, often, once a writer gets an agent, writers stop working quite so hard to move their own careers forward because now they have an agent, they believe the agent will take over the marketing stuff to move their career forward for them.

Wrong. A bad agent is not moving your career forward. A bad agent is letting your career flounder. Meanwhile, you have lost the only other person here who was working on your behalf, you, to "now I have an agent I can relax" syndrome. This is not a good scenario.

Writers waste time waiting on bad agents. Waiting for bad agents to return phone calls. Waiting for bad agents to get around to reading material. Waiting for bad agents to get around to giving feedback on material. Waiting for them to get around to submitting material. Waiting for them to get around to saying how submissions went. Or where submissions went. Or if submissions went. Waiting a lot. When writers could be doing something productive. Like sending scripts to a good agent.

And if you have a bad agent at a good agency? It gets worse. Because all the things you could normally do on your own behalf at a small agency, you can't do now because it just looks stupid when a CAA writer cold calls producers. You are with CAA. You are not supposed to cold call producers. Your agent is supposed to call and say what a great writer you are and set up a meeting. Producers know this. You know this. And if it isn't happening? You doing it will just tell the person you are calling that your agent doesn't think much of you, and if your agent doesn't think much of you, well, why should a producer?

Writers who have bad agents also quite often aren't looking for a good agent because (a) the agent is going to hear about it, if they do, and that could get ugly; (b) it is awful firing an agent; (c) it is seriously not fun looking for an agent; and (d) if you can just maniacally tell yourself enough times, maybe if you do this, or maybe if you do that, things will get better, it might actually happen and then you can avoid a, b, and c.

This can go on a long time. At some point, though, you will probably be forced to voice your concerns to a bad agent. Like when the electric company cuts your power. That is usually a pretty good indication maybe it is time to say something.

Bringing up concerns to an agent, however, is like asking a

husband whether he is cheating on you. People want the answer to be no. They want it to be no so much, they will often choose to believe a lie in the face of all evidence, rather than acknowledge the answer is clearly and obviously not no. That is how bad they want that answer to be no.

It's the same with the bad agent scenario. You bringing up concerns is basically you asking your agent if he is going to just seriously fuck up your career. And you want the answer to be no. And the agent will tell you no. He may cop to having let you down. He may be real sorry about that, too. He may promise he will change. Really. It is going to be different from now on, he promises, it is going to be better, he is going to be better, he will get right on it and do this and this and this and you will see, it's going to be great.

Most writers come out of that conversation relieved (thank God this is going to work out after all) and skeptical (it sounded good, but what if it was all talk?). Either way, now you have had this little chat, you will feel honor bound to give the agent time to follow through on those promises he just made. Which means you are (ahem) waiting around for your agent again.

Agents are good at the "go team" chat. They are charismatic and conciliatory and charming as hell, when they want to be. (Agents are salesmen in Hollywood. Where competition does not get much fiercer. Charisma and charm are job requirements. Remember that, the next time you are talking to an agent.) And agents don't like rejection any more than the next guy. They will turn it way up when a client says he or she is unhappy. They will turn it way up even when someone who is not a client, is just someone they make pocket submissions for once in a while, says they are unhappy. Because nobody wants to get dumped. So there you are with the full throttle "I don't want to get dumped" lever tripped in your agent's head, and you are now getting full wattage attention and charm and lots of promises, all the right things being said, because, well, they are agents, they know the right things to do, so sure they know the right things to say.

Agents will even do this with a new writer who they have not exactly signed, but have sort of mentored a bit along the way. A "pocket client" is someone the agent doesn't sign, but will send material out for. You don't get the agent's full attention or the backing of the entire agency, but it gets you submitted under a legitimate agency cover and then, if you make a sale, the agent will step up to the plate and negotiate the deal. It seems odd an agent would turn on all that charm for someone they don't value enough to actually sign (though sometimes that is not the agent's fault, that can be the "committee" in action). Other times, a new writer will have a "relationship" with an agent who isn't even submitting material for the writer, just telling the writer over and over "I can't send this out, but show me your next one." Well, here is the deal in both cases. Even though the agent isn't technically representing you, and sometimes isn't even submitting you, that agent does not necessarily want to lose you, because what if another agent were to pick you up and make a great big sale? Jeez! Then this agent would feel pretty stupid for not submitting that material and not signing you, right? So the agent will charm you too, if you're in this situation. Just because, well, first, no one wants to get dumped, and second, no one wants to risk discovering down the road they were wrong.

So you've just had this great big convo with your "agent." You've voiced concerns and he or she has said all the right things and made lots of promises. Great. If it happens, that's wonderful. But—

Agents don't always do what they say they are going to do. Sometimes that was just the I-don't-want-to-get-dumped talk. So you need to watch real close right now to see whether that agent actually does something now to follow through on all those promises, or whether the second the conversation ended, you went straight back to the ignore-at-will burner. And you should not wait too long before drawing your conclusions here. Because while you're waiting, if that agent you just talked to isn't doing anything for you, your career is going down the drain.

A lot of people say having no agent at all is better than having a bad agent. Signatory covers aside, this is true. For all the reasons above, but also, more importantly, it is true because a bad agent undermines your belief in yourself and your work. This is the one person who is supposed to be on your side. Your agent. The person who is supposed to be your cheering section in an industry second only to the music industry in harsh blows. The one person who is supposed to believe in you come hell, high water, famine, plague, or frogs. But a bad agent is not on your side. A bad agent is not cheering you. A bad agent does not believe in you. A bad agent is giving you the daily message "You don't matter." Every unreturned phone call says that. Every extra weekend it takes to read a script says that. Every submission not followed up on or not made says that. Day in and day out. You. Just. Don't. Matter. That is not good for writers. It is the most crippling thing anyone could do to you, telling you over and over again you don't matter, to the point you might begin to believe it, if you don't get away from him fast and now. So give him a week to see if he's following through on that pep talk. And if he is, great. Things may be looking up. But if he isn't? It's time to leave.

31 Leaving an Agent

THINGS TO DO WHEN YOU SHOULD BE WRITING #11: Make the potatoes in the pantry do tricks. Wearing interesting outfits. You know. Those interesting outfits you made last time you were supposed to be writing.

It's hard to leave an agent. I had a friend with an agent who had dropped the ball. Now my friend had an offer from another agent. Suddenly the agent who dropped the ball was conciliatory and interested in her career again and wanted her to stay and explained she, the agent, had been "a little overwhelmed," but that was fixed now and didn't she, the writer, want to stay?

It's too bad the old agent got overwhelmed, that's a shame, it's terrible when that happens to people. But it is also too bad she hid behind her answering machine and wouldn't return my friend's calls and was an asshole about it. It's too bad she made her problems my friend's problems. And it is too bad she only got interested in my friend's career again after another agent did.

When you are thinking about leaving an agent and suddenly the agent gets interested in you again and plays the loyalty card?

(The loyalty card: We have been together a long time, we are "friends," be loyal or you are not a good person.) Ask yourself this. Would she do it to you? She wants to keep you. Great, very nice. But if she didn't? How quick would she drop you? Would she even bother to drop you? Or would she just ignore your phone calls? Would she care if you were overwhelmed? Would she give you a second chance? Would she be "loyal"? An agent's problems should not be your problems. That's bad business. Can you afford to be in business with someone who practices bad business?

Don't stay because it is easier to stay. Stay because the answers to these questions are positive. If the answers are negative? Bite the bullet and get out. Staying with a bad agent (whether that agent is bad across the board, or just bad for you) is not being a good person, it is being a dumb business person. And writers cannot afford that. Fire the agent. Do it nicely, but do it.

"Nice" means say you gave this a lot of thought, and you like the agent a great deal and would like to stay, but you realize this is not a good business decision for you at this time and you must move on.

When you fire an agent, never give whys. Agents will argue with whys. It will turn into recriminations. Well you did this! Well you did that! Well you did that other thing! That will just leave everyone upset. So don't do it. Say you don't feel this is the best thing for your career at this time and feel you should move on. Repeat that phrase. It is your mantra for getting out of a difficult conversation. Say it when it doesn't even make sense. No matter what they say, that is your answer. Then say good-bye. Hang up. It's over.

And, in the freakish event you call and your agent doesn't return your calls? (You can laugh, but this has happened to me.) Fire the agent by fax.

Don't cheat. You have to call first. It is simply the right way to fire someone. Via voice. You are off the hook if the person doesn't take or return your calls. But anytime you fire someone, it should be "in person," as it were.

Unless you have an attorney to do the firing and talking for you. Even then, it is more polite to do it yourself, though.

Then follow up with a formal letter.

Besides calling being the courteous way to fire someone, calling allows you to pick your time. Not always. Sometimes you end up playing phone tag to fire someone. (Oh irony!) But if you fire someone by letter alone, they are going to call. I promise you. They *will* call. Which leaves you not knowing when the call is coming, just knowing it *is* coming, and dreading it. Whereas, if you reach the person by phone, you handle it on your time table, on your terms, when you're composed for it. Not when you're climbing out of the shower to pick up the phone and whammo, it's "the call."

When you can leave depends on your contract, how good your lawyers are, and when the last time is you got work or made a sale. The WGA contract says, basically, if you have not been hired and have not sold anything through your agent in the last ninety days, you may discontinue your working relationship with your agent, *i.e.* you can walk, contract or no contract.

So. If you're Guild and you haven't worked or sold anything in three months, you're in the clear.

If you're not Guild and your agent gave you a non-Guild contract to sign (which isn't supposed to happen, but does) and your agent gives you grief over leaving because your contract doesn't have the ninety day no-work-you-can-walk clause? Scream to the Guild. They may not do anything about it, but they should at least know it is happening. And walk anyway. What are they going to do? Sue? For what? A phone bill? Walk away.

It can be messy, if you have projects that have gone in under your old agent's cover and you change agents and now are trying to start over and resubmit. The first agent is entitled to commission on submissions made by the agency, unless there's a good deal of distance established between their submission and following submissions by a new agent. Sometimes the agents will work it out for a split commission. Sometimes, the original agent of record just gets the commission. And sometimes, there is enough distance created between the separate submissions it becomes clearly the second agent's submission and no one questions this. It depends and will be something to discuss with the new agent, who should be able to negotiate this with your old agent. (This is a small town. People try to get along. They have to eat in the same restaurants.) Bottom line, a new agent who signs you is making an investment in you and should pick up slack on projects even if they were submitted under another agent's cover because (1) it is important he/she be associated with your work in the eyes of the town, and that means all your work, regardless of past business associations; and (2) everything he/she negotiates for you, including anything submitted under someone else's cover, has impact on future projects and earnings, so it would be stupid not to pick up slack on older projects, even if someone else is getting commissioned on those, they will have impact on all future commissions the new agent plans to make off your work.

It's an odd place, changing agents. Especially if you are trying to make submissions and have any sort of down time between agents. If you know you're leaving, you don't exactly want stuff going out under the old agent's cover. That will just complicate things later. If you know where you are going, that simplifies everything. You just switch. If you don't know where you are going, that is a little more complex and it is real tempting to keep using the old agent's cover just to get read. Not a good idea. But tempting. In that position (and I've been there), I'd send stuff out myself, just say you're between agents and would they take it straight from you. Sometimes they will. Sometimes they won't. Other times, you are better off telling someone you are changing agents and will send the piece in under the new agent's cover as soon as you've signed.

This can be good, if the person you're talking to is someone you know who has read and liked your work. See, if they know you are leaving your agent, they may be able to give you the names of agents you should give a shout. And maybe give you a referral. (A referral, by the way, is that person calling the agent and personally suggesting the agent read you. The call has to come from them, or agents will sometimes just think you are making the referral up. Sigh.)

It can also be not so good, if you don't know the person well and/or don't know for sure you are going to be signing with someone pretty damn soon. You can only get away with saying you'll submit after you sign with someone new for so long, then if you don't sign with someone new, you could find yourself in the awkward position of having to call people a couple months down the road to say, "Well I haven't signed with anyone yet, do you still want to see the script anyway?" Which is embarrassing and takes the bloom off the rose for the callee, who is now thinking, Wow, no one wanted this, do I want to read something no one wanted?

These are chances you take when you leave an agent, but if you must leave, you must leave, so there is no point fretting. Just do it.

Leaving is not always amicable. I got yelled at real loud by one agent I was leaving. Another slapped me with a bill for back postage, office expenses, and phone calls. She told me that was "allowed" by the Guild. I said I'd allow as I wasn't going to pay it, I hadn't agreed to any such charges at the beginning of our working relationship and wasn't planning on paying someone for the privilege of leaving. These things happen and are not always fun. But they are more fun than sitting there day in day out getting that awful terrible message from the person who is supposed to be your number one fan, whose every action screams you are unimportant and negligible and nothing. So have faith, bite the bullet, and go.

32 Cheating on Agents

FROGS DON'T DO THIS #119: There are forty-two names on my buddy list's A-List. There are only five people on the A-List. Forty-two names????? You know who you are.

don't cheat on your agent. I'm serious here. Once you sign with an agent, if you send scripts to other agents, you had better be planning on leaving, because the message, when you send scripts to other agents, is you're shopping. Not a good way to start out with a new agent, saying "Sure, represent me, but I'm still shopping." And not a good way to keep your current agent happy, sneaking around with other agents.

Did I mention agent relationships are like marriages? Ask your significant other if he or she minds if you date a bit, just to see if anyone better is out there. See how well it goes over. It will go over just as well with your agent.

You have to consider business here, too. If you are shopping agents, it cuts your current agent's feet off at the knees. He can no longer negotiate for you. And any deal you have on the table becomes iffy or goes on hold. That is because this is a very small town. If you send scripts to other agents, everyone knows. I mean it. There are no secrets in this town. A lot of lies, but no secrets. So your agent can't negotiate for you because everyone knows you are shopping and no one has faith in any deals he is trying to negotiate for you. Everyone is just expecting him to get the axe any second here and they will hold off till you're definitely with someone new, before proceeding with negotiations, or, worse, they will go to another writer till after the smoke clears.

What this means is, don't shop around unless you are unhappy with your agent and plan to leave. There is no way to discreetly shop for a new agent. This is a small town and your agent will know. Everyone will know. The end. Assuming your agent is an actual Hollywood player. And if you are starting out and considering several agents, don't sign with one just to get your work out there while you flirt with others. It will backfire. It always backfires.

33 Managers vs. Agents

NOTES INTO THE ETHER #103: *Every time I turn something in, I have this feeling of doom, like, Well, that's it, my career's over now.*

managers generally, but not always, take a higher percentage than agents, about 15 percent versus the agent's 10 percent. If you have a manager and an agent, sometimes the manager will take less, say 10 percent, because (a) the manager is not doing all the work here, he or she has a partner, your agent; and (b) the manager is aware that 25 percent of your income is a lot to pay off the top for representation (and that will be thirty if you toss an entertainment attorney into the mix too) so will cut you some slack on the commission.

Managers are not, however, regulated by the Guild, and so have no boundaries on what they may ask for, in commission. Fifteen percent is standard. Personally, I would not go higher than standard. But mileage may vary.

Agents tend to have more clients than managers do and so less time for hand holding. Managers allegedly get a higher per-

centage of your income because they do have more time for you.
I have a manager and in his case, that's true. And certainly, if you
have fifteen clients instead of fifty, you should have more time for
individual hand holding. But—

The reason a lot of agents hang up their agent shields to become managers is they want to produce. As signatory agents,
they can't. That's not allowed by the Guild because it is seen as
a conflict of interest. As managers, they are not dictated to by the
Guild and can. This is when I start to wonder about the hand
holding bit. Sure they have less clients, but they are producing
movies, which might take up a little of their hand holding time.
Hmm.

Not every manager produces. Some of them just manage. So
ask a manager interested in you whether he or she produces *and*
manages, or is strictly a manager. It's a valid question.

That does not mean someone who manages and produces
can't be a perfectly fine manager. They can. I would still want to
know.

And I would also want to know, if they are producing,
whether they are planning on taking a producer's fee from the
studio on works of mine we set up. And if so, are they planning
on taking a commission from me as well on those projects? See,
a lot of managers who produce get a producer's credit on their
clients' work. That's how they set the deals up. And that's how
it goes down. That producer's credit doesn't always mean they
did much in the way of "producing" the film. (Though sometimes it does.) But it always means the studio paid them a fee to
go along with that credit. And when a manager is getting a producer's fee from the studio? It seems a little greedy to be de-
manding a portion of your paycheck too, in the form of a
commission. So ask about that. And see if you can't steer your
way into an agreement that says, if they set up a deal they are not

getting a producer's fee on? Well then sure, they get a commission. But if they're getting a check from the studio already on the basis of your work? Maybe they should cut you some slack on that little commission issue.

I have friends who have managers and love them. And I have managers and am pretty damn fond of them. And a manager is a real good fail safe, if your agent is maybe not doing everything he or she could for your career. A manager is one more person telling people in Hollywood you are a genius and they should hire you right away. In a town where name actors and actresses disappear overnight, the more people who are saying you are a genius, the better.

But a manager is also one more person taking a chunk out of your check. A check that shrinks with each member you add to the entourage. So—

If you already have an agent and are thinking about a manager as well, the big thing you have to ask yourself is, Is this person going to increase your hirability, will this person get you work, will this person justify the added chunk that is going to come out of each paycheck you get in the future?

Sometimes a manager will. At least two people I know rely more heavily on their managers for getting them jobs than on their agents. And they are working steadily. If that's not an affidavit, I don't know what is.

If you don't have an agent *or* a manager, and a nice manager offers to sign you, take it. Managers work hand in hand with agents, it is quite possible that manager can get you an agent as well. And you don't have an offer from a reputable agent, or you would have a reputable agent. So why are you wondering? Sign with a manager. You need someone out there talking you up to people who buy material and hire writers. That can be either a manager or an agent, who cares? A good person just offered. Take it. As long as we are talking about a reputable manager who is going to do some good for your career.

That's the drawback, however, that question: Is this person a reputable manager who is going to be good for your career? Managers (unless we're talking Warren Zide) aren't as high profile as agents. Meaning, while anyone who knows anything can name the top five agencies in town? A lot of people can't name the top five management firms. So knowing whether or not a manager is reputable or with a reputable firm is trickier than knowing whether or not an agent is. But don't panic. This is why you have been calling and hounding producers all this time. Producers know everybody. That is their job. When you need information, that is who you call. Producers. And you ask them about this person who just offered to manage you. Producers will know. They know everything.

34 Producers

EMBARASSING MOMENT #9,367,892: Um, guess what? The premiere is next week Monday the 25th, not last night Monday the 17th. I would like to say I realized this before I got dressed up and got in my car and drove to Westwood. I really, really would like to say that. . . .

i have said an awful lot about producers in other chapters. (Which, if you haven't read, you had better go read right now. I didn't just toss those in here for fun you know, what is wrong with you? Go read them.) One of the reasons for this is, producers are intrinsically woven into the fabric of every single part of Hollywood. Producers deal with studio executives, agents, managers, actors, actresses, directors, casting agents, and every writer in town, every day. That is because they are the people who put pictures together. And the people who get called, when those pictures start falling apart. And they have to talk to everyone.

There are a hell of a lot of different producer credits. I'll be damned if I know what all of them mean. There are two kinds of producers you are worried about, though. The executive producer. And the line producer.

The executive producer is the guy who picks up the Oscar. Sometimes he or she has a lot less to do with physically making the movie than he or she had to do with making the deal that got the movie made. Sometimes both.

The line producer may or may not have had anything to do with making the deal that got the movie rolling down the development track, but he or she is definitely on the set. Line producers are trouble shooters. They pay off the guy whose dog won't stop barking while you are trying to shoot a scene. They discover all those nifty palm trees you are planning on using in that nice sunset shot just died in a rogue frost, and find out where the hell you buy nifty palm trees in December when all the palm trees in California just died, and have them flown in. They troubleshoot so that the movie doesn't go to hell in a hand basket the way it would if no one on the set was trouble shooting. They are pretty important, and sometimes just happen to be the executive producer as well.

You are primarily interested in the executive producer, because that is who you are going to be dealing with setting up projects at studios and selling pitches and getting hired to work. This is the person you keep sending scripts to until he or she can't stand it anymore and yells, "Fine, all right already, I like it, let's go set it up." He or she is going to be the person you go into pitch meetings with, trying to sell a script or pitch to a studio. He or she is the person who is going to be taking a script or pitch to actors and actresses or directors or agents trying to make a package deal a studio might find more attractive than just a plain script or story, seeing as sometimes the studio won't see reason and sign you right on the spot. Producers are movie champions. They bring all the pieces together and shout encouragement and cheers until you have everyone together ready to make a movie. And producers are who you want to know most in Hollywood. Because producers know everyone and take no sides.

If you ask your friend the writer for an agent referral, your friend can only refer you to one agent. Your friend's agent. Why? Because, even if your friend knows lots of agents, if your friend's agent passes on your script and your friend calls other agents? Those other agents will say, "If your bud is so great, why didn't *your* agent sign him?"

Producers can refer you to a lot of agents. Producers know a lot of agents. They talk to them every day. And they are not expected to play favorites. No one will blink twice or say "How come your agent didn't read your friend?" They will just read your script, because their friend the producer referred you.

Producers can tell people you are a genius and people are inclined to believe them. It's your agent's job to tell people you are a genius. People know that. And while everyone likes to hear it, they also know your agent gets 10 percent commission on everything you make. That sort of puts your agent on your side by default. Not so with a producer. Producers don't make a commission off you. If they say you are a genius, they probably really think that.

Producers are founts of information. If you need to know who sends out good material and who doesn't, ask a producer. Producers read all that material. They will tell you which agents always have good material and get read first, and which ones are hit or miss. If you need to change agents or are just looking for an agent? Producers know which agents in town are maybe looking for new clients, and which ones are swamped and couldn't take you if they wanted to. Producers know who the managers are and which ones are getting work for their clients. Producers know which entertainment attorneys make good deals for their clients. (They were the first to hear the screams from Business Affairs, so for sure, they know this one.) Producers know if that actress you want to send a script to just got a new boyfriend and won't be reading anything for six months. Producers know all this stuff.

Studio executives know this stuff too. But studio executives won't tell you. There are too many politics going on at studios. Those are big places. With many power struggles. Just read the trades to see who found their furniture on the studio lawn today and you can pick that up. Studio executives have to be cagey. They can't afford to be founts of information. But producers are more independent, in smaller places that are just theirs and they do not have all those politics going on so they can afford to give you information.

In other words, producers are your friends. And when you are putting a movie deal together? Your best friends.

This does not mean producers won't throw you to the wolves to get a movie made. If you have a movie in the works and everyone else decides for whatever reason they need a new writer? Well, producers want to get things made, they are practical people, they will say so long. But give them credit. They helped you set that deal up in the first place. They championed it from the beginning. And now you aren't there anymore to champion that project yourself? Be glad someone else is and don't hold a grudge. Your final check is riding on them getting that movie made too.

How you get to know all these fabulous producers is up to you. Most of them are in the HCD (*Hollywood Creative Directory*). Some of them are on studio lots. Some of them aren't. But they're all mostly in there. Look them up. Pay attention to who has made your favorite movies. Call them. Write them letters.

Do not look producers up on the backs of videos you rent at

Blockbuster. The producer's credit is the most abused in the business, so it is not always exactly illuminating to read the Blockbuster rental box and you can't always assume the person listed there really made a movie happen. Maybe. But the producer credit gets passed around a lot, in screen credits. So. Check the HCD. Read up on projects. Look to see who really made the movie happen. The star's hairdresser? The star? Or that short guy with the beard in the background? Hint: probably the short guy.

When you query producers, it's always that. A query. You never send a manuscript cold. Don't tell them you have this great script you want them to "buy." And don't tell them it will "make them a lot of money." (Where were you raised? Stop that.) Tell them you like their work and would like to send them a writing sample. Got that? "Writing sample." Repeat it. Everyone knows, if this producer falls in love with the script and it is available, it is up for sale. But it is just more polite to say writing sample. So say that. Then, if the producer agrees to read the script, submit it.

All the same rules apply to producer submissions that apply to agent submissions. So don't be calling every day to check on a submission. If you've got too much energy, go call another producer. It won't hurt. The more producers you know, the better. And after a week or so, then call to make sure the script arrived. After a couple more, call to check in and see if anyone has read it.

Qualify producers, before you query them. Make sure you're sending to good people. That's only smart. You don't want to be calling up or submitting material to a bunch of Bozos. But don't outsmart yourself. I am always hammering people to check credits, to know who they're sending to, to make sure someone is viable, but—sometimes I say it too much and people take it too much to heart and then I see people filtering contacts for viability, as in do they send the script or don't they? And some of the precedents are too severe. For example, people look someone up and see they aren't in the HCD or see they don't have an office on a studio lot and decide that means the producer isn't a viable contact and then they don't submit material. Well, um—

Producers often have studio deals. That's a given. However, they also often do not, and other forms of talent, such as actresses and directors, more often do not. And are still serious players. And as often as not can also get a movie made. And many people on lots with studio deals spend three years butting heads with management over projects and never getting them made. So the consideration, can this person get a movie made?, while valid, is not answered simply by someone having offices on a studio lot and a studio deal. A studio deal does not guarantee someone can get a picture made. And not having a deal does not automatically mean someone can't.

Who can get a movie made, no questions asked, in this town? Tom Cruise. Everyone else has to work for it. Including people with deals on lots. Including people who work off lot.

So don't take an office on a lot as a guarantee someone can get a picture made. It isn't. And don't assume, just because someone doesn't have an office on a lot or doesn't have a studio deal, that means that person can't get a movie made. And don't always assume, just because someone has never produced a movie before, that means they can't produce and get a movie made. That is just wrong. You have to look at someone's track record, and ask yourself what they have done in the industry that might legitimize them, even if they've never produced anything. Ten years in the trenches working as a P.A. counts for something. Ten years showing up in front of a camera counts for even more. And—

Don't turn down offers of help in some paranoid assumption everyone in this town is trying to take advantage of you. That's not always wrong, that paranoid assumption, but it is also not always right.

I've seen instances where someone offered to help someone else, and the person getting the offer was so busy wondering what was in it for the person making the offer, he or she didn't consider the option this could simply be a nice person honestly offering to help.

Hey, it happens. Really. I've done it. With nothing to gain. Other than that I know how damn hard it is, when you're on the outside trying to get in, and I saw someone with talent and thought, I could help that person. And did it. People do still do that. Even in Hollywood. Do not get so into outsmarting the game you can't see a hand offered. It's called payback. People who get a shot and a blessing sometimes pass it on to the next guy. It is just good karma.

Be smart, yes. If someone calls you from Florida and says they are trying to get their junior college buddies to all pitch in to make them a big wig producer and they'd like to shoot your script but hey they can't pay you, that'll come later? Run away. But don't be so smart you're sitting on a script not letting anyone read it because you are waiting for Tom Cruise to come to Wisconsin and knock on your door. Get your scripts read. Take help when it's offered. Do not wear blinders that say "option/option" so loud you can't see any other paths or motivations. You *never* know what the path in will be. And while odds are it won't be that guy in Florida? And lots of people are big on talk and small on action in this town? You have to get read. And anybody who will help you do that is a person to consider sending material to. And any legitimate producer or show business professional, lot deal or no, is a valid consideration as well.

35 Bozos

NOTES INTO THE ETHER #97: Talk shows hold an important function in my life. I'm not sure whether this is God taunting me, saying Potato people find love, isn't it funny you don't?, or cheering me on, saying Look, these hose-oids did it, you will too, kid. It depends on my mood.

You always make judgments about where to send stuff and where not to. You always attempt to maintain some knowledge of where your scripts are going and where they aren't. But you also need to get read, so don't be too exclusive here. I'll tell a story.

Back in 1994, late September, when I went to L.A. and my then agent who was supposed to set up business meetings for me and didn't—oh joy, I'm in L.A. with no meetings—I got on the phone and called everyone in the HCD who would talk to me and told them I was in town unexpectedly for a week and how would they like to meet me? One of the places I called was a little office in Santa Monica set up by a features guy who'd been ousted by Fox, who was now developing TV stuff that would probably never get approval from Fox because, well, he had been ousted. And I talked to the woman who worked there and her assistant. And her assistant was great. We loved each other and talked hair and she read every damn thing I'd ever written. Including the plays and short stories. And we stayed in touch.

Back then, I was a no name writer trying to break in and she was an assistant to an assistant to an industry pariah. (No offense to industry pariahs.) Today, I'm a William Morris writer and she's a Disney executive. And she and I put together a feature deal Disney bought and I get to write the movie. We go to dinner and still talk hair, and I wonder sometimes how we got so damn important we have a deal and are making a movie. But I don't wonder too hard. Some things, like luck, you shouldn't question too hard. I just like to marvel at it.

I'm sure there's a moral in there somewhere. I'm not sure what it is, but I'm sure it's there.

I'm a real advocate of qualifying people you send scripts to. Maybe this is because I have sent scripts to a few too many weird people and just got a lot more careful at one point and think everyone else should be careful, too. Maybe it is because I have watched people send scripts to people even weirder than the people I sent scripts to, and have just pounded my head on the desk asking, Why?

But you have to use valid criteria, separating viable contacts from the Bozos. And not everyone you send to is going to be super powerful or the president of a studio. A lot of people will not even have studio deals. And sometimes you will be sending to someone's assistant, instead of the boss, because the boss won't read you, but the assistant will. And someday that assistant might be a big executive at a major motion picture studio and you might make a movie deal together. It happens. And then you will be glad you sent that person material and were nice when he or she was only "just an assistant."

Keep all that in mind. And know that most of the time, people who tell you they are something other than a producer or director are just what they tell you they are. And are probably not lying to you or misrepresenting themselves. And are probably good people to send material to. Because—

This business works, to a large extent, on word of mouth. If a person someone knows says, "I came across this good script," or "I came across this interesting writer," people will get interested. Because they know the person they're talking to and have a little faith in their opinion. People who can't get a movie made, okay, maybe they are an assistant or assistant to an assistant or a story editor someplace that is never going to make your kind of movie, and they can't get your movie made—but they can help you. By word of mouth. Because they can get you read.

And sometimes, when someone offers to show a script around, that is a favor. They are offering you their contacts. Contacts they worked to get and they could be using their time with those contacts to promote their own work, but they're offering to take time out and mention you. These people aren't going to offer to option your material. They often are not even producers. But they will show your script to a few people and say, "What do you think about this script? It's by this quirky writer in Utah who maybe you want to keep an eye on." And that is good for you.

It's also possible they have entirely scurvy motives and will march your material into CAA, claiming to be the producer attached, without a yay or nay from you. That happened to me one time. I was real surprised to get a call from someone at CAA telling me someone was there claiming to be the producer attached to my script and was that true?

Um, no. It wasn't. I made a mistake that time. I sent a script to the wrong person. That person was real chipper and helpful when she contacted me, too. Maybe a little too chipper and helpful. And I knew that. But I was in a hurry at the time so I ignored all that and sent the script pretty much just to be polite. And the end result was, this person and her partner walking around telling people they owned my material when, in actuality, they sure as hell did not own my material and maybe should have talked to me before saying any such thing. (I'm sure this person thought, too, that because I was out of state, I would never hear about it. Out of state writers have to be more careful, because they are more likely to be preyed on by these types, who figure how are you going to know, let alone do anything about it?)

You can't always protect against that. But you try. And notice this person claimed to be a "producer." Almost every time I have had things go seriously awry with a person in the industry, it has been with a person claiming to be a "producer." That is just a real easy claim to make. "Producer" is the most unprotected title in the industry. (It gets passed out like candy on films and I don't see the Producer's Guild doing much about it.) And even some of the people who actually have produced credits and can sound good on the phone can be scurvy dogs. You just can't always know. But—

You can know, if someone hasn't produced a movie in twenty years and is being too friendly to unknown writers, that person is way down the food chain and may do you more harm than good, attaching to your material. If someone is advertising in magazines or on computer bulletin boards for scripts, they are further down the food chain even than that. If some little company has a contest going and what you win is an option, and that's it, and it has a $50 entry fee, that company is paying its bills with disguised reading fees. If someone tells you they have twenty projects in "development," but that person has never had a produced credit in their life, it is time to wonder what all those writers getting developed are getting paid. And anyone making claims or promises too big or too early in a relationship is someone you need to watch. Because that's trying too hard, and if they were anybody of significance, they would not be trying too hard with you, an unknown writer. Those are givens.

And then there are people who actually do have credits, maybe even some recent, and are dogs too. They don't have the glaring warning signs, but you don't want to send them material. Those, however, are going to be very hard to spot. So—

You ask around. You call people you know. You join groups. You try to stay abreast. And you sift, and you listen to people talk. If a warning bell goes off in your head when someone is talking, that warning bell is something to listen to. I had one of those with that person who trotted my script around town. I just thought, Oh hell with it, I have to catch a plane here, I will just send the script and we will talk later about all this other stuff she is "promising" me—like to help me out finding an agent, in advance of even reading my script. Huh? That's a big claim. Watch out for people making "big claims" too early. No one's going to show your script to an agent before they even read it. Come on. Anyone saying so is trying a little too hard, and you should ask yourself, Why? But I thought it would be okay if I just sent the script out to be polite, and then asked questions later. Wrong.

I should not have sent that script. I knew that and did it anyway because it was easier to be polite than to say no. Um, don't do that. If you don't want to send someone a script, don't. You don't have to give a big explanation. You can just say you can't send the script out right now because you promised someone a certain reading time. Or you can say you are talking to agents and not sending anything out until you have signed with one. At which point you will give your agent their name and they can talk to him or her. (It's remarkable how fast most bad guys disappear when a real agent enters the picture. But this won't always work, because sometimes they will leap into that breach with, why don't you send the script to them so they can help you out showing it to agents? Crafty dogs.) OR, you can say you will send the script and then—just forget to mail it. That is a real easy one. It's lying. Okay, lying is wrong. I know that. I'm sorry. But it gets you off the hook. (Or at least buys you time to come up with a good excuse later for not sending the material, if they call you back to say they didn't get it.) And then just get off the phone and hope they are flaky enough they don't call again. And if they do call again? Tell them you are so sorry, you just flaked, wow. And flake again. Just keep flaking. And don't send anyone you don't want to your material.

Sending scripts to Bozos will only make for problems later. Like when they decide they have this great deal they want to make with you, um, for a dollar, and they are a Bozo and you don't want to make a deal with them even for ten dollars, but now you have to somehow graciously extricate yourself from this sticky situation with this person who wants to make a movie out of your script. Hmm. Or for more problems when they don't even tell you they want to make a deal with you, they just go out and tell everyone in town they did. Well. You can avoid all that. Just don't send scripts to Bozos in the first place.

36 The Free Option

SAFE RESPONSES TO REALLY STUPID SUGGESTIONS #34: "Let me think about that and get back to you."

There's something floating around out there called a free option. That is when you give a "producer" rights to represent your material as their own for—nothing. Nada. Zilch. You do it in a contract, too. You sign a piece of paper saying your script, something that is 100 percent yours because you conceived of and created it, is now, um, theirs?

I'm sorry. This sucks.

It also isn't legal. It doesn't break any laws. But it won't hold up in a court of law. In order for a contract to be binding, something of monetary value has to change hands. That is where the "one dollar option" comes from. At least the people who thought up the one dollar option understood contract negotiations and that something of value had to change hands for a contract to be deemed binding.

Yeesh.

I've never understood the concept behind a free and exclusive option. It's one thing for a person to say they want to show your script to a couple people, in a sort of test the waters scenario, and for you to say sure, show it to them. It's another for someone to say, "I want you to sign this contract that says I'm the only person attached to this project for a long time and I'm going to show it to everyone in town with myself attached and I don't want to give you any money for that privilege and you can't offer it to anyone else who might give you money for it in the meantime." Why would you do that? It's not in your best interests. It's in their best interests, sure. But not in yours. So why would you do that?

It doesn't make sense to me.

I've also never understood the principle behind a "nonexclusive" option. The point of an option is exclusivity. A producer doesn't want to bust his or her tail to set up a project and then, forty-eight hours before the deal closes, get scooped by someone else on something he or she just spent six months setting up. An option is, in essence, a commitment on the part of writer and producer that, by its very existence, implies exclusivity to protect both parties' commitment and investment of time, effort, and money. Why would you sign papers to say anything else?

Well, one reason. To allow the person who is asking you to sign those papers to negotiate low terms with you now, that you will have to honor later, no matter how much money they eventually sell the project for. They can't give you much money so they don't necessarily ask you not to show it to anyone else. But if they get you to sign that paper that says they are only going to give you so much, if they set it up? They can turn around and sell it to a studio to star Tom Cruise and make lots of money, and don't have to pay you any more than that paper you signed says.

That is not a particularly good reason for you to sign something. It's just not in your best interests to tell someone you agree to be paid a low ball figure for a project before you find out who they're going to sell it to. And for how much.

The more standardized, studio deal type options are monies paid toward a script's purchase price: We will pay you such-and-such option, against such-and-such purchase price that we will pay you if we make the movie (minus what we already paid you), and that gives us exclusive rights to *develop* the material. Rewrite fees are negotiated at that time too, and if you do the rewrites, what you get paid for those will usually be subtracted from the purchase price (if they make the movie) as well. Then bonuses are negotiated for things like sole or shared credit. Which you won't see unless the movie gets made and you get screen credit.

The option is a buffer for the studio. The studio doesn't want to pay full purchase price for the script, because studio people don't know how it will go during development or whether or not they can attach stars and directors to the script, or who might get hired next week at the studio and just nix the project from the top. They don't know any of that stuff, they just know they like the script. So the studio options the script now, and then waits to see if it can make it into a movie. *Then* the studio will buy it. In other words, the option exists to save the studio money while it plays God with your material.

Luckily, however, when studios are playing God, they usually give you a fair amount of change for the privilege.

Then there is the one dollar option. In general, this is not something you want to do. Before you option your material, it is all yours, 100 percent free and clear. You thought it up. You put it on the page. You own it. Once you sign a piece of paper and money changes hands, however, it isn't yours anymore, it is someone else's. And if the option expires and they haven't done anything with it, sure, you get it back. But if they decide to buy you out during the option term, under the terms of the agreement, it's gone, you don't get it back, they can sell it to their cat, if they want to, and you have no choice in the matter.

We aren't playwrights, who merely allow someone to rent their material during a production and then get ownership of it back when the production is over. We are screenwriters and we sell our material outright. And when you option your material to someone, they have the right at any time during that option to buy it outright for whatever terms you have negotiated at the time you made the option agreement.

That means they hand you a check and you don't own the script or story anymore. This can be great, if the agreement is fair. Or it can be not so great. For example, if the buy out terms say the writer will get $5,000 for the script, and the producer just set up a deal for $500,000. Then the producer pays you five grand and walks away with your script and the difference. Because that was the deal. Right?

Now maybe they are fair terms. Maybe you are optioning your script for just a dollar now, but there is a lot of money written into the agreement for it, if the producer sets it up later at a studio. That's fair. Then again, maybe they aren't fair terms. Maybe they are highway robbery terms. You should watch that. What exactly are the terms, and do they state a specific, flat out purchase price the producer can buy you out for? And is it low? Which isn't great. Or do they say you get paid a fair and reasonable sum based at least in part on what the producer sets the script up for at a studio? You want either big numbers on the back end, or a fair percentage of what a studio pays for the script, if it gets set up, named in the contract. Because you are taking a risk too.

You should also pay attention to who has the right to renew the option. Generally a producer is going to want the right to renew the option with or without your consent. If he is on to something, he doesn't want to let go of the material at option's close just because you say so. He will want to be able to renew whether or not you want to, so he can finish his negotiations and set up the deal.

This makes sense from the producer's standpoint. They get robbed too. Sometimes a producer will work to set something up, but everyone is a little skeptical of him or her, so the players wait out the producer's option on the material, and then option it themselves without him attached. Hey, it happens. This is the Old West out here.

A producer also doesn't want to work to set something up, only to be in the final closing stages of a deal when an option is expiring, and have the writer go insane and suddenly decide he or she doesn't want to make the deal. (Writers are not always insane for this, sometimes they have good reasons, but from the producer's standpoint, they are insane.) All of which means your producer will want the option of renewing with or without your consent.

You don't want to do that, though. You want to be able to say, "Thank you very much for your time and effort, but from what I have seen during our option period, this is not the healthiest place for me to be and I think now the terms of that option have been met, I will go home now."

Watch the fine print and see whose discretion the option may be renewed at. If it is solely at the producer's discretion, you want it changed. Otherwise, an insane producer (and producers are not always insane, sometimes they have good reasons for what they do, but from the writer's perspective, they are sometimes insane) can re-option your material no matter how much you want to run screaming from the association.

And if you're going to do a dollar option? There should be a good reason. Like you believe this person, though he or she doesn't have the bucks to pay you a reasonable amount for your script now? Does have the clout to get a movie made. He or she just needs time to set it up, and then you will all be in honey. You too, because the contract says, if someone buys it, you get paid a fair share. Otherwise, nasty little things happen like the producer gives you a small sum of cash and then, when they have a deal in place, buys you out low and sells to a studio high.

A long time ago people came to Hollywood and started making movies. Those people had had to deal with playwrights, and it was not a lot of fun for them because the playwrights were considered somewhat important in the theater and could push them around. This is because playwrights never relinquished ownership of their material. So in the new system, these people who were tired of getting pushed around by playwrights set it up so that they bought material outright. Now they owned the material. Now they could push the writers around. It's too bad. And it's why screenwriters are the girl. We don't own the material. Everyone justifies this by pointing out screenwriters get paid a lot more money than playwrights. I'm not sure that justifies it—but nobody is liable to change it anytime soon. We have to live with it. A dollar, however, is not a lot of money. A dollar doesn't justify anything. So pay attention to the fine print. And don't option your material to a Bozo for one dollar. If you're going to option to someone for one dollar, it has to be someone good.

37 What the Hell Do I Call This Chapter, or, Do It Right

THAT WAS A REALLY DUMB THING TO DO #3,492: I knew that.

i had a dance instructor, Barbara Wiley, who taught me more life lessons in the course of the two years I studied with her than I probably learned in the entirety of the rest of an errant childhood. One day we were doing a routine at the studio, and I was tired, slacking, just phoning in the steps, and Barbara stopped the dance and asked me what the hell I thought I was doing. And I said, "Promise, on performance day, I'll be on, but today I'm tired." And Barbara said, "Practice like you want to perform, because if you don't? Your body is learning right now what to do, and come performance day? This is what it's going to remember, what you practiced today."

Barbara was pretty smart.

See, you can look at today as a day when your career is not established and you are on some ill defined "beginner's tier" just "practicing." Or you can look at today as a day when you are a writer. And while a certain dose of pragmatism in dealing with people and an acknowledgment of reality, as in, "I haven't been doing this very long, I have a lot to learn," is not a bad attitude to have, the attitude you aren't a professional and so shouldn't behave or treat yourself like one or expect other people to treat you like one, I find questionable.

Can you, by writing for free, get the job, whereas someone who asks for money won't? Yes, if you're working with someone who only wants to work with people who write for free. But while you are writing for free, the person who won't is going on to find a person who will pay them for their work. As a paid professional. And it's a little tough to be out there pounding pavement for that person who will pay you, if you're spending the bulk of your time working for people who won't.

Situations will arise in which it's a realistic investment to work with a producer developing a script of yours, sans pay, on the basis that producer is going to take that script in to studios and attempt to set it up. But that's working with a bona-fide-real-credits-has-made-some-big-films producer. Not with just anyone who comes along and *wants* to produce. I have watched writers do this over and over, following every will o' the wisp that comes along, rewriting and rewriting a script to fit a multitude of expectations, telling themselves they're being good team players and they're showing people just how cooperative they can be (um, who are they showing, someone who *wants* to be a producer?), till they've run themselves clean into the ground doing work for people who don't have the clout, never had the clout, probably never will have the clout, to get a movie made. I've seen writers so wrung out by this process, they quit. And that makes me angry. That they were used, and used, and used some more, until they had nothing left to give and gave up in despair. But they cooperated with the process. And that makes me angry too. That they conspired in their own demise, and helped make it happen.

Don't need praise so much, you will prostitute yourself and

your work for it. Or worse, give it away for free. It would be nice if every struggling just starting out producer were Steven Spielberg in the rough. That's not the case. A lot of struggling producers in the rough are Bozos. And even if Bozo praises your work to high heaven, well, he is still Bozo. Get it?

There are hundreds of people in this town willing to give you an opinion on your work and overly willing to tell you how you ought to change it. There are only a few who will say, "Yes, I believe in this, this is wonderful, let's take it to a studio." And while it is unrealistic to believe nobody will ask you to make changes? (They will.) You are looking for someone who believes in the work so strongly, they can take rejection after rejection and still keep going, hear opinion after opinon that says it isn't quite right, if you just tweaked this little thing, or that little thing, we would go for it. And won't ask you to rewrite every time they get a new opinion. Because they know opinions really only count if someone is paying you money to pay attention to them. And they know what they've got is good, and they will set it up, when they find the right place. And they will keep going until they do set it up, because they believe in the original material enough to do that. And then someone will pay you to make changes based on their opinion.

Those are the people you want to work with. Not people who think it might be great, if only. Not people who think something needs a rewrite every time someone who doesn't want to buy it says, Well maybe this is why. The people who say, "It is great, let's find a way to break the damn wall down and set up a deal and make the movie." Those are the people you want to work with.

If you invest your time working with and for people who don't have that attitude? You will have no time or energy left to find the people you are supposed to be with. So treat yourself like a professional. If you don't, the day you do may never come, because you will have taught yourself too many bad tricks, come performance day, to be capable of performing to your own expectations of what being a professional is all about.

And treating yourself like a professional means, only get involved with people who treat you like a professional, too. And that means people who think you should be paid. People who do not put you on a treadmill doing free rewrites based on every Tom Dick and Harry's opinion they pick up along the way.

It is easy for me to say this now. People are generally nice to me because, if they aren't, I will rat them out to my agents and William Morris will be mean to them. But I didn't always have William Morris. And when it is just you, you have to weed through a lot of Bozos. And every time you say no, that little voice in your head asks, "Wow, did I just blow off the next Steven Spielberg?"

Well, stifle it. You can't know that. You have to go with what you feel and what you think and just do the best you can based on that. And if you just blew off a future film god? Well he is learning too and next time maybe he will make a better impression on a writer.

Meanwhile, if you're on your own talking to someone about your material and your ideas, ask about getting paid. I know writers aren't supposed to talk about money, and when you have a great big agent, you mostly won't have to. But you don't, you are on your own, so for now, you have to do that. Talk about the filthy lucre stuff. People are fast and quick to look at writers with that holier than thou you poor sap expression and inform us this is a "business." Well, damn straight, it is a business, and while they are happy to tell us that when they think we are being too starry eyed and "artistic," once in a while we have to remind them, when they'd just as soon keep us starry eyed and artistic. And that is when the subject of money arises.

It's not out of line, asking about pay. It has to be asked nice, not belligerent or aggressive or confrontational. And not whiney.

Just nice and up front and matter of fact. "Are you planning on paying me for this?"

I got into this sitch once, in which this other writer was very caught up with a supposed producer, some guy coming out of film school who wanted to finance a film using alumni contacts to raise funding. The other writer had told this guy about one of my scripts and said he ought to read it—which was a very nice thing to do. The problem was, I had very little faith in this scenario and didn't want to send the guy a script, if this was going to lead to one of those situations where someone dicks around with your work, but doesn't plan on paying you unless (ahem) they make the movie and the movie goes blockbuster and turns them into Steven Spielberg. Which is very much what this all felt like.

So. I talked to this guy some, and he planned to direct (wow, now that came as a surprise), and I said, "You know, I need to see something you've done." And he said well he couldn't send me a tape, he hadn't even read my work, why would he make that kind of investment, without even knowing if he liked my work? And I said, "Well, we are kind of at an impasse here, then, because you at least have heard my work is good, but I have no similar knowledge of you."

Now look. We weren't talking about a feature film. We were talking about a student short. I went to film school. Hell, I was in film school at the time. Short tapes are cheap. You buy them by the case. And if you're low on funds, well you ask people to return them after they're done and hope they will. If this guy couldn't even send me a tape? Which apparently he couldn't. It was probably time to bail. So I said now would probably be a good time to discuss whether or not he was planning on paying the writer.

Which of course he was not. And it ended there.

A lot of this comes down to, know who you're talking to. Do your homework. Ask people what they have done, ask people who know people what they have done, ask who they're associated with, ask to see samples of their work, and find out if they have financing, and where it is coming from. A lot of people are protective of their financing sources. That's okay, as long as they can tell you what they've got and what they need and at least legitimize the claim they've got financing—or even know what it is. Don't be afraid to ask.

If you're talking to Scott Rudin, well, you don't have to do all that, you don't have to even determine whether or not he is planning on paying you. It's a stupid question. Of course he is. That's the way business is done on his level. But if you're not talking to Scott Rudin, find out.

And don't work with people for a compliment and a prayer. If you have done five free rewrites post them sending the script to five people? They don't believe in your work. I don't care what they say or how pretty they say it, they don't. If they did, they wouldn't ask you to change it each time someone new reads it. Drop them. Go find someone who believes in your material. Right now.

Part of valuing yourself as a professional means being able to walk away. You will never, ever be able to accomplish anything in this business if you can't do that one thing, just say no and walk away. The business is too hard. There are too many people who will run right over you. Use you. Abuse you. And discard you. You have to be able to say no. And. Walk. Away.

Valuing yourself as a professional applies to the way you write, as well. If I see one more person tell beginning writers not to write "like the pros," that pros "can do that," *i.e.* write with exciting style and voice (in other words, well), but that beginners are supposed to do "something else," which I guess means what, write without exciting style and voice? I'm going to punch someone out.

I am not talking about format or using some aberrant font, I am talking about voice, style, verve, flair. If you read a writer's work whom you admire and you want to emulate that person, to learn from them, if you want to write with verve, voice, style, and flair, for God's sake, do it.

Why do you think that person sold in the first place? why do you think that person is a "pro"?

Because that person did something no one else could, like no one else could, and they did it exciting and fast and well and that is what people buy in Hollywood. Nothing sells like voice here. Nothing. It is what makes people stand out from the crowd. What makes them special. What separates them from the thousands of people who want to do this but can't. That shining voice that is recognizable and distinctive and says, "Here is a writer, a story teller, someone who will make you see things in special ways, who will take you somewhere."

Do not listen to anyone who tells you you are supposed to somehow write in a way that demonstrates you are not a pro until the day you become a pro. The idea you can do that and then one day magically turn into a pro is ludicrous. You will not cross some magical line and then suddenly be "allowed" to write well because you are now a "professional." If you don't write well, you will never be a professional. So whatever that line is, cross it now. Become a professional because you damn well wrote like one in the first place. Because you pulled out all the stops and were wonderful and daring and exciting on the page.

In other words, write like a pro and you will become a pro. Write like you are not a pro, and you won't.

38 Who You Want to Work With

L.A. MOMENTS #642:

ME (into phone): *I bought this gun from you guys and I don't like it.*
GUN GUY: *No problem.*
ME: *Can I bring it back and use it towards the purchase of something else? I don't know how this stuff works.*
GUN GUY: *Sure. What kind of gun is it?*
ME: *It's a Glock 19 with night stuff and an extended thumb thingy.*
GUN GUY: *Is this Max?*
ME: *Um, no, this is Charlene from Denny's.*
GUN GUY: *Max, we're open till six-thirty.*

Okay, I bought that gun six months ago, how did he know?

first of all, work with someone who can get the movie made.
Let me say that again, just in case it didn't stick. Work with someone who can get the movie made.

Everyone in town, all the producers, all the studio executives, will tell you, "We love new talent, we want very much to work with the original writer on material, this is your voice and your vision and that is what we fell in love with and we want to keep you on this project here, all the way through—really." And then the second you turn your back, you are replaced on your own project.

Never work with someone because they say they will keep you on the project. They are lying.

They all do it. They'll tell you they're different, but they aren't. They are just telling you what you want to hear because (a) they want you to like them and (b) they want you to pick them to sell your script to and (c) sometimes they honestly believe it. When they say it. Later they will say everyone gets replaced on material and why is the writer upset? He or she knew that.

Well, knowing it is likely to happen and actually having it happen are two different things. And of course writers get upset. That is their baby. Take any one of those executives' or producers' baby away and say, Well you did a nice job of conceiving and carrying and giving birth to this here baby, but we think maybe now we will raise the baby with someone else because we are just smarter than you and know how to do it better? They would be a little upset. But they don't see it in those terms.

And maybe you shouldn't either. Not always. There is this sort of conclusion writers jump to, that just because a producer or studio or director or actress or actor doesn't want to work with the original writer anymore, that means these people are automatically going to hack the piece. And that's not necessarily accurate. I mean, sure, sometimes it is *real accurate*. But other times, it isn't.

I worked with two different directors on separate productions of the same play. The first director was the director from hell. Seriously, he was such a jerk, I walked away from the production. This is a guy who knew I was not a morning person, so he would tell me there was going to be a rehearsal at 6 A.M. Thinking I wouldn't show up. And it was a lie. There was no rehearsal at 6 A.M. He made that up. I know, I called his house at 5 A.M. and woke his wife up just to check, because he was such an asshole I knew he was dicking me around and wouldn't be out of bed. I probably would have killed him if I had actually driven an hour through a snow storm to a 6 A.M. rehearsal that was made up, too. But—

The asshole director understood the material and did a good job directing it and the play came out perfect.

The second director was a sweetheart, really nice, very interested in my opinions, etc., wanted me there at every rehearsal, all that stuff—except she was blind. Not "blind" blind, metaphorically unable to see blind. She simply did not get the material, didn't hear the dialogue, was simply not, from my perspective, qualified to interpret or direct the material, because she didn't understand it.

The result was a production that stunk.

Given my choice, I'd choose to work with a wonderful director who loved me and got my material first. That is the best of both worlds. My second choice would be a jerk from hell director who threw me off the set, but still got the material. And God save me from "nice directors" who haven't got a clue. Just don't even go there.

When you make decisions about who to work with—and you won't always get choices, sometimes those choices are just thrust upon you and you have to do the best you can in an imperfect world, but when you do—there are three things you should be thinking about. And not one of those is, who will not replace me on the project? Because everyone will. And if they say they won't they are lying. The three things are: (1) Do I get along with this person? (2) Does this person get the material? (3) Can this person get the movie made? And not in that order.

I would love to tell you the most important thing here is whether or not you like the person and can have a fun time working with them. The problem is, in the early days, whatever choices you make had better be smart up front because you don't get many. And no matter how much you like someone? If they don't get the material, they will botch the movie. And if they can't get the movie made, well, they can't even do that right.

I would also like to tell you the most important thing is that the person gets the material. But if they can't get a movie made, that won't make any difference, you have no movie.

So, in our imperfect world, the most important thing going in is, can this person get the movie made? That is number one. Because being produced counts.

See, a writer with a movie, even a bad movie, gets a certain amount of respect in this town because, no matter how bad the movie turned out, anyone who has been around awhile knows that at some point, this writer created something that was so good, it inspired other people to spend the ton of money and time and effort it takes to make a movie. It may not have turned out so good, but by God, it had something going for it going in. People believed in it. And it got made.

That says a lot. And you need that produced credit. So ask yourself who can get this movie made. First and foremost. That is the most important thing.

And then ask yourself whether they get the material. You are still probably going to have to go with the person who can get the movie made, even if they don't get the material, simply because you need that produced credit. Then you just pray. But sometimes you have a choice, sometimes more than one person wants to make the movie, and then you weigh clout points to make a movie against do they get the material and go with the best combination of both.

Or try to. People can fool you. It will sound like they understand that script, they love that script, they just get that script. And then the whole group mentality thing of the movie making process starts and they forget what they ever loved about that script or got about it and "smart people individually sometimes turn into morons in groups" syndrome sets in and you are, basically, screwed. But you do what you can. Hope for the best. And sometimes you may actually get it right.

And after you have figured out who here out of this group of people all over your script can get the movie made, and who out of that group actually gets the material and might make it right? You get to ask yourself who you like. Try for all three. If you can't get all three, try for two. If you can't get two? Get the movie made.

Later, when you have made lots of movies, some even good because people got the material, you can work just with people you like. It will be a great big party. You will have a lot of clout. All the people you work with will be fun. Not only will you like them, they will get the material and can get a movie made, too.

But to get to that place? Get the movie made.

That is, of course, if you are selling material. There is another scenario. A project is already set up at a studio and there is a script or treatment or book already on the table, and now they need a writer and are thinking maybe that writer could be you.

This can be a very good thing. We all need the work. And especially good if you like the project and them and they like you. Everyone is happy, right?

Yes. If everyone sees the material the same way. That is important: If everyone sees the material the same way.

See, you'll go in to see the producers, and they will pitch you the book or treatment or existing story that needs writing or rewriting, and you will say, "Oh that sounds interesting, let me take a look." Then you'll take a look and if you like it, you'll figure out how you'd do it, and then you and the producers will get together and you'll tell them how you would do it, and if that sounds good to them, you will all go talk to the big studio honchos, and if that sounds good. You have a job.

Here's where you get into trouble. They like you a lot, but not how you would do it. This sets up a vortex of meetings, because you will go in and tell them how you would do it. And they really like you. They really want to hire you. But they can't quite convince themselves they want it done the way you are saying you would do it. So they say, "Can you flesh that out a little more? We are not quite getting it yet." Really what this means is they don't like it, but they want to like it. Because they like you. So you will go home and do lots more story work and then you will all have another meeting. "Can you flesh it out a little more?"

Look, this flesh-it-out-a-little-more stuff can turn into writing a 120 page treatment, which is a damn waste of effort because by now you could have just written the script and had done with. You have to see this scenario for what it is. You don't want to do the same things. They love you. They want to love your take. But they can't. And you can flesh it out just a little more till the cows come home, that is not going to change. You are all wasting your time. So pass. Say, "Thank you so much and I really appreciate all the time and energy you have put into this, but I think we are just going in different directions here and maybe you should talk to other writers about this and we should find something else for you and I to work on."

It will save everyone a lot of time.

The other way you can get into trouble in this scenario is, if you actually get hired to do the job. There was a book I was crazy to adapt, it was just a wonderful book, but someone already had an option on it so I was out of luck. Until they had gone through a couple drafts and were looking for another writer. And I was up for the job. Yay!

Well, maybe not yay. I had to go in and tell everyone what I would do and how I thought I would make the existing adaptation they had better.

So I did that. There was a director, there were producers, there was a big guy at the studio really interested in this project. We did a ton of meetings. Everyone was very excited. I was very excited. They hired me.

That is when I got into trouble. See, the reason I wanted to do this project was, I was in love with the book. I didn't like the script. I loved the book.

And that should have been clear to everyone in those meetings. But it wasn't. Not to the director. The director had never read the book. Just the adapted script. And he liked it.

This is something I should have found out, going in, but I was still pretty new and it didn't occur to me to even ask. You're making a book into a movie, you read the book, right? I just assumed. That was a bad mistake.

When I started writing "book" into the script and handed pages to the director, the response was not great. Okay, it was worse than not great. He hated those pages. It was a your career is over kind of hate. I know this because he told me so.

We had a very big problem. Or I had a very big problem. Someone I had told what I planned to do had not been listening. He had just been assuming that didn't matter much, he liked *me*, he thought it would be great to work with *me*. And I was a writer and could write whatever. Right? So I got hired.

Unfortunately, I can't write "whatever." I can write what I tell you I am going to write. But I can't write something that is totally not what I write. The message was clear, though: Write what you can't write, or your career is over.

I shut down and didn't write for two months. The phone was screaming with people asking me when I thought I would be finished. I couldn't "finish." I couldn't even write. That is very bad. Bad for your head. Bad for your soul. And bad for your career. In the end, I turned something in. It wasn't very good. Nobody was happy. Not me. Not the director. Not the producers. Not the studio. Hell, I think I'm blackballed at a studio now because everyone was so unhappy.

That is not good for your career.

I shouldn't have been working on that project. I should have seen the warning signs going in. I didn't because I was new enough I didn't know what to watch for. Well, now I do. And you should watch for it. See, people will give you jobs because they like you. And you might like them. But they don't always know what you can do, they don't always pay attention, and you must. Make sure everyone in that room is planning on doing the same thing. If they aren't, find out what they are planning on doing. If you can do that, great. If you can't do that, don't take the job. Another job will come along you can do. This one will only tie you up and hurt you.

39 On Writing That Works and Writing That Doesn't

MOMENTS OF THE SURREAL FROM HOLLYWOOD #102: *I'm going to Ralph's. I park beside the store and am walking through the parking lot. This kid comes around the corner. He's on a cell phone: "I don't care what Morty said. I want an answer on this. I get it today or the deal's off." That sort of stuff. The kid is talking about "the deal." He's nine.*

i am not going to tell you how to write. Frankly I don't have room. Just surviving and how things work on the business side is a lot. I've got a ton of stuff here about it. It just won't fit. And there are a lot of classes and books out there already that will all tell you how to write. There are scores of them. Writers telling writers how to write. The mind boggles.

I will tell you when and why a script works for me, and when and why it doesn't. Maybe that is a good starting place.

The first sign to me I'm into something good, when I open a script, is, I open that script and someone is telling me a story. This sounds simple. It can't be, or more people would do it. Have you ever been to a party, and there is a person there who is a story teller? You know who this person is immediately, because they laugh and are animated and there are several people around them, leaning forward, listening. They may be telling a joke, or they may be talking about getting pulled over on the way to the party, but they tell the story well? Those are the screenwriters. They are story tellers. They talk through metaphor and action and dialogue. And they hold an audience, because they deliver set up and pay off and punchline. (When they feel like it. Other times they are holed up being irascible in old pajamas with their hair sticking up. Try to catch them at parties.) When you open a script that does that, where someone is telling you a story, you know it, about five pages in.

I mean it, too. Five pages in, I know. Sometimes less. It's that clear.

When do I know a script isn't working?

Well. When it takes forty pages to launch a story, there's a problem. Sometimes this is the result of bad teaching. People go into these screenwriting classes and are told, Set up your story in the first thirty pages (and they're told they have all thirty pages to do that, too), set up your characters. Tell us all about them. So these poor writers set about the grueling process of telling you just who these people are by setting up all sorts of stuff, jobs, hobbies, vices, tax returns, Rudolph the red-nosed reindeer, who knows what all is in there—but it's all backstory and minutia. None of it has anything to do with the story. And then, forty pages down the line, a story actually appears. Don't do that. Just tell your story. Then worry about maybe how much information about the junior prom you didn't manage to cram into that love story about octogenarians.

I'll run through some of the other more glaring problems that sort of show up regularly. Let's go fast.

Too much exposition. When characters explain everything,

who people are, what the events are leading up to the story, all the details that maybe characters should be doing, instead of talking about doing? Think of the party person. How often does the party person say, "And then the character talked for fifteen minutes, and here's what he said." Not often. Because that's not how you tell a story.

Over-described action. Sometimes, these are screenwriting class victims, too. The instructor says, Don't just say a guy got out of a car, tell us this in a new and different way. So these people jump through hoops to figure out a new and different way to describe someone getting out of a car, which usually entails describing which arm he used to open the door, how his fingers were positioned on the door handle. Jeez. Knock it off! Look, what that really means? "Tell us in a new and different way"? Is "use good verbs." Saunter, strut, glide, sashay, trudge, stomp, are all other ways to say "walk." Use good verbs and you will be fine.

Writers being too much in their heads, not enough in the audience seat. This usually indicates a writer lacks the skills needed to express emotion through story events or action. The writer has imbued the story with a great deal of emotional content, but not figured out how to express it through action. So you get stuff like guys going to the cemetery five or six times and shedding tears, to show you just how much they miss this dead person, but that is repetitious and doesn't demonstrate an emotion, or elicit an emotion in response, it just shows a guy crying a lot. And usually says there is something in the writer's head the writer is trying to express without developing action within the story that will express it or elicit an emotional response from an audience in return. That's lack of craft.

Scenes that go nowhere. A scene ought to be doing something, but I've read a lot of scripts in which one third of the scenes went all over the place, and the other two thirds simply didn't move story. This is the question to ask yourself, when you read through a script. Read each scene separately, and ask yourself, What has changed? What do I, someone unfamiliar with the story (ahem), know now, having read this scene, that I didn't before I read it? There had better be something, hopefully involving story, at the very least involving character, or better yet involving both, new and happening in the story, or the scene shouldn't be there. I think a lot of new writers are blind to this, and just keep writing scenes, thinking well the scenes sound good, without recognizing the scenes must accomplish something—and maybe that is lack of practice. It takes time to learn some of this stuff. But now you've had all this great practice writing scenes, even if some of these are very good scenes on their own? If they aren't contributing to a viewer's knowledge of the story and/or characters in some way? They have to go. To make room for scenes that do.

That is scenes working as a group.

Scenes also have to stand on their own. Scripts are built out of scenes, and while sure, the scenes should all work together to create one work? Scenes should, individually, have a beginning, middle, and end. They have structure, turning points, an emotional peak, just like a movie. They each say something. And have a point. People get lost in the big picture sometimes and too often don't evaluate scenes as individual elements.

Scenes that are too long. Yikes. If scenes are too long? (Bear in mind a page of script is approximately a minute of screen time, how long have those people been standing by the woodshed whittling?) Knock the top and bottom five lines of dialogue off the scene and see if it still plays. Some people are not good at entering and leaving a room, this is a "kill the long good-byes and hellos" trick. If the scene still works? Do it again.

Personally, I think writers are born. Or had that piece of them at birth that was potential writer already inside them and then it was crafted by circumstances until one day there they were, full blown writers. Wow. There they are.

Writers have to learn craft, though. Craft is important. It's your toolbox. It will help you do what you want to do. Everything I was talking about up there, all those problems in scripts? A lot of those are craft problems, writers just didn't have the tools to do what they intended to. So what they wanted to achieve stayed locked in their heads. Well, that's because they lacked tools.

When I said one day, "Okay that's it, I'm writing," and set out to do that? Nothing in my head looked the same on paper as it did in my head. The emotions, the images, they were not there. It was pretty frustrating. Not to mention annoying. So I took classes. I studied other writers, what they did, how they did it— for a long time. And sometimes, now, I get what I want on the page. Not always. But sometimes. And that's craft. The ability to mechanically manipulate language to create an intended emotion or image in another person's head. And it can be learned. It's not talent. Talent is pretty much something you have or you don't. At least in my opinion. But craft is the technical ability to focus talent using techniques that can be learned. Not everyone studies. Some people, I am sure, don't have to. But I did. And I don't think it could hurt anyone, not even people who get along fine without it. It can only help.

All that said, the only real rule I know in writing is, *Don't be boring.* Sleeping people don't read a word you write or hear a thing you say. How can they? They are asleep. So don't put anyone to sleep, and you will probably do okay. Put people to sleep, and it is all over.

40 On "Visual" Writing, or, Your Lit Professor Lied

GROUCHY MOMENT #167: *Tell hubby it is not about directors. It is about films.*

if you are here because your college Lit professor told you you should maybe try screenwriting because you are such a "visual writer," you may be here by mistake.

Anyone who would like to see "visual writing" in literary terms can pick up an Anne Rice novel. Anne Rice is a "visual writer." She will spend three paragraphs describing ivy curling around, over, and under an iron fence. That's lovely. But that's not screenplays. That is never screenplays. Screenplays don't work that way.

Many prose writers make the mistake of thinking because they're good at that, at writing intriguing and long descriptions of objects or environments, or because they are prone to that descriptive element of prose writing, they should take a crack at screenplays. Often because someone who has never read a script and doesn't know a thing about screenplays told them so. Like that Lit professor. Well. He knows nothing about scripts. He is making it up. And he is wrong.

That doesn't mean, if you're a prose writer and want to try scripts, you can't or shouldn't. You might be a bang up screenwriter who just has to sit down and write a script to find that out. You won't know till you try. But there are a couple things you should know, going in.

Scripts are 120 pages long. Give or take a little. That's how many pages you get to tell a visual *story*. Emphasis on *story*. That is the mistake the Lit professor made, in interpreting "visual" in relation to scripts. He was thinking visual "passage" or visual "description." We are in actuality talking visual "story," when it comes to scripts.

Screenwriters do not write long elegant descriptions of curling ivy on iron fence posts. We write verb driven action sentences, free of clutter, that move story. The *story* is "visual." The people, places, scenes, and events. The movement. All that is "visual." Not the paragraphs. We really don't write in paragraphs. Not paragraphs in the classical sense of the word. We write in something that could almost be defined as sub-paragraphs.

One word sentences.

"Silence."

One sentence paragraphs.

"The branch moves."

Three lines of scene description is a lot, and then, most times, we hit return and are off and running.

Not all screenwriters. There are a couple pretty great screenwriters who write blocks of text. But they're rare. (I'm not even going to name any for fear I'll get shot for even suggesting anybody wrote larger than normal blocks of text.) And they aren't describing ivy. They're describing (a) action or (b) emotion. Almost always.

If you don't believe me, pick up a script. In most cases, you will see just as much white space on the page as you do words. And that's how scripts, in general, are written.

So. If you want to take a crack at scripts, go for it and good luck to you. But please ask your Lit professor to stop telling prose writers already prone to overwriting descriptive passages they should be writing scripts. Before he hands out any more advice like that, he should read a few scripts.

41 Parentheticals and Other Lies

L.A. MOMENTS #49: Some kindly soul decided to fill my new trash cans with their trash—I guess they didn't think I could do it on my own—so none of my trash fit. Now, having managed to dispose of my trash, their trash, miscellaneous trash from about the galaxy, in fact, if anyone else has trash they would care to drop off, feel free (jeez!), someone has decided to gift me with a cast off baby blue Tupperware atrocity occasionally mistaken for a trash can. Baby blue? Who're they kidding?

In every book and every class, they hammer away at you about parentheticals. That is that cue in brackets below the character's name, above the character's dialogue, that suggests what sort of mood a character should be in, delivering the dialogue. (Angry!) (Breathless!) Instructors and gurus will say don't use parentheticals, that it is insulting to your actress or actor to put those in, that your actor or actress will have their own ideas about how they should play the scene without any suggestions from you. (You bet they will, and not all of them good, either. Ahem.) So you are not supposed to use parentheticals. Right?

Well. Maybe.

I had an interesting meeting. Going over a script in a development meeting with the producer's people, prior to sending a script to the studio. I write spare scripts. I almost never use parentheticals. That's the way I write scripts. But I'm in this meeting, and I'm getting pounded for this line of dialogue. It is a pretty simple line, and the person who is delivering it is pretty specifically in a certain type of mood. I don't remember the specific line, but it was something like "No problem" being said in a pretty sarcastic way. And this dialogue appears way into the script, if you've come this far, you should probably know this smart ass character in this situation would be being sarcastic. And someone in the meeting is asking me to make the dialogue more *tone* specific. (Tone really means tone here, just like a writer would use it.) And I say, "Look, I am not going to cheese up the dialogue, this is delivery specific, any actress can do this and will do it right and well, because she knows the character and has read the dialogue preceding this (hopefully) and the scene (hopefully), and if she is too stupid to get it, the director can tell her, because he's no slouch either."

The producer person looks at me. It is one of those oh-she's-being-difficult looks. And says, "I know that, but these are studio big shots we're handing this script to, I know them. They won't get it, they are in a hurry, they have to be hand fed."

So we went round and round. And finally I said, "Okay, I'm not going to third-grade my dialogue here, I can't do that, how about if I put in a parenthetical? Will *that* work?"

And everybody sighed in relief and she said, "Yes."

So. I have been told by a producing entity to put parentheticals into a script.

This is funny to me, because when I was coming up through the trenches, people were always yelling you weren't supposed to use parentheticals. And I am sure they are still telling people the same thing, "Don't use parentheticals." But—and here is the big "but"—they are telling you not to use parentheticals for the wrong reason. Parentheticals are not for the actor, or the actress, or even the director. Parentheticals are for studio big wigs who have to be "hand fed."

I said "hand." Not "shovel." If using a couple parentheticals will clarify an ambiguous line of dialogue? Great. Use a parenthetical. Just don't plow the script under with them.

Likewise, people will tell you in lots of cases, "Don't use flashbacks! Whatever you do, flashbacks will just slow down a plot, bog down a story, they are no good, don't use them!" Quite a few people feel this way or think this way and will tell you this. The thing is, I watched *The Fugitive*. Now that is a pretty good movie. Fast paced, action packed, wow, that plot moves. And that movie is (guess what?) full of flashbacks. Rent it on tape and count them. They are all over the place. Flashbacks galore. But the movie moves. How come, if flashbacks are such a tool of the devil and slow down plots and mess up films, flashbacks worked in *The Fugitive*?

Well, um, because flashbacks aren't bad. They are just a tool. And if they're used well, they work well telling a story on film. If they didn't, no one would go see movies with flashbacks in them and smart actors like Tommy Lee Jones and Harrison Ford wouldn't star in them. And that means, those people telling you flashbacks are bad are just plain wrong. I don't care how, I don't care why, they just are. Don't tell them that to their faces, we don't want to hurt anyone's feelings, but know that and don't tie your hands up, if you are writing a script and flashbacks would make it a better script. Flashbacks are a tool. Use them, like any other tool, wisely.

The next biggy is voice overs. "Wow, don't use voice overs," people will tell you. "That is just a lazy writer's way of telling an audience what is happening when a writer should be showing what is happening on screen." Well, sometimes. But not all the time. Voice overs worked pretty well in *The Accidental Tourist*. They worked okay in *Bull Durham*. Call me crazy, I think those are good movies. They weren't ruined by voice overs. I can't imagine them without them. Because—tell me if you've heard this before—voice overs are tools. Used right, they can be effective. Used wrong, they can be defective. The key point is, how they are used. Right? Or wrong?

And that is where people who tell you that voice overs, or flashbacks, or parentheticals are not something you can use, if you want to write a good movie, are wrong.

Those are all tools you can use and write a perfectly fine movie. Even a great movie. Maybe one that might even get made, if you put the parentheticals in so the studio big wigs who have to be "hand fed" get the story. (And any actors or actresses out there, please stop making scenes about parentheticals, they are not for you, they are for dummy big shots, we know you're smart, settle down.)

Tools only work, however, if you use the tools well. And maybe these people who keep telling you parentheticals or flashbacks or voice overs are devices of the devil have just seen them used one too many times *not well* and decided they had to go, all of them, lock stock and barrel. (Or maybe they just heard someone else say it and are playing parrot today, ahem.) That doesn't make them bad tools, though. That just makes them maybe harder-to-use-right tools. Use them wisely.

42 What You See On Screen

SAFE RESPONSES TO REALLY STUPID SUGGESTIONS #742: "Can I call you back? Someone is at the door."

What you see on screen is not a script. Quite often, it is not even a close approximation of a (the original) script. It is a movie.

Do not mistake the two. Especially if you are writing scripts on speculation. I'm not kidding. I am so tired of a writer asking me to read something, and then when I say, "You know, you have a problem here?" Saying, "Oh I know, but it's good enough, I mean, did you see that trash at the box office this week? That is as good as I have to be."

Um. No. That is not as good as you have to be. The movie is never as good as you have to be. Your competition is not movies. Your competition is scripts. Don't ever tell yourself what you write only has to be as good as what's on screen. What's on screen didn't sell to a studio. A script sold to a studio. And was probably pretty good, to do that, too, probably. Before it got "developed."

You don't hear a lot of writers saying, "Wow, they took that script of mine that wasn't very good and sure made a great movie out of it." Now that could just be writers hogging all the credit for that poor under-appreciated director's work. Or it could be a lot of scripts started out better than the movies they eventually became. A lot can go wrong making a movie, and while everyone is trying to do the right thing and make a good movie, not everyone knows exactly what that is or should be. Things get confused and a lot of writers get involved, one after the other, taking notes from a lot of different people who are not always all pulling in the same direction, and the outcome, after all the chefs get done, does not always exactly look like the cake everyone thought they were baking.

Then a bunch of trying-to-be-writers go watch it and say, "Wow, that is pretty bad, I can write something that bad," and that is what they shoot for. "Something that bad."

Don't shoot for mediocre just because some of what you see on the screen is mediocre. In most cases, it did not start out that way. It started out a really good script. It is just hard to make a movie and sometimes things go wrong and when you see a mediocre movie on the screen, that is probably what happened. Things went wrong. Between script and screen, a lot can go wrong.

A spec draft is different from a shooting draft. A bunch of what you write in a spec draft, you wouldn't even put in a shooting draft. (For example, those parentheticals. Ahem.) See, it's hard for readers to make all the story connections, without visuals on a screen in front of their noses. A lot of those readers are grouchy and reading in a hurry because they have all these other scripts to get through. They are not paying as much attention as maybe you need them to. So you put extra stuff in a spec—where visuals will carry the information in the movie—so readers will *get it,* during the read.

It's a weird game. You have to overwrite the spec, to give the readers a full idea of what's happening in the story—but at the same time, you have to write in such a way everything looks like it absolutely has to be there.

Or, looks like it was meant to be there, but is really just there so someone can fight with you later about taking it out. Losing it will not be a great loss, but making you take it out will maybe make someone feel like they have done their job and then maybe they will leave the good stuff alone. (Delicate cough.)

And you have to do this all really well. Because if you don't, no one is going to buy it. They don't buy mediocre scripts. They buy great scripts. They just sometimes make them into mediocre movies. (And we all wish it was the other way around.)

If you sat down and transcribed one of those mediocre movies people are fond of comparing their scripts to, and compared it to the spec draft that sold? You would get a clear picture of what I'm talking about. So that's your homework. Pick a mediocre (in your opinion) movie that started out a big splashy spec sale, track down the original spec, read it, then watch the movie. And then you will know the difference between what is on screen. And what you have to write to make a sale.

And never, ever, when you are writing a script on speculation, say, "I could do better. But this is good enough." If you could do better, it is not good enough. It is only good enough when you can't do better. So just go for it. Write to sell. Not to be as good as some movie you saw. To sell. If it doesn't sell, well, that's the nature of the beast. But always write for it, like there's no tomorrow and this is it, the real thing. The worst that can happen is you fail, people laugh at you, and you're forced to leave the country. Big deal. Switzerland is nice. The best that can happen is, you'll sell. And there's a good feeling that comes with REALLY trying. Instead of hanging on that limb between fear and failure, you can sit back, breathe, and say, "Okay, fine, I gave it my best shot, at least if I get hit by a truck tomorrow, no one can fault me for not trying." There's something to be said for that.

43 High Concept

GOOD ADVICE NOT TAKEN #15: "Don't turn the script in till the studio hires a director."

high concept, in a nutshell, is a story idea so novel, the concept alone will lure audiences into the theater. (The irony being, when a script is high concept, quite often a lot of important people get involved, so the idea alone almost never ends up being the only lure. But I digress.)

The Last Action Hero is high concept. A little boy's favorite action hero comes off the movie screen into his world. The movie didn't turn out so great, but it was a great idea. High concept.

Groundhog Day is high concept. A man must relive one day until he gets it right and wins the woman he loves. High concept. (And I bet a bitch to execute.)

Jaws is high concept. A rogue shark terrorizes an island community and some poor schmo—afraid of water, no less—must get on a boat and go kill it. And (I love this) the shark is bigger than the boat. No one had ever seen it before. High concept.

Jurassic Park is high concept. Recombinated dinosaurs in an amusement park run mad. No one had ever seen it before. High concept. (Most of Crichton's stuff is high concept. I wish I had that guy's head for story.)

Sometimes people confuse "box office" with "high concept." That's fine, in hindsight, but just because a movie makes a lot of money, that doesn't mean it's a new or novel idea. Someone the other day was saying *Grease* was high concept. *Grease* had just been re-released and I guess was making big box office, which is great for the owners of *Grease,* but *Grease* is about a boy and girl from opposite sides of the tracks who fall in love. That is not new or novel. Big box office, sure. But not new and novel. The concept predates Shakespeare. And is not high concept.

When people hear a high concept idea, they know it. And it sells. That is sort of the point of trying to think high concept, people call you high concept in advance of making big box office and you sell. If you think high concept, you are blessed. You will sell scripts no matter how well or badly you write, because people will buy your scripts for the ideas alone, and then hire someone good to rewrite you, if you just aren't the prince of execution. (Well, you could be so bad, I guess, they can't find the concept, in which case you won't sell, but let's pretend that couldn't happen.) If you think high concept and are good? You're a god and I need to put a hit out on you because I don't need that kind of competition.

44 That Genre Is Dead

SAFE RESPONSES TO REALLY STUPID SUGGESTIONS #849: "That's the stupidest thing I've ever heard in my life!" (Just kidding.)

my first script was a supernatural thriller. (Stop laughing, it was.) Also known as horror. That was the first time I was going to hear a genre was "dead." I was talking to this semi-bored, very filled with ennui man on the phone, I think he was an agent, and he said, "Oh don't write horror, horror is dead."

I could just hear him settling back in his chair and the little God wheels turning, too.

Interestingly, years later, Wes Craven seems to be doing okay.

The next genre I would hear the death toll for was science fiction. "Science fiction is dead." I am fascinated by how well *Star Gate* did. How well *Species* did. How *Fifth Element* rocked the house. Seeing as science fiction is dead. Hmm.

Next it was the Western. "The Western is dead." After which *Dances with Wolves* and *Unforgiven* seemed to do pretty well. (Doc Holliday was resurrected in two films. Count 'em. Two.) And then, the kicker, I was sitting in someone's office, and he looked at me with a straight face and said—

"The romantic comedy is dead." Which I am sure accounts for why *Jerry Maguire* did so poorly. (Cough-cough-cough-are-you-out-of-your-mind-cough.)

No genre is ever dead. Anyone who tells you so is stupid. It may be out of vogue. It may not be what everyone is buying this very second. It is not "dead." Genres exist for a reason: People like them. People like them so much, whatever it is about the genre that is intrinsic to it has become a God damn story telling tradition. In other words. A "genre."

And saying romantic comedy is dead, to a screenwriter who is known for romantic comedy, takes balls. What is the proper response to that? "Well gee, I guess I had better pack for Des Moines? Thanks for your time?"

What it amounts to is terrorizing writers. This is not like saying, "The Tom Cruise vampire movie didn't sell so hot so right now no one will look at vampire stories." That's honest, it's the times, it'll pass. This is different. This is saying something is *dead*. Which of course it isn't. And it only tends to get said to writers about the types of projects writers either write or just wrote. And the only reason I can think of for a person to even say something that dumb to a writer is, either the person saying it is a congenital idiot, which is not his or her fault; the person is talking too fast and not thinking, and they should know better; or the person is taking way too much pleasure in telling you the way things are in Hollywood that is not good for you, and that is definitely his or her fault.

That third bunch?

Just don't talk to people like that. Smile nice, walk out of their offices, wipe the dust off your feet, and never go back. You are not here to make tin gods feel a little more in control of their surroundings. You are here to write.

45 Teen Girls Don't See Movies

L.A. MOMENTS #54: *Would it be un-neighborly to put a sign up—I'm thinking neon with flashing lights and maybe a nice flamingo—informing fellow dwellers the next person to touch these trash cans will be shot for trespass?*

i write girl movies. They aren't necessarily for girls. I think guys will like them too because, well, guys like cute sexy girls in movies. That's why they all went to see *Clueless*.

Writing girls (sometimes my protagonist is even—shocker—a girl) can get you in tricky water, though. See, for a long time, people kept telling me the people who went to see movies were all teenaged boys. And teenaged boys, they told me, didn't want to see girls (which I guess explains why teenage boys have those sassy magazines stashed under their mattresses, hey, I have a brother), they wanted to see car crashes and action heroes.

Um, right. Did I mention *Clueless* yet? And I'm pretty sure that is why all those teenaged girls went and saw *Titanic* fifty times running. Because there is no girl audience, right?

Thank God for James Cameron. Who (and I don't know

whether this was on purpose, but it sure happened) tapped into the teen girl audience with *Titanic*.

There has always been a teen girl audience. And a twenty-something girl audience. A thirty-something girl audience. There is probably even a forty- and fifty-something girl audience. Someone went to see *Driving Miss Daisy*. Any way you slice it, there is just a "girl audience." You can see it in old black and white clips of women screaming and fainting for movie stars and singers. I have no idea who told the knuckleheads in Hollywood different. (No offense to knuckleheads in Hollywood.) It has always been there. It just didn't get tapped for a while.

If push came to shove and I was asked why people ran around so long *saying* there was no teen girl audience, I would have to guess it is because a few too many of the people wearing suits were once teenage boys, are drawn to teenage boy flicks, understand them, and do not have a clue what teen girls like (um, here is a hint: teen girls like cute guys under thirty), and for that reason, bumped their noses a few times trying to make movies for teen girls and decided there simply was no market.

Well, James Cameron and Leonardo DiCaprio just blew the roof off that one, didn't they?

So I have been thinking about this whole teen girl audience dilemma and here is what occurred to me. Hire more girls! Right now. Immediately. Girls know what girls like. They were teen girls. They have it all figured out.

Nifty idea, huh?

Better yet, hire me. I'm a girl. And I have a shoe bill you would not believe.

46 Writing for Ratings

THAT WAS A REALLY DUMB THING TO DO #3,493: Oops.

no one rates spec scripts. Seriously, I've never had anyone show up at the door, demand a spec, and stamp "R" on it. It just doesn't happen. Ever.

But people worry about ratings when they write specs. Um, why? I can see it, if someone is worried about outdistancing the intended audience. No one says "fuck" in *The Little Mermaid*. You would probably not use much harsh language in a movie for a *Little Mermaid* audience. That works. But if you're writing a mainstream feature film intended for an adult audience, why worry about ratings? Shouldn't you be worrying about what works best in the script instead? (Okay, I am not saying go "close up, carnal act." That's porn. But you know what I mean.)

In a film, you can change things right up till release. Many films have gotten harsher ratings than their makers wanted and the filmmakers went in and made changes to lower the ratings, everything from cutting scenes to dubbing dialogue, got a lower rating, and then went into release with the film. And that is after the movie has been shot. That is how malleable film is. If it isn't in a theater, you can still change it. And, in fact, you can still change it after it goes to the theater. That has happened too. A film has been released, pulled, and re-released after changes.

Now if film is that malleable, think just how malleable a script is. A script is so malleable, they will throw you off it and hire someone else to rewrite it.

That's pretty damn malleable, don't you think?

Don't worry about ratings when you write a script. Worry about what will make the script so wonderful it will leap off the page and smack someone around the room till he or she agrees to buy it. And if you have to say "fuck" to do that, say "fuck."

47 Don't Write <u>Batman</u>

THAT WAS A REALLY DUMB THING TO DO #3,494: Stop saying that.

Okay, I have to bring this up. One too many times, someone has wandered in and announced they are writing *Batman.* On spec.

You can't write *Batman* on spec. *Batman,* the comic book, the TV series, the movie franchise, belongs to someone else. The city, the characters, the Bat Cave, the Batmobile? *All* belong to someone else. *Someone* who made them up and/or *someone* who paid that person to make them up and/or *someone* who later bought the privilege to use what those *other someones* made up. Do any of those someones look like you? No. They are not you. You did not make it up. Not the world, not the characters, not the Bat Cave, not the Batmobile, not the Penguin, not the Joker, not the bat suit and certainly not that nifty tool belt. You lifted all that from someone else's work and the only thing left that could possibly be called your own is the story's plot, and even then, a plot in a made up world created by someone else probably could only arise in that world so isn't all yours either.

This applies to all the comic book characters. Batman, Superman, Spiderman, Conan, Wonder Woman, Fantastic Four, Red Sonja, Silver Surfer, Green Lantern, all of them, every single one, and more. This applies to all the franchises. *Lethal Weapon, Alien, Terminator, Gremlins, Jaws,* all of them and more. And if you write a movie using someone else's world and characters and only your situation/plot and one new nifty character you decided to make up and throw into the mix, you can't sell it. Because the world and characters belong to someone else. And that someone else is the only person legally entitled to make a movie using that world and those characters.

And a script written using someone else's world and characters isn't a great feature writing sample, either, because while it might demonstrate you can write dialogue and action, it will not demonstrate you can create characters or a world. Those were already created by someone else. So this does not demonstrate you can do that. It might demonstrate you can copy. But it won't demonstrate you can create.

Here is the only time any of this might not apply. If you are trying to convince the owner of a franchise you are the writer who should write the next sequel. If you are trying to get hired on to write the next sequel, well, this is a pretty brash way to go about it. Because you only have one person you can sell that script based on someone else's world and characters and idea to. The owner of the franchise. And it is only a good sample for one person. The owner of the franchise. I actually spoke to a guy who pulled that off once. He had been crazy mad in love with *Halloween* since he was a kid, and he wrote *Halloween* specs. And he actually got to the owners of *Halloween* and ended up writing

Halloween VI. Which is pretty remarkable. And a real nice story, don't you think? I like it. But—

I don't know how that writer is doing today. And if you want a career here? And you write a *Batman* spec? And you can't get to the owners, or you do get to them, but they say no? (And *Batman* has a bit higher budget than *Halloween*, and the bigger the budget, the less inclined people seem to be to hire untried writers.) You can't take that spec anywhere else. Nowhere else. Period. Finito. The End. It's a dead script.

Feature scripts are a lot of work. It would sure be nice if, after all that work, you had a few more places to take the script and a few more people to show it to. Think about it.

48 Writing "Marketable"

DELIRIOUS COMEBACK #938: *"That's out of my jurisdiction, better consult the Magic Eight Ball."*

I know two people who set out, purposefully, to write "marketable." Andrew Marlowe, who wrote *Air Force One* and is another Nicholl Fellowship winner, and myself. As I understand it, and I am playing fast and loose with details here because I don't know all of them, Andrew decided it was time to break out of the pack. Doing that meant writing something someone would have to buy. Wouldn't be able to say no to. Would *have* to buy. So he looked around, and what was hot was *Die Hard*. Everyone was crazy for *Die Hard*. *Die Hard* on a boat, *Die Hard* on a train. *Die Hard* on a bus, *Die Hard* on the moon. There was even a story around at the time that someone, obviously unfamiliar with *Die Hard* but catching on to the concept fast, had pitched, *Die Hard* in a building. Bottom line, everyone was mad for *Die Hard*. That's what was selling. So Andrew thought, what hasn't anybody done yet? And came up with *Die Hard* on Air Force One. I don't know how many scripts Andrew had written at the time. I know he's a damn good writer. I've read him. And he was an award-winning writer. He won that fellowship from the Academy. But now he is an extremely well known and well paid writer. Because he got methodical about it, looked around, saw what was selling, and came up with a concept for an idea that was hot at the time. And better than anyone else's because it went just one step further than anyone else's. And it sold.

I wrote eight scripts to get "discovered." Script number seven was done and people were reading it. It would go on to win the Nicholl. I was thinking, Hell, seven scripts, that is a lot. maybe it is time to sell something here. And that is about the time a person at a production company said to me, "You're a good writer, but everything you write has some sort of mystical or supernatural element. If you write something that doesn't, I think you will sell."

Most times, when I sit down to write, I write what comes into my head and stays with me. I wrote a play about dogs that perform exorcisms one time. To give you an example. That came into my head and I wrote it. After this talk with this person, I had to think about it. I hadn't thought about it in those terms before. What is a concrete story line I could work on that does not include mystical or supernatural elements? Then I wrote a script about a girl who stages her own kidnapping and it sold. That was *Excess Baggage*.

A lot of people try to sell last week's hit at the box office. I hate that. I don't think anyone should do that. But if you have been working at this for a while and people like your writing, but you are just not making that sale? Maybe it is time to sit down and get methodical about it and look at your writing and see what it is in there that is always there that might be holding you back. For me it was things mystical. For Andrew, I don't know what it was, but it was probably something. For you, what is it?

What is it that you keep doing that is stopping that crucial sale from happening?

If you can find that, that one thing, and try something different, it might make a difference.

Me, I figure, if you're going to write on spec, you might as well write about what you want to write about. We're all crazy optimists to be in this business in the first place, so run with it. But there are a lot of things you can care about. *Excess Baggage* was not about anything I hadn't written about before. It was a story about someone alienated and alone dealing with family issues. That is a thematic in a lot of my work. And the characters were not people I hadn't written about before. I write a lot of outsiders. The only thing that was really different was, plot. It was plotted both feet on the ground. No supernatural elements. Well, except for a priest, but they cut him. Bastids.

But think about it. Think about your writing, about the content, the themes (um, don't tell executives I said theme out loud here or I will never work again), and the plots. Give it some thought. And then think about how you can bring what is special about you into an arena that is possibly easier to sell. You make that one sale, it all gets easier. But you have to make that one sale, first.

49 Why You Do This

NOTES INTO THE ETHER #53: *It takes more effort to not write than to write. I am exhausted from not writing. I keep staring at myself and wondering, What is the pay off to not writing? You are wearing yourself out here, not writing. Wouldn't it be easier to give yourself a break and just write?*

People forget sometimes why they do this. Everyone has a reason. It tends to be different for different people, but one time, a long long time ago, you decided to do this. And now you're here, doing, or trying to do, this.

It's not easy. It's hard. You call people and you send out material and you get read and people say no to things no one in their right mind should say no to for reasons that make no sense because, well, they are just dumb excuses that don't make any sense so why should they make any more sense to you? And you keep going and make more calls and hit more walls and do more lunches and dinners and meetings and write more and send that out and hit more walls and—

Sometimes people get so caught up in that, in the mechanics of building a career, they forget why they started out in the first place.

That is called burn out. It hits a lot of people. Some of them quit. Even people doing pretty well. People with Oscars and big contracts. They just quit—

Because, I think, they forgot why they cared about doing this in the first place. It's easy to do. Your head feels all emptied out like there are no more beautiful words in there, and staring at a hostile computer gets to be too much and your vision is black and white 'cause the color has all bleached out of everything and reality appears petty and nondescript and the dogs bark too damn much and the blasted phone ringing might be important but probably isn't and instead will just slow you down worse and—

That's when I do odd things. Like read poetry. Which is kind of embarrassing. It is not like I am a particularly poetic person. But I like Charles Bukowski. I keep "Love Is a Dog from Hell" in the kind of spot my eyes will hit, when I am staring blankly into space.

Or sometimes I just rake leaves. Raking leaves makes me sweat and makes my shoulders sore and there's something about that that brings me back, and sooner or later I feel better and remember why it is I do this and I take a big breath of air and look around and remember—the world is a wonderful place.

It is easy to forget that sometimes you have to stop. Look around and just stop. And do something else, whatever else it is you do that will remind you who you are and why you started out to do this. What it was that mattered to you so much the only way to express it was by spinning words into forever to build stories for other people. Not the dumb mechanics of getting here. Why you chose to get here.

It will make a difference if you just stop and remind yourself.

And when it is time to stop, you will know it. And then. Stop. Go do whatever it is you do to clean out your head. When you're all better and alive again, come back.

Come back and take no prisoners.

50 The Green Light and Turnaround

THINGS TO DO WHEN YOU SHOULD BE WRITING #13: Reshape your eyebrows. (Do not do this too many times, or you will be drawing new eyebrows with Magic Marker.) Draw new eyebrows with Magic Marker.

a "green light" is a mythological thing. Okay, I'm kidding. Really it is official sanction from the studio to roll cameras. There are funny stories about green lights. One story goes, a film was on location, cast and crew, everyone waiting for a "green light." Which didn't come. And didn't come. Finally, they looked around and said, "Hey, we have cameras, we have people, we're in another country, for crying out loud, who's going to stop us?" And just rolled. With no go ahead. And (the story goes), no one at the studio knew it. Sure they knew cameras were rolling, but everyone assumed someone else had green lit the picture, so nobody asked questions, they just paid the bills as they came in, and that's how the picture got made. (I don't know what picture this was, by the way, I just like the story.) I am not even sure, in some instances, who has the authority to green light a picture and who does not. People talk about green lights all the time. They sure seem to know. To me, it is this nebulous thing, the green light, which somehow materializes from on high. Nebulous or not, however, the benefit of a green light on your end as the writer is substantial. Now the picture is green lit and cameras are rolling, the studio actually has to buy the script.

They will really keep you waiting that long, too. The script was optioned, it was re-optioned. You can know it's going to be a movie. Everyone can know it is going to be a movie. There can be one star, more than one star, a director, a whole cast, a production date, everyone can be on location with equipment and licenses and the whole shebang, and the studio will still not want to pay out for the script until cameras roll, because (they will tell you) there is this fear at the studio the film could still fall apart, and then they would be out cash for the script. (I think if they had it their way, they wouldn't pay for the script until the film was shot and in the can, I mean, stuff can still go wrong during production, face it, but they can't figure out a way to standardize that so are stuck paying when principal photography begins.)

How do you get to a green light? Well, you get a producer and you option to the studio and the studio likes the script and they start looking to cast the project and to attach a director, and everything is rolling along. But there is this meeting you have to survive at a studio. It is the annual "we all vote on the projects we have in development" meeting. Your script is one of the "projects in development." Now the studio is going to have its big meeting. So all the projects in development get copied off to all the studio executives, and the executives all go away for a "retreat" and read all the projects, and then they all vote on what's going to move forward onto the production slate, and what isn't. There can be a hundred scripts in development, but only about ten to twelve of those are likely to move onto the production slate, so this is a big deal. And this is the point at which the executives who are chaperoning your script at the studio start praying, because they need that vote, or your script is going to get shelved, *i.e.* the studio will drop the option or, if they commissioned you to write a pitch into a script, you will go into turnaround.

If you survive the pow wow (and I have always wondered if some people's votes counted more than others, but no one seems inclined to tell me), the studio will move forward with casting and attaching a director and hiring people to rewrite you to "improve" the script. And, with support from the whole studio backing the project, it has a much better chance of getting put together and actually made, *i.e.* the green light.

If you don't survive that meeting, and it's not an original spec that comes back to you once the option expires, you go into turnaround. Which means you (or more commonly your producer, who, by virtue of bringing the pitch or project to the studio with or without you attached, more often than not holds the legal keys to the material) go hunting for another studio to buy your project off the studio that doesn't want to make the movie. The new studio must reimburse the old studio the initial investment the first studio made in your script, *i.e.* option and writing monies and development costs and whatever producing fees they paid out to the producer, etc., and at times pay an additional fee for the privilege of taking the material off the first studio's hands. That fee, I have been told, in the old days could be huge, since a studio that doesn't want to make a movie also doesn't want someone else to make the same movie into a blockbuster. That tends to indicate the first studio is full of blockheads, when that happens, and nobody likes to look like a blockhead. But there has been some reform, I'm told, and they can't just hold anything they don't want to make for ransom anymore. And, once the new studio has paid up and owns rights to the script, the new studio can move ahead to make the script into a movie.

That is assuming, of course, that after surviving turnaround, you survive the next studio pow wow to come your way. Me, I am just learning about this animal called "turnaround," so all I can say is good luck, and once I have a clue, I'll get back to you.

51 What You Really Get Paid

FROM THE FILES OF "PEOPLE I'M GOING TO WRITE ABOUT SOMEDAY": I had a friend in Texas, Jimmy Lee, who got arrested carrying four guns. Do not ask me why one man needs to carry four guns. And nobody found them. So in booking, he pulled them out, laid them on the counter and said, "You'll be wanting these." Apparently, there was a good deal of excitement over that. . . .

What you read in the trades, "New Screenwriter sells spec script to Big Bang Studios for a mid-six figures," is a little misleading. The suggestion being that person just got handed five hundred thousand dollars. It happens. All sorts of things happen. But it is not the norm.

Studios, in general, do not like to buy scripts outright. They option scripts and sign a contract with the writer that states what the purchase price will be, if they make the movie. The contract further specifies what the writer will get paid for any revisions and/or polishes. (Polish is usually a polite term for "rewrite we will pay you a lot less money for." Technically, it is supposed to be smaller and easier than a real rewrite, but I haven't seen this yet.) And says what bonuses, if any, the writer will receive if, after the film is completed, the writer receives screen credit.

So the first thing you have to be discriminating about here is the difference between a purchase and an option. The trades don't always discriminate between the two. But you need to know, most of the time, when a spec script from a newcomer gets "bought," it is not really being purchased, it is being optioned, by a studio.

I am not good at math. (I'm from the humanities, leave me alone!) So I called my attorney for this part (which was at one time beautifully written out and all explained, but no one can find that damn post), and said, "Hey, I want to present an accurate portrayal of a contract breakdown so people can see actual numbers to get a clear picture what is going on here."

He told me ten different breakdowns, all radically different, and said, "Max, make it up, we do."

Uh oh. Well. Okay. For example purposes *only,* and bear in mind a humanities major is *making it up* and it is *math* (!) here is a sample breakdown:

The studio will option the script and specify terms for two rewrites and one polish in the contract. The contract will also say what bonuses you will get for sole credit or shared credit, if the movie gets made and you get screen credit.

You get the option money up front. It will be subtracted from the total purchase price of the movie, if the movie gets made and the studio has to pay you for the script. As you complete each writing stage in the contract (if you complete each stage), the price of that writing stage is also subtracted from what the studio still owes you. (All together, the writing stages tend to equal the total purchase price of the movie, so if you complete all the writing steps, the movie has been bought and paid for. Sometimes. Not always. But this is an example.) Screen credit bonuses are extra, they are not part of the total purchase price, which is why they are called a "bonus." And are dependent on the movie getting made and you receiving screen credit on the film.

Let's say someone just sold a script for $500,000. Here's how that might look on paper.

Option:	$100,000
1st Revisions:	$200,000
2nd Revisions:	$125,000
Polish:	$ 75,000
Sole Credit Bonus:	$200,000
Shared Credit Bonus:	$100,000

So, what you have in your pocket is actually $100,000. That is a decent chunk of change. But it is not $500,000.

The studio will have a certain amount of time in which to execute their option, and if at the end of that time, they want to renew, they'll have an option to renew for another fee. But what you see above is a basic (made up) contractual agreement between a studio and writer for the purchase of a spec in the mid-six-figure range.

As you start each writing stage, you will get half up front, the "commencement" fee. When you turn it in, you will get the other half, the "completion" fee. (At least in a perfect world, you will, there have been cases of writers holding scripts hostage for their commencement fees. "Um, I've finished, if you'd like to see it, you will have to pay me to start it.") So you'd get paid $100,000 to start the first rewrite, and you'd get another hundred thousand when you turned it in. Etc.

But you start off with the option, $100,000. Now how about what you put in the bank?

You got $100,000 up front. Out of that, you pay your agent 10 percent. You're now at $90,000. You pay your attorney 5 percent. You're now at $85,000. If you have a manager, that's at least 10 percent. $75,000. The Guild gets $2,500 to join, if you're new. $72,500. If you've got an accountant on commission (some people do) that'll be another 5 percent, but we'll leave that off, most people starting out don't, and the fun part is coming. Uncle Sam. Uncle Sam gets up to 55 percent. *Kaching.* You have $17,500 left over. That's what you put in the bank. It's nice, but it won't buy a Mercedes.

If you want to break it down further, count the years it took a person to perfect their craft, make their contacts, and make their first sale. Say it was five years. $3,500 per year, back pay. Big bucks, huh?

It's not all bad. You will probably have write offs to save some of the money from Uncle Sam. You will probably go on to do at least one of the writing stages in the contract. That will pay (half up front, half on completion, and you get to keep what's left over after paying out commissions, Guild fees, and Uncle Sam). If the movie gets made, whether or not the writing stages were fulfilled, you'll get the full purchase price (minus whatever monies have been paid to you already, minus commissions and taxes, etc.). And if you get screen credit, you'll get that bonus (minus commissions and taxes). Slowly, but surely, if you keep working and getting jobs, you will pull ahead on the back pay issue and eventually even start to feel a little flush. But remember this rule: For every quarter you spend in Hollywood, you need to earn a dollar.

52 The Guild

SAFE RESPONSES TO REALLY STUPID SUGGESTIONS #598: "Let's ask your boss and see what he thinks."

What the Guild, *i.e.* the Writers Guild of America, West, will do for you, if you are not a member, is not much. The Guild is not entirely friendly to outsiders. It has a mentor program, but that is only for members. It has a "get writers read by agents" program. But that is only for members. It has a "get writers read by producers" program. That, too, is only for members. Which makes a certain amount of sense. The Guild is a union. It exists to help its own.

If you are not a member, you are not "its own" and pretty much out of luck. I've known non-members who called the Guild to ask for information and were asked if they were members and summarily dismissed when they said no. And that was just asking for information. However, the Guild will provide you with a list of signatory agents (not all of whom are screened too carefully for ethical business practices, so be wary) for a couple bucks and a SASE. It will provide you with contact information on members, if you call. And it will provide you with a list of what jobs/sales/options accrue what points toward Guild membership, if you'd like to know just what you have to do to qualify to become a member. (Selling a spec script will get you the points to get you in.)

This is not a club you gain entrance to through application. You don't call the Guild. The Guild calls you.

When I got my first contract, I got a call from the Guild telling me it was time to join. I was startled, I didn't know I had the points to join. Each piece of work you do professionally is considered so many "points" toward membership in the Guild. When you have accumulated a specified number of points, you are required to become a Guild member or you can no longer be employed by signatory companies, i.e. studios and production companies that have signed a contract with the Guild to be nice to writers—and that contract specifies how nice they are required to be. I had an option, but not an outright sale. And an option, as far as I knew, did not rack up enough points to qualify you to join. A sale did. An option didn't. I also, however, had a contract that said what I would get paid to do a certain number of rewrites, but I am skeptical of "woulds," and figured I had to do the work to accumulate the points and then I would be qualified to join. Wrong. Apparently, if you have contracted for the work, you have the points and it is time to join. So I did, which cost $2,500 (ow) and went to the Guild "orientation meeting."

If you can't pay that up front, by the way, I was told the Guild will let you pay in installments. That's not far fetched, that pay in installments plan, either, since $2,500 is about half the minimum basic amount a signatory can get away with paying a writer for an option on a feature script—or was when I joined—and the other half would pretty much go for taxes.

Also, it might be good to point out, you can't join the Writers Guild without the minimum number of points, but you can sell, without the points, to Guild signatories. After the sales equal out to the number of points needed for Guild membership, however, you have to join, or you can't work for signatory companies anymore (which is almost all companies in features, and definitely all companies in television).

The first thing that happened, when I went to the orientation meeting, was I showed up on time and was told to wait in the hall.

After some waiting around and a few cigarettes in the garage, the meeting started. It was run by a woman who didn't like me. On sight. Okay, that is not putting it strongly enough. She despised me. On sight. During the entire meeting, if I would raise my hand, she would ignore me. It was so obvious, other people started raising their hands to tell her I had my hand up. One of the people "orienting" us held up a black binder-type book and said, "This is your book that contains all the rules and regulations as well as rights you're entitled to as a Guild member, you'll get this, if you haven't already, and you'll receive updates." Then someone pulled his coat tail, there was muttering and whispering among the "old hands," and someone else said, "Er, we don't provide that anymore."

That was the last I heard about documentation the Guild provided members until I got into a sticky situation in 1996 and had to call to say I didn't know fuck what to do about it because I never got "the manual." So, going in, I had no information, no booklets, no manual. And no one was too damn friendly. I did get a small plastic ornament that said "Writers Guild '95" at the next meeting, a "come see a film clip about your Guild buddies on strike" sort of affair. A bargain, I guess, for $2,500.

I hear rumors active Guild members can't understand why

new members aren't more involved or active. Well, I don't like showing up on time and being told to sit in the hall and wait like I'm some little kid. I don't like being chucked under the chin and told "You're so cute, you must write romantic comedy." (I said, "Yes I do, but everybody dies.") I don't like being condescended to. I don't like being ignored. And every piece of information I was given at the "orientation" that I might have found useful was either contradicted there, or, on follow up, was inaccurate or contradicted later. Oh, and while we're at it, I'm sorry so many Guild members are out of work, but I. Am. Not. The. Enemy.

If every new member is sharing my experiences, I would say the reason new members don't know their rights is, it's damn hard to find out what they are. And the reason new members aren't active or sometimes even interested is, they are disenfranchised from their Guild going in.

It got better. Um, over a year later. Probably because I mentioned my dilemma to someone in an open forum. At which point someone who was someone at the Guild heard someone was real unhappy and talking about it in public and I got e-mail and people started being a little more helpful. There are some helpful, nice people at the Guild, too. You just have to find them. And that is the problem. If you are new, you don't know how to find them because you don't know who they are. And let me tell you, the welcoming committee is not . . . welcoming. (You know who you are, Bun Woman.)

I am probably never going to be a great Guild member. My early experiences also include being told I was not Max Adams by a woman who tried to bar me from a Guild screening, and finding out from a producer (who had had a little trouble finding me, ahem) that every time people called the Guild for contact info, they were told I was a sixty year old man who wrote *Go Navy* and didn't have an agent. Because I was not listed in the damn computer. And no one was in a hurry to fix that at the Guild. I had to yell at three people to make them even consider fixing that.

(There is another Max Adams. If that happens, if there are two of you, whoever comes second—or third or fourth—has to come up with a variation of the name that distinguishes them from the first person to join bearing the name. That is why I am Max D. Adams. The "D" stands for Dammit, because Max "The Younger" Adams did not seem particularly polite. Though the impulse was there.)

Other than that, the Guild is a great place. I think. There are helpful people there, once you find them. People who will fix computer databases that don't list you or your credits (though I still get congratulated once in a while on *Go Navy*, quit it, smart asses) and will send you manuals and will go over arbitration procedure on the phone with you and explain stuff you don't understand. And the Guild has accomplished great stuff to make life better for writers. I'm a member and therefore entitled to that great stuff—better treatment, better pay, better response times, health insurance,* dental coverage, retirement funds—great stuff accomplished through long strikes that cost people jobs, houses, and sometimes careers. I appreciate that. I'd better. They showed me a film about it when they gave me the plastic ornament. Right before they told me to look to my right, that person would be rewriting me. (Um, I thought it was supposed to be us against

*To date, Guild Industry Health Fund benefits are only accumulated under the auspices of "work for hire," *i.e.* work done under contract to a studio. They are not accumulated through the sale and/or option of "original" material. This means any writer whose income is derived solely from the sale and/or option of original material loses all benefits. I know this, because I did lose all benefits. While I was making some pretty good paychecks, too. Likewise, any writer not under contract to a studio by virtue of unemployment will, after a short period of time, lose all benefits. You work for the man, or your union will not insure you. Nice system.

them, what is this us against each other crap?) I would like, however, to see a little reform in the manner in which people are inducted into and introduced to their Guild. In my experience, it is not a friendly place for newcomers.

The Guild does, however, for about $20, provide registration services for scripts. For members and non-members. Registration lasts five years and while the Guild does not guarantee content, it does store and date material, which carries legal ramifications.

The Guild also publishes a periodical, *Written By,* which can be informative reading, moreso for television writers than feature writers, but there is stuff in there for feature writers too. This is provided to members for free and costs $40 for a one year subscription for non-members.

And the Guild publishes a yearly members directory, which lists members and (sometimes) their credits and representation. This can be a good place to look up who is representing whom, doing agent research. The directory is available for about $10.

For information on Guild publications and/or services, contact The Writers Guild of America, West. It is listed in "Resources."

53 Screen Credit and Arbitration

L.A. MOMENTS #50: The L.A. trash guys keep leaving the baby blue mystery trash can by the curb. I guess they think it is just festive and scary enough you might own it on purpose. If I put a sign on it, will they take it then?

What you get paid, after all is said and done and you finally have a movie up there on the screen, is dependent on what screen credit you get, because "bonuses" are attached to screen credit.

So, when you negotiate your contract, you place bets. This is standard. The studio is figuring in bonus stuff on top of whatever deals it cuts for straight writing. And the studio can be generous with everyone, negotiating bonuses, since only three writing entities, more than likely, are going to get actual writing credit. It can pass bonuses out to everyone, on paper, and only have to pay out those few, in the end.

So you take a look. And say, well this is what I think I will get, this screen credit, so I would like a big bonus for it. In the off chance I don't get what I think I'll get, I'll take a lesser bonus there, which is what would come next. And this here won't happen, so I'll give up any bonus on that for a bigger bonus on those other two. You spread the bonus out that way. Based on what screen credit you think you are going to get. And then you hope you were right.

If you are the first writer on the project, you will negotiate for a big bonus for sole writing credit, a medium bonus for shared credit, and not much if you get no credit. And that goes double, if the project is your original spec, because it's hard to write the original writer off a spec. Not impossible. But harder than it is, say, to write a writer off an adaptation, because you have to change more of the material of an original script to throw the writer off the screen. About 20 percent more.

That's the standard. And odds are in the first writer's favor he or she will get some credit, even if it's not sole, even on an adaptation. It's the first script.

If, however, you are coming to a project late, you may negotiate for a big bonus if you are the last writer on the project. Screen credit may not look too likely. There may have already been five writers on this project. You may take a look and assume you're not going to get a screen credit. So you give up the screen credit bonus in exchange for a bonus if you are the last writer, *i.e.* the writer who gets this piece of material up and running to a point a studio is willing to roll cameras.

Betting against screen credit, however, is a little unusual.

There is a lot of money riding on screen credit. Because there is so much money riding on screen credit, writers are in a position in which it's healthy for them financially to kill their own.

And it doesn't look like this is going to change anytime soon.

Before a movie is released, the studio looks at everyone who has written material for the project, draws up what they think should be the screen credits, and submits that to the Guild. There are only so many slots for screen credit. Three for "story by," three for "written by." A writing team can share one space. (You know it is a writing team on the screen if the names are joined by an ampersand, "&," and that it isn't, if "and" is written out.) You could have six writers' names up there under "written by," if it were three teams, and another six up there under "story by," if you had another three teams come up with the story. Then there is some sort of "based on" thing, but that's it. Everyone else is out in the cold. No matter how many writers worked on the film. There is just no more room.

You know *The Flintstones* purportedly had something like thirty-five writers on the project? What do you suppose all the writers who don't get credit tell their parents? "Well yeah Mom, I worked on the movie, it's just no one thought it was important enough to mention it on screen"? Hmmm.

When the Guild gets the studio's proposed writing credits, it sends copies to all the writers who worked on the film. Anyone who thinks they got unfair writing credit can complain at this time, and then arbitration is automatic. All drafts of the script are gathered together and sent out to an arbitration committee, which is a group of qualified Guild members (meaning they have seen these shenanigans before) who then have to read all the drafts and decide who gets credit.

Meanwhile, each writer on the project is required to write a letter to the arbitration committee, saying why they think the studio's decision is fair, or why they don't.

The arbitration committee reads those too.

Arbitration appears to be turning into a status quo. People who shouldn't ask for arbitration ask for it all the time. Not necessarily because they are entitled to or deserve more screen credit, but because, in the off chance they win, they'll get more money.

It's insulting to be asked to write a letter to strangers justifying putting your name on your work. But failure to respond could cost you your credit. After all, someone else is writing up a storm to say why they deserve more and everyone else should get less.

If you win, you get your bonus.

If you lose, you lose your bonus.

You write the letter.

This is a bad system. I cannot imagine what hell it is to be on an arbitration committee and have to sort through who knows how many angry letters from writers, on top of twenty-six or more draft copies of a script. I do not even want to contemplate that. The arbitrators lose valuable time they could be spending on their own careers, sorting through this mess. Sometimes because someone has honestly been wronged. But I tend to think more often because someone got greedy.

Meanwhile, every writer who worked on the project has to stop whatever they are doing, sort through all those drafts, and write a letter (and a good letter might be a good idea) to the arbitration committee. Or at least every writer who has anything to lose. If you just walked in off the street and did a polish, figuring you were getting no credit, you can just whistle Dixie and walk away. (You definitely want to sort through those drafts, too, because the time I had to do this, someone at the studio had forgotten to put the original spec script every other draft was based on in the box. Um, that was mine. I thought it was an important oversight.)

Meanwhile, all the involved writers' lawyers and agents and managers are involved as well, because they want their clients to win and get their money. If the writers don't get their money, neither do the agents and managers and attorneys. They have a vested interest here.

Everyone is losing time here. Because it is a bad system.

It is not a bad system because an arbitration system is in place. Arbitration is, in theory, a good idea. It allows a writer to address wrong or unfair treatment from a studio, and it is a way to keep studios honest about giving fair credit where credit is due, instead of maybe to whomever they are pals with. That's a *very* good idea. I can't imagine the hell that would ensue, if there was no watchdog system in place to keep studios honest with credit.

And if you feel for any reason a studio's suggested credit is unfair and wrong? I was talking to a writer who told me she was getting wronged, but was wondering about whether or not to make a fuss. My reaction was, What? Are you crazy?

Look. If you are getting wronged? Make a fuss. Always. That is exactly what the arbitration system is in place for, to arbitrate credit and make sure it is not granted at the sole discretion of the studio. To make sure that in the end, writers are in charge of who gets credit on what and when and that credit is therefore granted in a fair and impartial manner. (Well, as fair and impartial as human beings get.) That is important, it makes sure no one at a studio can arbitrarily give credit to Joe Bob because he cooks such a nice barbecue. Don't ever deny yourself access to that, merely because you don't want to "make a fuss." That is what the system is for. To help you, if you are in trouble. So make a fuss.

The problem is, all those bonuses tied up to screen credits limited to less slots than the number of people who work on pictures these days. The bonuses pit writers against writers. And while the "only so many slots" rule, I can only guess, was invented to protect writers, it has ceased to function, under the pressure of the desire to get those bonuses. It isn't protecting writers anymore. It is damaging them. We are killing our own. Regularly. With malice and aforethought. And that's got to be reformed. When I figure out the best way to do that, I'll get back to you. Till then, count on arbitration sometime in your lifetime and pay attention to what bonuses you negotiate for.

54 Separation of Rights

HELPFUL TITLE SUGGESTIONS FROM THE PEANUT GALLERY #38:
"The only thing that leapt to mind is . . . How Not to Get
Ass-Fucked by Evil Bastards. Whoops. That one iust slipped
out. What I meant was—"

When I got into arbitration, "separation of rights" came up.
I was not clear on what "separation of rights" exactly
was, but everyone said "yes you want those" so I said "yes I want
those." And somewhere a piece of paper says I have them.

Later (like just recently because I am writing this blasted
book that wasn't supposed to require research), I asked around
to find out what "separation of rights" is. Well. For starters, 80
plus pages of fine print and legal jargon. Yikes! The basic
premise, however, is that original material has a creator who is
entitled to certain specific ancillary rights post the sale of that
material. Original material. *Original material.* This would not
apply to an adaptation or work for hire.

That is something writers who adapt their own material
should pay attention to. If you adapt a book that you wrote, and

say "based on the novel by" on your script? You lose your rights, as the author of an original "script" here, or that is how I understand it, because your script is not an original work, it is an "adaptation." Think about that before you claim a novel as the source of your material. Even if it's your novel. It works this way in arbitration too, basically, even if you adapted your own novel, your script is not seen as an original work, it is seen as an "adaptation," and it is easier to leverage the first writer off an adaptation than it is to leverage the first writer off an original spec. Food for thought.

Certain rights to original elements of an "original" work are held separate from a script's purchase. The studio owns the script, sure, but if the studio was going to make a toy based on an original character or creation in the script, the writer would be entitled to separate payment for that, over and above what the studio paid for the script. (Unless you got so much money for the script, you just wouldn't care anyway and wouldn't be reading this book in the first place, so we'll leave that out of it.) If the studio wanted to release a book or form a television series or create a Broadway musical based on characters or elements originating in an original script, that would also entitle the writer to additional payment. And if the studio were to publish the script itself, say in book form, the writer would also be entitled to payment above and beyond the purchase of the original script. You still have rights, you see, to your original creations. To a point.

You don't still own the characters outright, so you couldn't, say, go publish a book with those characters in it without striking some sort of deal with the owner of the script, *i.e.* the studio. It is a partnership of sorts. The studio, however, can't go dancing tra la la into the future building empires on your original creations without recognizing your rights to monetary compensation for use of the material other than as a script.

Original elements in the original work, however, have to be *identifiably* original elements. For example, if you wrote a script with a robot in it, and you just said "the robot," without being too descriptive? Well, that is not an identifiably original robot, it is just "a" robot, and the studio can market a generic robot without paying you for the privilege. However, if you said "the robot is built on a chromium alloy chassis and covered with human flesh just like a human and when he takes his eye out you see a cool glowing red orb," etc., you have been pretty descriptive and that is your robot that is different from just any old robot and you have special rights to payment, if anybody wants to rush out and make an action figure out of it.

Separation of rights is mostly something for lawyers to worry about, but if you write sf or horror and are in the habit of creating different or scary or unusual creatures, you might want to be descriptive, just in case. And if you are adapting your own material? You might want to just change everyone's name along with the story line and maybe create a new and "original" work. It could just simplify things down the line, both with separation of rights and arbitration.

55 Entertainment Attorneys and Business Affairs

PITCH MEETING #9,456:

EXECUTIVE: *What if it was more about them on the road instead of them forming a band?*

ME: *Then it would be another movie.*

EXECUTIVE: *But could you make it more about them on the road instead of them forming a band?*

ME: *No. Then it would be another movie.*

EXECUTIVE: *You don't want to sell this pitch very much, do you?*

ME: *I want to sell "this" pitch plenty.*

There are different reasons for having an entertainment attorney. One is, if you can't find an agent, sometimes you can submit through an attorney instead. That does not always work, I've been turned down by companies who said they wanted the submission through an agent or not at all. (That actually meant they didn't want a submission at all and would come up with excuses to block my every move unless I signed with a big agency.) But in many instances it will.

Once you have an agent, however, you still need an attorney.

Because attorneys understand contracts. Agents are deal makers, very good at negotiating up front. But they are not lawyers. And fine print can cost you a lot of money. And every time you cut a deal with a studio, you are going to run into Business Affairs.

I hate Business Affairs. I'm sorry, if you work in Business Affairs, I just do. A studio has decided to hire you. You are happy. The studio execs are happy. The producers are happy. Your agents are happy. Your lawyers are happy. Even your dogs are happy. And then the negotiations begin with Business Affairs. You negotiate. They argue. You negotiate some more. Everyone argues. Finally, after days of negotiation, everyone comes to an agreement on *the deal*. What you are going to get paid, what your bonuses will be based on credit. How they will fly you somewhere if you have to do research. How much time you get to complete each stage of the project. What you get for the first draft. The second. The third. (If you're still around that long.) What you get if the movie gets made. All of that has been hammered out. Up front. And then the contract shows up.

And the contract looks nothing like the deal everyone just argued for days to come to an agreement on. Argh!

That's Business Affairs. I don't know what else they do, but they sure manage to piss me off with just that one little thing—a contract that bears no resemblance whatsoever to the initial agreement.

So it starts all over again. Everyone has to read the contract. And then someone has to fix it, put it back to what is was when it was initially a verbal agreement. And then that same person has to decipher and work out and qualify and correct all this other stuff that just magically showed up on the contract without anybody talking about it at all, that just appeared between the time you made a verbal agreement and the time this thing that is not that agreement showed up at your door. (Those are all additions by Business Affairs designed to stop you from getting paid what you agreed to do the job for in the first place.)

The person who does all the fixing and deciphering and correcting is your entertainment attorney. He knows how to do that because he is smart and went to law school and read lots of books about it and goes to seminars. It is a damn good thing, too, because I sure as hell don't know how to do that. And don't exactly have the time to learn.

In addition to duking it out with Business Affairs and fixing your contracts and getting rid of all that weird stuff that appears on your contract from out of the blue that you never ever agreed to and just how stupid do these people think you are that you would maybe not notice that?

Attorneys are also one more person to go around Hollywood telling people you are a genius. Yay!

Attorneys will also contact people about material you might want to option and will negotiate terms for you and check all the paperwork and draw up new paperwork, if you need it, and tell you whether something looks reasonable in their opinion. Their opinion is usually better than yours, because this is what they do every day and you only do it once in a while. And attorneys know how to do things like options in a professional way, whereas you are a writer, what do you know about formalizing options and negotiating with agents for them? Okay, you might know it all, but I don't.

Attorneys keep an eye on your agent (upsetting one lone writer is one thing, embarrassing yourself in front of another powerful entertainment entity in Hollywood by behaving badly with a client is another) and are back up if things between you and your agent go south. Attorneys can do all the talking for you if you have to leave your agency, and negotiate your way out of your contract. They review agency contracts you get from new agencies, and fix them too. Basically, entertainment attorneys are just very good people to have on your side.

Entertainment attorneys generally work one of two ways: either on commission (5 percent is standard); or by the hour. With an attorney working on a commission, if you don't get paid, he doesn't get paid. And if you do, so does he. The plus to this is, when funds are running a little low, you still have an attorney working for you full-time. The minus is, he takes a big chunk of your check, and the bigger the check, the bigger the chunk it is he takes, regardless of whether or not his work load on your behalf has increased. It is just the opposite with an attorney doing piece work by the hour. If you aren't working, he still gets paid, regardless, anytime you need anything lawyerly done. But he gets an hourly fee, so his bill stays constant with his workload, even if your salary goes up.

I like working with the attorney who takes a commission. If I get somewhere in this business and start making a whole lot of money, well he stuck it out with me to get there when there was pretty much no money in it for him, and his faith in me and efforts on my behalf during down times is enough to justify his payoff in the end. That is what working on commission boils down to, in the end: faith.

And attorneys, at least the attorneys I have worked with, make you back the 5 percent they cost you. All those lines they strike out on contracts, all those things stuck in there by Business Affairs when no one was looking? All those things add up, I figure (though don't ask me to do the math here), to 5 percent in the end. Unless someone strikes through them. And the person who strikes through them is your attorney. So I look at attorneys as paying for themselves. Without them, I wouldn't get that extra 5 percent anyway. And with them, I get a lot of good advice, one more person telling people I am a genius, and some nifty paperwork drawn up on the side. What a deal.

56 Death and Taxes

FROM THE FILES OF "PEOPLE I'M GOING TO WRITE ABOUT SOMEDAY": Jimmy Lee had two women, a wife and a mistress, living one on each side of a duplex. They said he'd get home and stumble on the steps and that was how he decided who he was going home to. And he was game for a third. Funny guy. I'd get out of the club, we'd go have breakfast, he'd make his pass, and I'd say "Go home, Jimmy Lee, and hope one of your girls doesn't shoot you."

if you're writing for profit, you are in business as a writer. If you aren't making much money at it, well, that's not your fault, you are trying. And just because your business isn't making money, that does not mean it is not a business. Lots of businesses don't make money. Lots of businesses lose money. The IRS knows that.

That does mean "writing" for profit. You can't tell the IRS you are a writer, take a bunch of deductions, and then when they show up say, "Well, I am planning on writing." You have to be actively writing and submitting material, *i.e.* attempting to sell, to take deductions.

Phone calls, faxes, paper, ink, computers, software, membership dues, Guild dues, commissions, seminars, books, movies, tapes, scripts, trade publications, directories, maps, plane fare, hotel bills, research materials, business related lunches, business related dinners, business related breakfasts, business related coffee, photocopies, classes, contest entry fees, postage, envelopes, home offices (don't put a bed in there and use it as a guest room, it does literally have to be an office), filing cabinets, gasoline, your desk, your calculator, your clock, even your Day-Timer, all that stuff is tax deductible.

And it adds up.

The IRS gets a little cranky with writers. People will tell you putting "writer" on a tax return is a red flag. That the IRS is not too fond of creative types and thinks we cheat so is more likely to scrutinize our returns. Well fine. Some things you can't change. Like death and taxes. Save your receipts. Save old correspondence. Keep records of submissions. Keep records of phone conversations. Write the name of whom you met for lunch or breakfast or dinner or drinks or whatever on your restaurant receipts. Write something on the back of movie ticket stubs. Leave a tiny trail of lead marks all over every receipt you've got. If the IRS decides to give you a run for your money, show them. Be honest. Don't deduct pet food because you have decided to write a story about a dog and now think maybe you will just write off Fido. That doesn't work. But fair is fair and if you have a legitimate expense, there is no good reason you shouldn't deduct it.

It is a lot of work wearing all hats at one business, though. If you are a writer working out of your home, you are research and development, production, the office manager, the receptionist, the bookkeeper, the marketing director, the cleaning staff, the sales force, the facilities director, and the accountant all in one. That's too much work.

Hire an accountant. Specifically an accountant who works in the entertainment field with writers and is familiar with and stays abreast of specific tax laws that apply to writers.

Accountants in this field work two ways. Either on a fee by fee basis, or on a commission basis. Standard commission for an accountant in the entertainment industry is 5 percent. If you make money, he makes money. If you don't, he does your taxes for free. You aren't going to get one of those accountants unless you're making income in this business, however. Accountants need to put dinner on the table too. And unlike attorneys, they trust numbers, not talent.

There aren't really standard fees for accountants who work on a fee by fee basis. You negotiate your fee up front with this accountant on the basis of how much work he thinks doing your taxes is going to be. But it is worth the money.

There are special rules that apply to us. You have a lot to do besides going out and learning every tax law that applies to creatives and keeping up with the yearly changes that are so popular with the IRS. Accountants have to go to seminars for this stuff. And read trade publications. And special books and manuals. Thick books and manuals. Tomes. Just to keep up. That is how much there is to know. So do yourself a favor. Hire an accountant. That is a write off too.

57 Reading Fees and Consultants

HELPFUL TITLE SUGGESTIONS FROM THE PEANUT GALLERY #42:
"Terri says how about Hacking Hollywood?*"*

guild signatory agents are not allowed to charge reading fees. Some of them get around this by opening a business on the side which is specifically a "consulting firm." At least that is what one agent told me, and assured me it was okay. I wonder how many lines that crosses. If a writer sends you material and you offer to work on the script for a fee through this "other" business, is that really okay?

Agents also sometimes tell you they can't read you without a professional recommendation, and then tell you about this script doctor you can send the script to who might give you that professional recommendation.

When that happens, you don't always know whether someone in the office decided to take initiative and make a little reading money on the side, or the agent is helping out a friend who "consults," or what. I am not too thrilled with the idea of agents sending ads for script consultants to writers who query them.

Then there is the agent who reads a script, says it has problems, and suggests the writer send it to a consultant. Personally. Not just returning a little slip of paper to you in your mail. Telling you, in person, on the phone, maybe you should go see this consultant. A specific consultant. One agent in town was notorious for sending writers to an expensive script analyst. The writers tended to be under the impression, once they made changes suggested by the consultant, the agent would sign them. That didn't tend to happen.

I can see the agent's perspective. The agent is sending writers to someone who could maybe help them, but hey, just because they get good advice from a script doctor, that doesn't mean they will automatically turn around and write a slam home dunk 'em script. So the agent can't guarantee to sign them just because they go to the analyst.

That sounds good on the surface. But agents and script consultants should probably not mix it up in business. It smacks of conflict of interest. Which is something everyone should want to avoid. Conflict of interest is the same reason the Guild won't allow signatory agents to produce. Because it is hard to fairly represent your client's interests, when you are the producer and want to buy low and sell high. And asking for money from potential clients, or asking potential clients to spend money on this consultant friend of yours, before you will consider them as a client, smacks of conflict of interest too. It is too much like a reading fee. Too much like milking the fatted calf. It probably just shouldn't be done. Period. The end.

Then there is this new cottage industry, "agents to the agents." These companies claim to have agency contacts and the ability to refer you. First they have to read and critique your material. For a fee. Then if you are a swell writer with a swell script they will shuttle you in to their agent pals. This boils down to a reading fee you pay someone who isn't even an agent. Hmmm.

If you are even considering going any of these routes, ask for sample coverage and references. You want to see what sort of notes these people gave writers. Both positive and negative responses. You want to talk to happy clients. You want to talk to writers who got referred to agents and signed with agents on the basis of the company or consultant's recommendation. (They are claiming they can do that, there better be living proof that claim is true.) If you've been referred to this service by an agent, you want to know how many of this agent's clients came via this referral service. Then, and only then, if it looks like the $150 or so these people and places charge, and it gets a lot steeper than that from time to time, might be worth it, well, sleep on it.

A lot of times, an agent saying "I can't read you, I'm busy and don't know if you can write, but go to these people and if they say you're good, then maybe" is a case of misdirection. The agent, instead of telling you "no," which is not fun to do, has tossed the problem back at you. "Here is something else to think about, instead of the fact I just turned you down." Then you walk around wondering whether or not you should send money to these people to get read by this agent, instead of being mad the agent wouldn't read your script. Simple, huh?

It's misdirection.

And the ultimate question, when you get this from an agent, is, How many of your clients did you sign on the basis of a referral from this service you're suggesting I use? If the agent says, "Based on recommendations from this service, I read and signed three writers," you've got a possible avenue. If the agent has never signed a person whose work got referred via this service, it's smoke.

Personally, I think people should skip the "referred for a fee" places entirely and get free reads from every producer they can talk out of one. Producers give you feedback and, if they really like your work, refer you to agents—for free. And all those agents who refer you to script consultants? Well, bless their little hearts, maybe they just don't know what the term "conflict of interest" means, but I would steer clear of them as well.

Then there are script consultants who are independent of agents and don't make claims they will refer you to agents or industry professionals, they just read your material and give you feedback and work with you on your script. These are essentially private teachers. I was one of these. And I was decent at it. But I sure hated the work.

For one thing, I don't like telling people their material isn't working. That's one of the hardest things in the world to do. You can't lie to people. But you don't want to be the straw that broke the camel's back, either. So you walk this fine line between telling someone the truth, which is often, "There are quite a few problems here," and telling them the truth in a way that is maybe less painful than them getting run over by a Mac truck. And that's not fun.

Also, it's time consuming. You eat up a lot of the energy that would go into your own writing, putting it into other people and their material. It is educational. You learn as much from figuring out what is wrong with other people's stuff as you will ever learn figuring out what is right with something that works. But it is toil.

And, I am not a patient person. It takes twice as much energy for me to calmly explain something that to me appears real simple, as it does for maybe a normal person who is less inclined to grab someone by the lapels and just give a quick shake.

A lot of script consultants are writers making ends meet till they hit their stride. If you get one of the good ones, that can be lucky, because they know a lot about the business they can share with you before they go. Others are honest to God teachers. They like working with other people. They are not impatient and do not want to shake you about by the lapels. Everything for them is not "learn this now because I am not going to be around much longer to help you" for them. But they do not always have a grasp of the business the way the writer types do.

Consultants are a huge issue of contention among the "ranks." Some industry professionals are crazy against them. They'll tell you consultants take advantage of writers, consultants are people who don't know anything about what is really marketable, that they can't write themselves, so go around telling other people how. That you shouldn't be sending your stuff to a consultant, you should be joining writer's groups and getting feedback from your peers. It's a serious rant. I've heard it. It's silly, though.

A script consultant is a private writing teacher. Some are good. Some are not so good. Nobody ever said people who can write can also critique, that's not always the case, and people who can critique can't necessarily always write. That's just silly. Everyone on earth should not rush out and hire a consultant. Some people have access to objective perspectives from people knowledgeable about craft who won't charge them money for an opinion. And there are some enormously talented people who just write so damn well, a consultant would be useless, they'll never need help, ever. But not all places on this earth are swimming with talented writers who know how to critique. And not everyone will never need help. And good writing instructors, private or otherwise, speed up the learning process. (I said "good," pay attention to that qualifyer.)

See, in order to learn from a mistake, you must be cognizant of it. But, presumably, if you made it in the first place, you aren't.

How do you learn from something you can't recognize? Generally, either someone else points it out to you, or you keep on struggling and sooner or later a blast of insight catches you off guard and you get it on your own, or you never figure it out and keep on making the same damn mistake over and over forever until you give up or die.

Teachers, good teachers, whether they're on a college campus or operating independently out of the Eiffel Tower, can help. They can show you what you can't yet see yourself, what is wrong.

Don't go to consultants for basics. You can get basics out of any class or book. Don't go to consultants if you have access to professional quality reads or insightful input that won't cost you money. Don't go to consultants if your area is swimming with good classes and instructors for one third the money. Think about consultants if you live in Truck Stop, Arkansas, and the nearest library is one hundred miles away and Zelda The Dog Faced Girl just isn't giving you the feedback you need on your scripts.

If you consider a consultant, it is important you know, is he or she any good? You won't learn anything from a bad teacher. You have to have a good teacher. So get credentials. Professional experience. Educational background. Find out how much he or she charges and what you get for that. Get at least two sample critiques, a positive response and a not so positive response. Get references. Ask how his or her clients are doing. If this consultant is helping people, someone should be winning contests or getting optioned. This is private instruction. It costs money. Make sure it will be worth what you pay.

58 Classes and Seminars

Classes won't teach you to write. If you say you want to write and don't, you are going to have some problems being a writer because no class in the world can teach you to put down words. That's called drive. And classes cannot teach drive.

Classes won't give you talent. You are either blessed by God and have talent. Or you don't. I could be wrong on that. But that is sure how it looks from here. People are born with it, or they aren't. And classes can't teach it.

What is left is craft and inspiration.

Craft is knowing ways to make things happen on the page. It either springs from some innate inner story intuition; or from so much practice you know something has to work because you have damn well tried every other way that didn't; or from studying and taking apart the way other people write till you amass a knowledge of ways to accomplish something on the page that you can use in your own writing and build on to develop new ways of doing things. We call that craft. Or skill. That ability to accomplish something on the page through sheer mechanics. And craft is where classes help. Because, while classes won't give you drive or talent, they can give someone with drive and talent mechanical tools with which to focus the written word to make it accomplish what that person set out to make it do.

And craft is what gets talented writers out of trouble. It is all very well to be born with talent and drive. You can get by a long time on that alone. Sometimes forever. But, if you do this long enough, sooner or later it's likely you are going to be trying to accomplish something on the page and it is not going to be happening. You are going to be stuck. And you won't know why it isn't working, you will just know it isn't and you don't know how to fix it. That is when you need tools. So that, rather than pounding your head on the desk, you can take apart what you just put together until you find the problem. If you've got the tools, you can do that. If you don't, if you've been writing on blind instinct, you don't know how you did what you did on the page in the first place, so you don't very well know how to take it apart and fix it. And that is a problem.

I am very big on classes and craft and tools. I suggest everyone go take a writing class right now.

I will say though, as far as craft goes? In general, most screenwriting classes I've taken concentrated so much on the "three act structure," they tended to leave out stuff like scenes. And openings. Few of them ever went into in depth writing mechanics like story versus plot, or who what why when where, get it out there in the first breath type stuff, the way fiction writing classes and playwriting classes do. So I advocate writing classes in general. Which include screenwriting classes, but take other kinds of writing as well. You can learn craft in a lot of places, and what works in one medium will often work in another. And you can use it all. If you know what works. And what doesn't. Knowing that might bail you out next time you are rattling down the page on instinct and hit a wall. And it is a lot less stressful than banging your head on your desk.

Classes can also help in the inspiration department. Feature writers work alone. Or, in partnerships, with one other person. Day in, day out, there they are. Alone. The dogs laugh at your jokes. But you feed them, so they have to. Once in a while spending all this time alone, just you and that hostile computer—or I suppose just you and a hostile computer and a hostile writing partner, I've never worked with a partner so am not sure, but suspect I would get real hostile from time to time—you get tired and out of energy and your drive falters and you are just out of inspiration.

Going to a class, a seminar, a workshop, will at least get you out of the house, and may get you around people who, for whatever reason, make you feel recharged. Dave Trottier's classes always did that for me. I walked out of that guy's classes feeling like it was all about writing and I just wanted to get home and rip it up on the page. All teachers are not like that. All classes are not like that. I've gone to some seminars and classes and just sat there listening wondering when we were going to get to something good. If we were going to get to something good? But some are. Look for those. Seek them out. They will get you through a lot of pages.

Classes can also get you feedback on your work and sometimes allow you to hear your work out loud. In roundtable classes, people bring in work in progress and everyone takes a role and reads through a scene aloud so you can hear it and get a feel for how it is sounding. Screenwriters write words to be spoken. It doesn't hurt hearing your stuff spoken. Outside your head. (Well, not unless the reading goes very very badly.) Afterwards everyone critiques the piece, which is feedback, and that can be good. Not always, it depends on whom you are getting feedback from, but you get with a smart group of people and the feedback will generally be good and help you.

I'm an advocate of writing classes. I better be, I got a degree in this stuff, that is a whole hell of a lot of classes, if you don't think they're worthwhile. But I do. Some are better than others. Almost all of them will help you in some way get where you need to go. The only time this is not true is when you get into a toxic teacher class. You can spot toxic teachers right off. They are all eaten up with ennui and disdain and they encourage malicious critiques. Toxic teachers almost always have a little group of toxic students following them around. These kids have been "stamped" and believe in malicious critiques too, and watching them might be funny, if you didn't feel so bad for the poor SOB they were picking on. Don't go to these kinds of teachers. Go to teachers who are inspirational and don't need carbon copies of themselves surrounding them. Go to teachers who talk about writing things you've never heard of. They can teach you something.

There is one last thing classes can do for you. I don't have a lot of experience with this one because, well, doy, I went to school in Utah. But film schools, the bigger ones, are full of people who are going to be working professionals in the industry. USC leaps to mind. There are a ton of USC alumni working in this town. At agencies. At studios. USC alumni are just all the hell over. That means, if you take classes at USC, you rub shoulders with a lot of future industry professionals. That's called contacts. Contacts are not a bad thing to have in this town.

Some of the bigger seminars are like that too. Robert McKee's seminars are huge in the industry. All sorts of people take that seminar. It is a nifty seminar, too, I took it and liked it a lot, though I was cross eyed and stumbling by the time I got out. (McKee covers a *lot* of material in one weekend.) That seminar is full of people who work here. Contacts. Those are good to have. Think about classes and seminars from that standpoint, too.

59 Workshops and Critiques

FROGS DON'T DO THIS #83: Emily Dickinson showed her poetry to a writer friend, who promptly told her that her work was unpublishable. So she never sent anything out. And she wrote in solitude for the rest of her life. . . .

There are two types of workshops. One is an instructional workshop. Participants pay to attend the workshop and it is led by someone who is (hopefully) a professional in their field and can teach a specific aspect of craft or marketing or whatever the focus of the workshop may be. The other, also known as a "writer's group," is a group of people with a common goal, to improve their writing, who gather regularly to exchange work and critiques. In general, the latter is free, unless there are dues for refreshments or something.

Workshops are one of the fastest ways to get opinions on your work in a short time from a lot of people. They are also a way to hear how your work plays out loud. You roundtable scripts (*i.e.* everyone at the table takes a role and you read the script out loud), and it may not be Laurence Olivier, but you know how your work sounds. Workshops are also places you get together with people who are trying to do, or doing, exactly what you are trying to do or doing. Places to swap scripts. Swap information. Share encouragement. They can be great.

Or not so great. It depends on who is in the workshop. I was in a fiction workshop with a writer who was prolific. Every week the group met and anyone with new work passed out copies. You went home, read it all, the next week you handed everyone's work back and did roundtable comments. This one person was writing a book. And she could crank out chapters. I will give her that. New chapters every week. No matter what. But those chapters were not so good. And never, ever got better. So every week, I would take her chapters home, and have to read them. And every week, it was the same problems. And every week I would have to go back and tell this person, "This is not working, and here is why." She was always real nice about notes, too. She'd say thanks and smile.

And hand you new chapters.

With the same problems you had pointed out every week, week in, week out, for the last half a year.

The same problems everyone had pointed out every week, week in, week out, for several years. (This was an old group, I was starting to crack, I asked.)

Those chapters became the nightmare of my week. The thing I dreaded most. The one thing I couldn't bear to face. They were the reason I quit the group.

You want to be in a group with talented people. It's painful for me to tell someone their work isn't working. If I have to do it every week, to the same person? Week in, week out? I can't do it. I have bad dreams. I have to leave.

So that's rule number one. Make sure people in the group are at least moderately okay to read. And moderately okay to critique. And if they aren't? Find another group.

Rule number two is, make sure everyone is nice. Toxic commentary does not belong in a writer's group. (Nothing pisses me off worse than people who savage other writers in critiques.) Writer's groups are supposed to be supportive, and toxic commentary is not supportive. It is toxic.

When critiquers start getting the impulse to be harsh or insulting, it's a sign of critiquer burn out, and burned out or not, it's not an impulse that should be indulged at the expense of another writer you are (allegedly) attempting to help. You can't help someone you have insulted and put on the defensive. It's a destructive act and clouds the reviewee's ability to hear or utilize any *good* suggestions in your critique because, once you attack, he or she can't see past the nastiness of the delivery and it's a wash.

I've heard people get pretty self righteous post maliciously delivered "help," saying "Hey, I was being helpful there, it doesn't matter how I delivered it, this was for their own good." Um, you're not being helpful. You're being an asshole. Knock it off.

When you critique another person's work, look for the strongest, and weakest, aspects of the work. And open with the strongest. It is a lot easier for someone to hear criticism, if you have just said something nice. "The characterization in here is strong, you did a good job on that. I think the structure is weak during the second act." That is easier to absorb than "Your second act sucks." If you can only give someone two things, that is what you give them, the strongest and weakest aspects of the work. And you lead with the strongest.

And if you are so busy being helpful telling someone what is wrong, you never get around to mentioning what is right? Um, why are you assuming they know what is right? You are sure assuming they don't know what is wrong, or you wouldn't be going on about it so much, so don't assume they know what is right. Tell them. If you only hammer away at what is not working, it is very easy for a writer trying to address that to lose sight of what they had going for them in the first place and lose it, trying to shore up weak spots. Tell someone what's good. Take the time. Hopefully they'll do it for you.

Try to say "the script," or "the material," or "the story," instead of "your script," "your material," or "your story." When you say "your," it personalizes criticism. It makes it about the person. When you say "the," it distances criticism from the person and focuses it on the work. Getting told things are wrong is not fun. It helps if you're being told things are wrong with the work, not you.

If you're part of a group, don't indulge any impulse to pull someone aside and give them private commentary on the side.

First, you could be wrong. Especially when addressing technical aspects (hey, even Cole/Haag is wrong in some spots), but if no one else sees or hears this "private" advice you suddenly feel the urge to inflict on someone, you are not going to know you're wrong, and the person you're talking to is not going to know you're wrong either.

Second, when you start indulging impulses to "get private," it's easier to forget to curb harsh delivery. And harder to remember to critique in a politic and constructive manner. Well, if it's so bad you can't say it in front of other people, why the hell are you saying it to the writer? Public statements are generally better thought out in advance of speaking, and the better you think out a critique, the more help you will be. Which is the whole point of a critique. To help. And if you're saying something nice in private? Um, why are you sneaking around about it? Say it out loud. Where other people can hear it. That doesn't happen enough.

Third, in a workshop, the purpose of sharing critiques is not merely to receive critiques of your work from others. It's also to learn by critiquing. And by hearing other people's critiques of the same material you critiqued and seeing what they perceived as strengths and weaknesses that bolster, or undermine, your opinions. If you go private, the workshop as a whole loses a voice, and so an avenue of perception, a point of view, and knowledge. And so do you.

If you're not part of a group, and are swapping scripts privately with another individual, the critique is just going to be private, but try to apply the same rules. Start with something good. Say "the script," not "your script." Don't be so busy telling someone what doesn't work, you forget to say what does. And be polite. Taking criticism is hard.

And if you're not the critiquer, you are the critiquee? Sit down. Shut up. Listen. Learn. If there is one thing tiresome, it is someone who addresses every statement out of your mouth, as it comes out of your mouth, while you are just trying to get through a simple critique. If you are receiving a critique and your mouth is open and words are coming out? You are not listening. So what is the point of someone saying anything to you at all? It is not your job to argue with a critique. It is your job to listen, think it over, weigh what was said, decide whether or not the problems brought up are real problems, and if so, address them on the page. Not in the critiquer's face. On the page. Period. The end. And say thank you. Someone just spent a lot of time reading your material, thinking it over, concentrating on your work, when they could have been concentrating on their own. Even if they are so wrong you wonder if they are maybe from Planet Zampf, say thanks to them for taking the time. Then—

Take the good advice, don't take the bad advice, and hope like hell you know the difference. That is about the only rule of thumb there is for taking advice. There's no magic formula. You do your best and hope you're right.

When you are the critiquer, you have two goals: (a) figure out what the writer was trying to achieve; and (b) help them

achieve that. That's your job. Try to do that. That means not su-
perimposing your thoughts and impulses or likes and dislikes on
someone else's work, but instead attempting to see the writer's
goals and help the writer get there.

This approach will save your tail if you are reading something
that is not your type of material. See, you can on the one hand
be sitting there saying, Wow, I really hate this kind of humor. Or
you can be sitting there thinking, This isn't my type of humor,
but it is what the writer is trying to pull off, so from an objective
viewpoint, how are they doing? And how can they do it better?

Critiques are supposed to be objective.

It's important to tell someone what you thought they were
trying to achieve, before you tell them how you think they have
missed the boat or can better achieve it. The reason you do this
is, if you are completely off base and wrong about what they are
trying to do? It helps them to know the motivation for your suggestion. "I think you are trying to establish that this character is
a nice person, by showing her helping orphans. I think that
might be better achieved if she were kind to animals and didn't
kick that dog in the first act." Now they know why you think the
character shouldn't kick the dog. Whereas, if you just say "This
will be a better script if she doesn't kick the dog," well, they
don't. And that's important. Because—

Maybe they weren't trying to establish that the character was
a good person. Maybe they were trying to establish that the character was a bad person. They set that up with the character kicking the dog, and were building on it with the character helping
orphans in a self serving way. (Look, this is just an example here,
I'm not writing a script about orphans and dogs, it's just *an example,* jeez.) Only you didn't get that it was a self serving way,
you just saw "helping orphans." If the writer knows your motivation for the comment, the writer can say, Hmm, that helping

orphans in a "self serving way" is not coming through, I had better fix that. If the writer doesn't, he or she may just think you don't like characters kicking dogs and ignore the comment. It was an important comment though. The writer needed to know the self serving way wasn't coming through.

Sometimes, you won't get someone's material. Even the smartest person on the planet sometimes just doesn't get something. It happens. Okay, not to me, but (I am kidding). If you can't comprehend a script or find any merit in it, you are not the person to critique it. Period. The end. If that happens, say you don't get it and move on. Just because you don't get it, that doesn't mean no one else will. And it's not going to do anyone any good if you try and tell someone how to make something better that you don't get. So move on. Graciously. But move on.

I mean it. Sometimes, even after you say, "I'm sure someone will get this, but I don't and can't help because I don't see the perspective or what it is trying to achieve"? Sometimes a writer will still try to drag a critique out of you. The writer will say, "Oh well would you just tell me what you maybe didn't get?" Believe me when I tell you, if you start telling someone everything you didn't get in a script you didn't get, it is going to get ugly. Very quickly. So say no. Say maybe you would like to listen to the other critiques. Say anything, but get out of it and—

Just. Don't. Do. It.

Finding workshops and writer's groups is a hit or miss proposition. They are out there. But you sometimes have to look. Mostly you find them through word of mouth. Which means you have to meet and talk to other people who are either pursuing, or know people who are pursuing, what you are pursuing. Subscribe to publications, pick up film flyers on campuses, check out local film organizations and talk to people there, look up educational workshops in your area and attend them, you will meet other participants at those. Pay attention to who sounds like they know what they are talking about. Ask if they know of any groups in your area. Get out there enough, and you will stumble across something. And if there's really nothing in your area? Get on the internet and start hunting up newslists. There are a lot of online critique groups these days. You just have to find them.

60 Clubs and Memberships

L.A. MOMENT #212: What I Learned Bowling: Even a novice can get a strike. Bowling shoes come in more attractive colors in smaller sizes. Copernicus did not design the bowling scoring system. Bowling balls are not fingernail friendly. French fries and bowling do not mix. And, after staring at a nine pound bowling ball, not to mention repeatedly lifting and hurling it down a long, wooden macadam at wavery, distant pins, I am convinced I never, ever, want to give birth.

if I was trying to break in, I would join IFP. Actually, I did join IFP when I was trying to break in, so there is your recommendation right there.

IFP is the Independent Feature Project/West (there's an East, as well). They're based out of Santa Monica and sponsor the Spirit Awards as well as independent film screenings and they put out a monthly newsletter and calendar of "events." They sponsor a continuing producer series, which included the New Line Acquisitions luncheon I attended. That was a luncheon IFP members could attend to meet people from New

Line and hear about what New Line was doing and looking for. At the luncheon, they had tables that sat about eight people each, and there was a New Line representative at each table, so everyone got a chance to talk to a representative of the company. That is not bad to do, and IFP sponsors those sorts of luncheons with different companies. IFP also has a monthly "Member Mix," where members can meet members, schmooze, pick up gossip, make connections, share information, etc. IFP sponsors a Breakfast Series, that filmmakers, writers and agents attend to discuss subjects like "the agent/client relationship"—and you can maybe meet an agent while you're there. Which is a good thing.

The luncheons and breakfasts are not free, membership dues entitle you to attend and then you pay for lunch or breakfast in addition. Sometimes you pay quite a bit, the New Line luncheon I attended was at L'Orangerie, which ain't cheap. But is a nifty way to meet people. And annual membership is under a hundred bucks, so it is worth looking into. Their main line is (310) 392-8832, and their events hotline (a recorded announcement of upcoming events) is (310) 392-8553.

IFP is probably not the only organization in town providing industry mixers to promote its members. There are probably others, I just didn't belong to them and can't tell you about them. But I would look around, if I lived here and was beating on doors, because—

Hollywood is a people town. Nothing gets you read faster than word of mouth, and if one person says, "Wow, I just read the greatest script," ten other people want to read the script too. And referrals are the way to go. That's why I stress IFP. When I was starting, I could only partially benefit from membership, because I lived out of state, but people who live in L.A., well it is on your doorstep. And if you're here, you might want to make an effort to join organizations and participate and meet people. Because people get you in doors.

There is a lot of angst about how hard it is for outsiders to break into this business. And it's true, nepotism abounds in Hollywood, people are more likely to hire people they know. Even if you're better than someone they know, they are still more inclined to hire the person they know and/or have worked with before.

Well. There is a reason for that.

Making movies is hard. I mean really hard. Long hours. Long weeks. Long months. Getting up too early, staying up too late, everyone having to work together. And get along. Did I mention days, weeks, months? Sometimes in the heat of the Mojave Desert? With no running water? With equipment breaking down and people falling over from heat stroke and lights popping in the middle of a perfect shot so you have to shoot it over and then the daylight is going and the boom doesn't work and the orang-utan is being uncooperative and its trainer is (where the hell did he find a bottle in the middle of the desert?) drunk and someone who you thought was perky turns out to not be perky without help and their stash just ran dry? And by the way could we all have a shower now? No, the hot water just ran out at the bad hotel you are all staying at. That is the only hotel within a one hundred mile radius. Assuming you are optimistic enough to write a hotel into this scene.

If you were stuck on a desert island, who would you want to be stuck with? Someone you'd never met? Or someone you had been in a trench with and maybe knew wouldn't go insane and start thinking you were a bottle of Dom Perignon and trying to uncork you?

Think of movies like that, as desert islands. And you are stuck with these people, on this movie, for better or worse, till the movie is over. And movies that go bad last longer than movies that go good. Invariably. Now think who you want to hire.

And don't lie. You know it is someone you know you can count on in a crunch.

If you are coming in from outside, you are an unknown entity. If something goes wrong, people who've never met or worked with you don't know whether you will hang tough, flee for cover, or worse, go insane and start screwing up the whole damn project. That's why people hire friends. That's why they're leery of strangers. That is why it is a big deal for someone who's never worked with you to take a chance on you. That is why you need to join clubs and organizations and get out there and meet people and keep in touch. So people know you, so people trust you, so people know they can depend on you if they give you a job. Especially so they know they can depend on you, if that job turns into the job from hell. Go make some friends.

61 Competitions

NOTES INTO THE ETHER #9: Never believe your own press. They can take that away, and if you're counting on it, that would hurt.

i was asked once by an interviewer, was I surprised I had won a writing competition? I thought that was a dumb question. I have never in my life entered a writing competition I didn't think I could win.

Now I have *not won* a lot of contests. I entered the Nicholl competition for the first time in, I think it was, 1991. And lost. Entered again in '92. And lost. Lost in '93. Not even a place or show. Just plain lost. You might think that would put a damper on my estimation of my ability to win a writing contest.

But I don't think you can enter a competition thinking you are going to lose. You might be delusional, but you had better believe you can win. Because why else enter?

You are not going up against Huey, Duey and Louie here in this business. You are going up against William Goldman and Carrie Fisher and Shane Black. (If you haven't read a Shane Black script, go get one right now, I learned how to write reading that guy's scripts.) These people can write. That's why they get hired. They are good at what they do. That is who you are stepping into the job pool with, every time you send out a script. Those are the people whose work your work is compared to, has to compare to, every time you toss it in the ring. You better think you are that good. You better be that good. And if you are, you can probably win a writing competition or two.

You enter competitions primarily for two reasons. The most important is, to get read. It is not easy to convince someone that a person they have never heard of has written a screenplay they should spend an hour or two reading. They already have scripts on their desk from Carrie Fisher and Shane Black and William Goldman to read. And telling them Mom thinks you're great doesn't help because, oddly enough, they tend to think Mom is biased. But win a competition or two, they might take you seriously. Might. And you need that, you need them to take you seriously, because the goal here is to get read. Nobody is going to make that movie if they don't read your script. You must get read. So, on the one hand, competitions are industry door openers. Wins add up on a query letter. Even if no one has heard of the contest or knows much about it, if you get two or three or four of these things together into a letter, they add up to push the odds in your favor getting read.

The second reason is validation. Winning makes you feel good. Feeling good and positive, in the face of so much rejection, is good for the soul and can keep you going those days you're staring at a wall wondering what in hell you're doing and why you keep going. The wins are bursts of appreciation, moments of encouragement that tell you yes, the work is good, you can do this, you will make it, you should keep going. That counts. For a lot.

After getting read and validation come press and prizes.

Press is good. It gets you read. Not all competitions get you press. I've won competitions that did zero for me in the press department. But they still worked on query letters.

Prizes are good. The money I won in the America's Best competition went toward tuition, ink, and paper. (Thank you America's Best People.) The money I won at Austin paid for plane fares and hotel bills. (Thank you Austin People.) And I wouldn't have made it through the first year in L.A. without a Nicholl Fellowship from the Academy. (Thank you Mrs. Nicholl.) Prizes are good. They pay for stuff. But don't forget the prize is not really the prize. Getting read is the prize. Because you want to make a movie here and getting read is how you will set that script up and do that.

I am an advocate of competitions. Which only makes sense. They have been good to me. And if you win, they can lift you out of obscurity and drop you smack in the middle of the limelight.

Not everyone gets to win, though. That is the nature of competitions. And I know people who get real discouraged when they don't win. Well. Knock it off.

If you don't win, it doesn't mean you aren't good. It means it wasn't your day. It is pretty hard for a bad script to win a competition. There are a lot of readers. You go through levels of reads. But it is not that hard for a good script to lose. One reader who doesn't get it and wham, you are out of there. Which does not mean you aren't good. It means you got the wrong reader on the wrong day who maybe got hit by a powder blue van this morning and well, that's it for your script, you had the wrong color cover. Oops.

But don't get depressed. Don't get discouraged. It doesn't mean you aren't good. It just means it's not your time. And competitions are numbers games. Just like reads. If you can write and you enter enough competitions, you have a good chance of winning. Believe that. Or don't enter.

Also know, even with a contest win, quite often a spec won't sell. Or, it will sell, but it won't get produced. This happens in the industry at large. Why would it be different with contests? It isn't. So know, while the purely perfect scenario is to sell the winning script and get the movie made? A more pressing issue is, does the notoriety of the win help you get read? And does the script people are reading get you work? In other words, does the competition win get you there, career-wise? It does. I can vouch for that. Does it do it for every winner? No. Some of them slip through the cracks. Which is terrible, but it happens. Partly, I think, because some people think winning is enough, and it is not, you can't just sit there, you have to keep pressing. And partly because of pure bad luck. Bad luck sucks. But the bulk of the competition winners I know made it through to the other side and are working in the industry. Do you know who they are? Probably not. Screenwriters don't get a lot of recognition across the board. But they're getting paid.

The big dogs on the competition circuit are the Austin Heart of Film Festival, Chesterfield, Disney, and Nicholl Fellowships in Screenwriting. Those are the four competitions that appear to have the most positive impact on people's careers. Nicholl and Austin go crazy in the press department, doing as much to publicize winners as humanly possible, including circulating lists of winners to industry professionals. Disney hires you for a year, puts you in a mentor program, and introduces you to the town at year's end. Chesterfield I do not know as much about, I don't know any Chesterfield winners, and their sponsorship has appeared to shift about some recently, but I hear they have a mentor program and rumors are mostly good.

After that you have Sundance, which to all appearances is geared mostly towards people already in the industry who wish to move from one arena to another (if I'm wrong about that, my apologies, that is how it tends to look from here); America's Best (the year I placed in America's Best there was no awards ceremony or press, but I got a check); Christopher Columbus Discovery Awards (the fine print there tends to indicate you are optioning your script to them, as opposed to "winning" prize money, watch that kind of stuff and know what you are getting into, if you win, *i.e.* an automatic option); Houston Worldfest (which is hella expensive so I've always shied away from it); there's also the Warner Bros. Workshop, but that's for TV writers and I'm focusing on feature stuff here because that's my field; and then there are regional competitions around the U.S. too numerous to list—unless you win. Then put them in your query.

If you're using competitions on a query letter to get attention, pay attention to how you say things. Say you place tenth in the Idaho Corn Growers Screenwriting Competition. "A competition dedicated to promoting films and screenplays about Idaho Corn Growers." (Hey, it could happen.) Okay, tenth is not so good, maybe, and no one in Hollywood has ever heard of the Idaho Corn Growers Association, let alone their competition. So maybe you do not want to list that. Unless it's all you've got. If it's all you've got, list it, but list it in its best light: "Top ten in Idaho Screenwriting national competition." Or just "Top ten in national screenwriting competition."

This is, essentially, a résumé you are building in that letter. You want everything you put down to stand in its best possible light. And as you build up big stuff, you take off little stuff to keep it as simple and hard hitting as possible.

Also, be discriminating about competitions. Get the guidelines. Read the fine print. Find out what you win, what it's going to cost to enter, and what they get from you, if you win. (I don't like competitions that automatically "option" winning material under the guise of giving you a cash award, that has always looked suspiciously like the entry fee is a disguised reading fee to me.) Find out who is sponsoring and running the competition and who is judging it. You would really be better off getting read by working producers and agents, as opposed to getting read by corn farmers. (No offense to corn farmers.) Do all that. it's called homework. And then?

You never know where good things are going to come from. With Austin, it was a small competition, it was in its first year, it was in Texas. I hesitated, but then thought what the hell, go for it, and entered. In my wildest dreams, I did not imagine winning a screenwriting competition in Austin, Texas, would launch my career. It did. But who would have thought it? A small competition in its first year at a conference in Texas? Well. You never know where the break is going to come from. So enter competitions, (1) because a win is inspirational and can get you read; and (2) because the wider you cast your net, the more avenues luck has to come back at you.

62 Where to Get Scripts

SAFE RESPONSES TO REALLY STUPID SUGGESTIONS #34: "Look over there, isn't that Cher?"

if you are writing scripts, I sure hope you are reading them. Or have at least read one? Because writing scripts without reading them is sort of like writing symphonies when you have never seen sheet music. It's a dumb idea. And I strongly advise against it.

If you live in L.A., scripts are easy to come by. They are all the hell over. Go down to the Academy, go down to the Guild, raid a production office, raid an agency, go to your local college campus film department, they all have libraries. And if you can't borrow them, swap them, or steal them, Book City sells scripts in format. And Larry Edmunds and Samuel French and Book Soup all sell paperback and hardback scripts.

If you don't live in L.A., it gets a little trickier, but the local campus may have a script library. You want to talk to the dean of the Film Department (if there is a Film Department) *and* whoever is teaching screenwriting, both, because sometimes one, but not both, will know where the scripts are stashed.

If you live near a film commission, which is an office set up by the state to promote filming in that state to bring in revenue, film commissions all have lots of scripts. Every script that ever shot in the state, they have. They have lots of other nifty stuff too, so look up your local film commission.

You want to read scripts in script format. That means three hole punched on standard letter sized paper with brads. That's where you're going to pick up a feel for how the writer made the script move on the page, not to mention how to format. It's important to be reading scripts in virgin format.

Scripts that are printed hardback or paperback are good as well, but you will not pick up a feel for pacing and presentation reading book bound scripts the way you will reading formatted scripts. So go ahead, read paperback and hardback scripts, but also read formatted scripts.

If you can't get those from your local college campus or film commission or library or supermarket parking lot, then order them. Book City has just about any script for any film ever released for about $18 per script including postage and handling. Formatted. Book City is listed in "Resources," give them a call.

Scenario magazine publishes three complete scripts in each quarterly issue. A one year subscription runs $39.00, so that is twelve scripts for cheap, compared to a place like Book City, and the scripts they publish are all prestige scripts, meaning all good. Which means you won't get to pick your own titles, but you will get good scripts. Unfortunately, you won't get formatted scripts. For some reason, *Scenario* editors think it is more aesthetic to publish the scripts in play format. Don't ask me why. But hey, they are publishing scripts, which is a step in the right direction. *Scenario* is listed in "Resources" as well.

And you might think about working as, or volunteering as, a reader. I did that. Since there were just not a lot of places to find scripts in Salt Lake City, I volunteered at Writer's Workshop, a place in L.A. that gave inexpensive consults and, when they found something good, did staged readings for industry types in L.A. And, for free reading services, would ship scripts out.

If there's one way to learn a lot fast about scripts, it is analyzing other people's material. Especially imperfect material. And we did reports, not for agents or studio execs, for writers. Doing that makes you think, about what works, what doesn't, and how to fix it. And makes you think maybe a little harder, since if you don't, you are dicking around some poor writer who just paid WW to get their script analyzed. It is good exercise, and if you can spend some time as a reader, it will be good for you as a writer. And the scripts are free. Not necessarily always good. But free.

63 Do You Have to Live in L.A.?

L.A. MOMENTS #42: One day I came home and the trash cans were gone. Just gone. I had to order all new cans from the City of Los Angeles. This means a green one for leaves, a black one for take it somewhere toxic, and a blue one for miscellaneous recyclables. Does anyone know how complex it is to order anything from the City of Los Angeles?

There is no such thing as the impossible in this business. Every rule anyone will ever tell you has been, or will be, broken at some point. Including that you have to live in Los Angeles. So there aren't "rules." But there are guideposts. Some things help. Like living in L.A. Living in L.A. gives you greater access. To studios. To people. Just to plain old copy stores that know how to bind scripts. That doesn't mean it can't be done from outside Los Angeles. It can. But more people make it into the business from the inside than from the outside. And you should know that, going in.

I made it in from outside. I was living in Utah. That is about as far outside Los Angeles as you can get. And I broke in. Which

I guess makes me a living example it can be done. At least in features. TV I'm not so sure about. The way I pulled that stunt off was, I got read by the president of production at Columbia Pictures and he optioned the script. And eventually made the movie. Why he read me was, (1) I won two national competitions in one week; (2) a producer whose opinion he valued was a judge in one of those competitions and talked up the script; (3) he had a long plane ride ahead of him with not much else to do besides read my script. So I got lucky. Then I got more lucky, because he messengered the script to my then future (and now past) agent and said, "Read this now." And the agent did, overnight, and signed me. So, by the grace of God, I jumped coverage at two important places, Columbia Pictures and CAA. Got read by people who were big enough and important enough they could actually say yes to things and did. And Columbia optioned the script. And CAA made the deal. And my career was born.

After all that, I still moved to Los Angeles. I had the attention, the agent, and the option at that point. I still thought I had better be here. Because, while at the beginning of a career, it's extremely difficult to break in from other places? It is equally difficult to keep a career going from other places. Especially a new career.

Living here, you don't pay long distance on every call to a studio. You can go to pitches at the drop of a hat. If you talk to an agent and make a reasonably good impression, you can go to lunch without worrying whether that plane ticket is going to take you over your credit limit. If someone wants to see a script in a hurry, you don't have to pay Federal Express to lose it on the way and, if push comes to shove, you can drive it there yourself. When you get invitations to events, you can actually show up. Meetings are simple to plan because no one has to cough up plane fare to discuss a simple idea with you. If the meeting time has to move, it does not involve changing a plane ticket and hotel reservation. And meetings don't all have to be set in a one week block of time. If you live here. If you don't, things become a little more difficult.

You can write in other places. Nobody has to be here to write. And half the time it is better and cheaper to be somewhere else, just to get the writing done. But you can't be there for the business and personal sides of the business, other places. And the business and personal sides of the business are myriad. And it is very easy in this town to slip out of sight. And in this town, out of sight is, in most cases, out of work. Literally.

Of the forty plus Nicholl winners when I won a Nicholl Fellowship in 1994, there was only one winner living outside Los Angeles with a career (and he lived in NY, not Utah). There were a number of winners living in Los Angeles working in the industry. I took a hard look at that. And—

Moved. Because one contest win does not a career make. Hell, two contest wins does not a career make. You win a contest, you get attention. You must use that, while you've got it, to get your work and face out there so people know who you are and what you do and think of you when jobs come up. And attention fades. This is a fickle town. You don't have forever to use that. It is a window that will close. And, post winning a competition, you still have to get the script set up (read option/sale), and then you have to get it made (read movie). And in between and post all that, you have to keep a career going (read find your next job). And none of that is easy. Not in Los Angeles. And not outside Los Angeles. But in Los Angeles, it is a damn sight easier.

So. I will not say you have to be here. You don't *have* to be anywhere. There is just no such thing as rules in this business. They all get broken. I will say, life is a hell of a lot less complicated if you are here.

64 The Last Word

ENCOURAGING COMMENTARY FROM THE PEANUT GALLERY #32:
"Truman Capote said that finishing a book and sending it out is like taking your child out into the backyard and shooting it. (Or something to that effect.)"

When I started this book, it was by accident. Now, nearing the finish, it damn well isn't by accident anymore. (Jeez, why didn't someone tell me how much damn work books are!) Six years of posts and letters. Cripes. There was so much information. What to keep, what to dump, what was repetitive, what wasn't, and what just wasn't anywhere around and needed to be filled in, those were all questions. Many of the original posts and letters were personal, to specific people, they had to be rewritten to include everyone, or at least as many everyones as possible, to be broader in application. And originally I thought I would end this with a note I wrote once about the writing profession itself, that it is hard, that it sure as hell isn't for the faint of heart, that it will break your dreams so fast they will end up colorless as over laundered socks. That you should think twice. Think hard. And think well.

But you know? I have heard that at one too many conferences. Kurt Leudtke, God bless the man, he has saved me more than once when I would call in big trouble for help and advice—and that advice was always good, whether or not I was always smart enough to take it—gave one of those speeches at the first Austin conference I attended. "Writing is hard, no one should do it, etc." And after he was done telling everyone that it was hard and terrible and we shouldn't even do it, I said, "Well that is very nice Mr. Leudtke, but I am committed here and don't have much choice in the matter and can't quit so telling me not to do it won't do me a whole hell of a lot of good, why don't you tell me something I can use that will help me avoid some of the problems instead?"

He's a good sport. He did. And maybe that is what this book is about. This is a hard business. But some people are committed. Stuck with it. They can't quit. So this is for you. I hope some of what I have put down here will help you, the kids that cannot quit, and maybe lighten the path and ease the road.

Write like God.

RESOURCES FOR SCREENWRITERS

Recommended Books for Screenwriters

Callan, K., *The Script Is Finished, Now What Do I Do?* This book talks about breaking in, what to do, what not to do, and is full of excerpts from conversations with agents, producers, and executives—*i.e.* your basic players. It is very useful reading.

Cameron, Julia, with Mark Bryan, *The Artist's Way.* You might wonder what this is doing in a list of film books. Two things. First, Pooks suspects it's the origin of her mystery quote, and it's only fair, if it is, to give it a plug. Second, there's more to writing than putting words on paper, and this book has saved three people I know from writer burnout. That's as good a recommend as you will ever find.

Cole/Haag, *The Complete Guide to Standard Script Formats; Part I: The Screenplay.* This covers all aspects of formatting; however, it has two areas you should ignore:

First, the book tells you to signify sounds and specific viewpoints by writing "we SEE such and such" and "we HEAR such and such." Ignore that: It's outdated. If something makes noise, write a normal sentence and capitalize the sound: "The stereo plays soft MUSIC." If something is of interest within the scene, don't write a "we SEE" cue. Write what's happening in the scene—"Tom crosses the room"—and leave it at that.

Second, the book tells you to include whoever (characters) or whatever (a brooch, etc.) the camera is on in scene headers. This is not a good idea. A lot of readers skim scene headers and won't thank you for forcing them to go back and read them. Put people and objects in scene direction.

Aside from that, this is the format bible, use it.

Froug, William, *The Screenwriter Looks at the Screenwriter*. This is a collection of twelve interviews with working screenwriters.

Goldman, William, *Adventures in the Screen Trade*. This is a witty, candid look at Hollywood, written by one of Hollywood's more (perhaps most) famous screenwriters.

Long, Rob, *Conversations with My Agent*. The book opens saying "this is half true." It's true enough. A "semi-memoir," this is funny, educational, and although Long works primarily in television, it translates to features.

Rabiger, Michael, *Directing: Film Techniques and Aesthetics*. The book is for directors and/or aspiring directors. It explores story in depth and actually talks about scenes like they have their own structure—which they do, although you won't hear about that in many other books. The only thing wrong with the book is Rabiger tells you to capitalize characters' names continuously throughout a script. Don't do that. Everything else is good.

Seger, Linda, *Creating Unforgettable Characters*. Seger is one of the best, if you're looking for a book about the mechanics of writing. She occasionally mixes movie stuff up with script stuff (oops), but otherwise she's all good.

Seger, Linda, *Making a Good Script Great*.

Trottier, David, *The Screenwriter's Bible: A Complete Guide to Writing, Formatting, and Selling Your Script*. To be honest, I haven't read this. (Which is a disgrace, because I have a signed copy.) However, David Trottier is one of the most inspirational teachers I ever had, and knowing him, I am sure it is worth a look.

Whitcomb, Cynthia, *Selling Your Screenplay*. This is informative and one of the most encouraging books out there. It is full of interviews with producers and directors who talk about what they look for in material, what they look for in a writer, and what makes an impression on them.

You should be able to find any of these books at Samuel French Theatre & Film Bookshop, (323) 876-0570, Larry Edmunds Cinema & Theatre Book Shop, (323) 463-3273, or Book Soup (310) 659-3110. Call for phone order information.

Additional Books Recommended by the Academy of Motion Picture Arts and Sciences

Egri, Lajos, *The Art of Dramatic Writing*. This is a pretty good book, but concentrates on theater.

Field, Syd, *Screenplay*. I'm not fond of Field's books, they emphasize writing by page number; other people swear by him.

Field, Syd, *Selling a Screenplay: The Screenwriter's Guide to Hollywood*.

Hauge, Michael, *Writing Screenplays That Sell*. I'm not crazy for anyone who says you can write a script without ever reading a script; however, people swear by him too.

Root, Wells, *Writing the Script*. Haven't read this.

Walter, Richard, *Screenwriting: The Art, Craft, and Business of Film and Television Writing*. Written by the director of the UCLA screenwriting program. His advice for people trying to get read is blasé and I don't trust his numbers, but other than that a fast read and good book.

Recommended Scripts for Screenwriters

If you want to write screenplays, read screenplays. Preferably good screenplays in standard industry format. These are all good and cover different genres:

Black, Shane, *Lethal Weapon*. Action/Drama.

Black, Shane, *The Last Boy Scout*. Action/Drama.

Cameron, James, with Gale Anne Hurd, *The Terminator*. SF/Action/Horror.

Ephron, Nora, with Rob Reiner & Andrew Scheinman, *When Harry Met Sally*. Romantic Comedy.

Esterzhas, Joe, *Basic Instinct*. Thriller.

Thomas, Diane, *Romancing the Stone*. Action/Adventure/Romantic Comedy.

Wallace, Earl, with Pamela Wallace & William Kelley, *Witness*. Drama/Suspense.

You can purchase scripts from Book City, (818) 848-4417 (Burbank), (323) 466-2525 (Hollywood). Scripts are about $18 with postage and handling. Don't expect great copy, but they're legible.

Publications for Screenwriters

Hollywood Reporter. Subscription Department, PO Box 1431, Hollywood, CA 90078. (323) 525-2150. Annual subscription: $219. Similar to *Variety,* this publication covers the business end of the film industry. See also hollywoodreporter.com.

The Hollywood Scriptwriter. PO Box 10277, Burbank, CA 91510. (818) 845-5525. Annual subscription: $35. The newsletter features interviews with industry professionals (especially writers), market updates, and agency bulletins. See also hollywoodscriptwriter.com.

Scenario: The Magazine of Screenwriting Art. For subscription information, call (800) 222-2654. Annual subscription: $39.00. Each issue reprints three feature scripts in their entirety (albeit in play format). If you're paying for scripts, this is the best deal you will find.

Variety Daily. Subscription Department, PO Box 7550, Torrance, CA 90504. (800) 552-3632. Annual subscription: $219. Like the *Hollywood Reporter,* this publication covers the business end of film. Opinions vary on which is the better publication; they cover the same information, so it tends to be a personal choice issue. See also variety.com.

Variety Weekly. Subscription Department, PO Box 710, Brewster, NY 10509-9864. (800) 525-3632. Annual subscription: $219. The weekly, condensed version of *Variety Daily.* If you're short on time, I'd say opt for weekly; it will keep you up to date and not kill you trying to keep up. See also variety.com.

Written By (formerly *The JOURNAL of the Writers Guild of America, West*). 7000 West Third Street, Los Angeles, CA 90048. (888) WRI-TNBY. Annual subscription for nonmembers: $40. *Written By* tends to be television oriented but addresses feature writing as well. See also wga.org.

Contests for Screenwriters (The Big Dogs)

America's Best: The Writer's Foundation, Inc., 3936 South Semoran Blvd., Suite 368, Orlando, FL 32822. Entry fee: $40.

Austin Heart of Film: The Austin Heart of Film Festival, 1600 Nueges, Austin, Texas 78701. Entry fee: $35.

Chesterfield Film Company—Writers Film Project: Writers Film Project, 1158 26th Street, Box 544, Santa Monica, CA 90403. Entry fee: $39.50.

Nicholl Academy Fellowships in Screenwriting: Academy Foundation, Nicholl Fellowships in Screenwriting, 8949 Wilshire Blvd., Beverly Hills, CA 90211. Entry fee: $30.

Sundance Feature Film Program: The Sundance Institute, 225 Santa Monica Blvd., 85th Floor, Santa Monica, CA 90401. Entry fee: $25.

Walt Disney Studios Fellowships in Screenwriting: c/o Fellowship Program Administrator/The Walt Disney Studios, 500 South Buena Vista Street, Burbank, CA 91521-0880. (818) 560-6894. Entry fee: none, but requires notarized application.

There are many more competitions. For more listings, check out http://www.moviebytes.com.

Directories for Screenwriters

Film Directors: A Complete Guide. Another Lone Eagle Publishing directory, this time feature directors cross-referenced by film title. Comprehensive, but current editions are not always perfectly up to date. $85. Contact Lone Eagle Publishing, 2337 Roscomare Road, Suite #9, Los Angeles, CA 90099. (800) FIL-MBKS. See also loneeagle.com.

Film Writers Guide. A Lone Eagle Publishing directory of feature writers cross-referenced by film title. This is a more comprehensive listing of credits than the WGA provides in its directory, but current editions are not always perfectly up to date. (Neither, however, is the Guild's directory.) $70. Contact Lone Eagle Publishing, 2337 Roscomare Road, Suite #9, Los Angeles, CA 90099. (800) FIL-MBKS. See also loneeagle.com.

Hollywood Agents & Managers Directory. A trademark publication listing agencies and managerial companies, their staffs, who to contact, and what associations (WGA, for example) the companies list. If you're looking for an agent, you should have this directory. $49.50. Phone (310) 315-4815 or (800) 815-0503 outside California. Address: 3000 Olympic Blvd., Suite 2413, Santa Monica, CA 90404. See also hcdonline.com.

Hollywood Creative Directory. Another trademark publication by the same people who publish the *Hollywood Agents & Managers Directory.* It lists over 1,200 production companies, studios, networks, their addresses, phone numbers, credits, staffs, and titles. If you're trying to get read, you should have this directory. $49.50.Phone (310) 315-4815 or (800) 815-0503 outside California. Address: 3000 Olympic Blvd., Suite 2413, Santa Monica, CA 90404. See also hcdonline.com.

Spec Screenplay Sales Directory. A listing of recent spec sales. You can get small versions, updated regularly, listing more recent spec sales, or the deluxe version, which spans years. Loglines are not always perfectly accurate, but it's good to flip through to see what is selling. Published by In Good Company Products, 3250 Olympic Blvd., #79, Santa Monica, CA 90404. (310) 828-4946.

Writers Guild of America Directory of Members. A publication of the WGA, this lists Guild members, their credits (the short list, optional), and who represents them. If you want to know who is repping whom, take a look. To order, contact the Writers Guild of America, West, 7000 West Third Street, Los Angeles, CA 90048. (323) 951-4000. See also wga.org.

Zagat Survey/Los Angeles So. California Restaurants. A listing of Los Angeles restaurants. When you're doing lunches and dinners, it's helpful to have. $10.95. (212) 977-6000. (In any L.A. bookstore.) See also zagat.com.

Note: The Writers Guild of America, West, also prints a list of signatory agents, available for about $2 with SASE. Contact the WGAw for more information. See also wga.org.

Organizations for Screenwriters

IFP, West (Independent Feature Project, West): 1625 Olympic Blvd., Santa Monica, CA 90404. (310) 392-8832. See also http://208.215.132.160.

WGAw (The Writers Guild of America, West): 7000 West Third Street, Los Angeles, CA 90048. (323) 951-4000. See also wga.org.

Registration and Copyright Services for Screenwriters

United States Copyright Office: Library of Congress, 101 Independence Ave., S.E., Washington, DC 20559-6000. (202) 707-3000. See also http://lcweb.loc.gov/copyright.

WGAw (The Writers Guild of America, West): 7000 West Third Street, Los Angeles, CA 90048. (323) 951-4000. See also wga.org.

Additional Websites of Interest for Screenwriters

Done Deal (catch up on book reviews, movie reviews, other sites of interest, and chat with strugglers and pros on the message boards): http://pub4.ezboard.com/bdonedeal.

Drew's Script-O-Rama (free script downloads): http://www.script-o-rama.com.

Internet Movie Database, aka IMDB (every factoid you ever wanted to look up about a movie, and most of them are right): http://www.imdb.com.

Screentalk (international webzine for screenwriters with pro articles and interviews): http://www.screentalk.org.

SeeMaxRun (you knew this was coming, right?, yes, it is the author's evil shrine): http://www.seemaxrun.com.

Simply Scripts (more free script downloads): http://www.simplyscripts.com.

Wordplayer (read—very good—articles on the business and craft of screenwriting by pros and chat with strugglers and pros on the message boards): http://www.wordplayer.com.

Date: (FILL IN DATE)
Proposed Title of Material
Submitted: (FILL IN TITLE OF MATERIAL)

Big Wig Producer
BIG WIG FILMS
10000 W. Big Wig Way
Hollywood, CA 90000

Dear Big Wig Producer:

I am submitting for possible use by you my material identified herein (hereinafter called the "Material") in accordance with the understanding, and subject to the conditions, set forth. I acknowledge that the Material was created and written by me, (INSERT YOUR NAME HERE), without any suggestion or request from you that I write or create the Material. I have attached copies of the Material, (INSERT SCRIPT TITLE HERE), a feature film script for motion picture, and a brief description of same. I am executing and submitting this letter in consideration of your agreement to review the Material with the express understanding I limit my claim of rights to the Material specifically synopsized and attached.

1. Except as otherwise specifically stated, I represent:

   a) that the Material is original with me;
   b) that I have the exclusive right to grant all rights in the Material;
   c) that I have exclusive rights in the title as regards its use in connection with the Material.

2. You agree that you will not use the Material unless you first negotiate with me compensation for such use, but I understand and agree that your use of material containing features and elements similar to or identical with those contained in the Material shall not obligate you to negotiate with me nor entitle me

to any compensation if you determine that you have an independent legal right to use such other material which is not derived from me (either because such features and elements were not new or novel, or were not originated by me, or because other persons have submitted or may submit material containing similar or identical features and elements not derived from me which you have the right to use).

3. I agree I must give you written notice by certified or registered mail at your address (set forth in the address portion of this letter) of any claim arising in connection with the Material or arising in connection with this agreement, within the period of time prescribed by the applicable statute of limitations, but in no event more than ninety (90) calendar days after I acquire knowledge of such claim, or if it be sooner, within ninety (90) calendar days after I acquire knowledge of facts sufficient to put me on notice of any such claim, as a condition precedent to the initiation of any legal action hereunder. I shall further withhold filing any legal action for a period of thirty (30) calendar days after said written notice to allow you time to investigate any claim.

4. I have retained a copy of the Material and I release you from any liability for loss or other damage to the copy or copies submitted to you.

5. I hereby state that I have read and understand this agreement; that no oral representations of any kind have been made to me; that there are no prior or contemporaneous oral agreements in effect between us pertaining to the Material; and that this agreement states our entire understanding.

6. I further submit I am of legal age, being over eighteen (18) years of age, and my signature on this contract and release is binding and legal.

Sincerely Yours,

(PRINT YOUR NAME HERE)

Signature:_____

Date:_____

Your Address:
City:
State:
Phone:
Fax:

*SEE ATTACHMENT

*ATTACHMENT:

TITLE OF MATERIAL SUBMITTED: (INSERT TITLE HERE)

FORM OF MATERIAL: Screenplay for motion picture.

SUMMARY OF THEME AND PLOT OF MATERIAL SUBMITTED: (Put "what your story is about" here. Add details, you are outlining what it is that makes your material unique and protectable by law.)

PRINCIPAL CHARACTERS: (Name principal characters and characteristics that make them identifiable and therefore protectable by law.)

OTHER IDENTIFYING CHARACTERISTICS: (Name distinguishing factors in the script that might make it new or novel or protectable.)

WGA REGISTRATION NO.: (INSERT WGA # IF YOU'VE GOT ONE)

Signature:_____

Date:_____

"GREATEST SCREENPLAY ON EARTH"

Written by

Greatest Screenwriter

Represented by: WGAw
Greatest Agent
At Greatest Agency
310-555-5000

```
SCRIPT TITLE

FADE IN:

INT.   OFFICE - NIGHT

Max, hair askew, one sock on backwards, glares at the
computer screen.  What the hell should she write?

She shrugs, types --

EXT.   MAX'S YARD - NIGHT

The office window spills light across a dark patio.  A
squirrel pauses.  Eyes the lighted window.  Nervous, flees
into dark --

INT.   MAX'S OFFICE - NIGHT

Max types.  Type.  Type type.  Pause.  Type.  The phone
RINGS.

                    MAX
          Shit!

She grabs it up.

                    MAX
          What?

                    INCREDIBLY SEXY BOYFRIEND (V.O.)
          What are you wearing?

                    MAX
          I am trying to finish this book.

She slams the phone into its cradle.

                    MAX
          Sheesh.  Incredibly sexy boyfriends are
          so pushy.

(Stop laughing, I'm writing it, I can have an incredibly sexy
boyfriend if I want.)

                                        FADE OUT:

                    THE END
```

Note: "fade in" and "fade out" are used only to open and close a
script. They are not used to open or close scenes.

August 25, 1994

Joe Producer
Big Film Productions
c/o Big Dog Studios
5000 Big Dog Way
Hollywood, CA 9000

Dear Joe Producer:

I'd like to submit EXCESS BAGGAGE, a feature length screenplay, for Big Film Productions' consideration. I have professional writing credits in fiction, non-fiction, humor, and theatre, recently graduated with a film degree from University of Utah, placed in the top five of the America's Best '93 national screenwriting competition, and am a current semifinalist in the Nicholl Fellowships in Screenwriting competition '94.

EXCESS BAGGAGE is a dark romantic comedy about an heiress who stages her own kidnapping and the car thief who derails her plans. The story's set in Portland and Seattle.

If you'd consider taking a look, please contact my agent, (Agent's Name), at (Agent's Phone Number), or call me direct at (My Phone Number).

Best,

Max Adams

This letter, written in August 1994, got me a lot of reads. It is simple. It tells someone I have a script, I want them to read it, why they should read me, and what the story is about. Simple works. Good luck to you.

ALSO AVAILABLE FROM WARNER BOOKS

ADVENTURES IN THE SCREEN TRADE
A Personal View of Hollywood and Screenwriting
by William Goldman

No one knows the writer's Hollywood more intimately than two-time Academy Award-winning screenwriter William Goldman. Here he takes you into the dream factory's inner sanctum, behind the scenes of such classic films as *Butch Cassidy and the Sundance Kid*, *All the President's Men*, and others. Delving into his own experience in the crafting of screenplays, Goldman gives you a firsthand look at why and how movies are made.

"This is that big, sad, funny, incisive, revelatory, gossipy, perception-forming book about Hollywood that publishers have been promoting for years—and now the real thing is finally here."
—*St. Louis Post-Dispatch*

WHERE DID I GO RIGHT?
You're No One in Hollywood Unless Someone Wants You Dead
by Bernie Brillstein with David Rensin

The consummate dealmaker, Bernie Brillstein was one of the first great Hollywood agent/manager/producers—and he has the legions of friends and enemies to prove it. Now for the first time the outspoken legend pulls back the curtains on a star-studded, roller-coaster, five-decade career and shows you how to survive and prosper in Tinseltown. From Elvis Presley to Jim Henson to John Belushi, Brillstein sets the record straight, telling you who he loved, who he hated, and what Hollywood's major players are really like.

"Great tales . . . an intriguing history of deals and damage."
—*People*